Nick Dear

Nick Dear's theatre credits include *The Art of Success* at the Royal Shakespeare Company and subsequently at Manhattan Theatre Club, New York. It won him the John Whiting Award for 1986, and he was nominated for Laurence Olivier Awards for both this and *A Family Affair*. He was Playwright in Residence at the Royal Exchange, Manchester, in 1987–8. Other plays include *Summerfolk* (after Gorky; National Theatre, 1999); *Zenobia* (RSC, 1995); *The Last Days of Don Juan* (after Tirso de Molina; RSC, 1990); *In the Ruins* (Royal Court, 1990); *Food of Love* (Almeida, 1988); *A Family Affair* (after Ostrovsky; Cheek by Jowl, 1988); and *Temptation* (RSC, 1984). He has written the libretti for two operas, *A Family Affair* (1993) and *Siren Song* (1994), both premièred at the Almeida Opera Festival. His screenplays include *Persuasion* (1995; BAFTA Award); *The Gambler* (1997); *The Turn of the Screw* (1991); *Cinderella* (2000) He has also written extensively for radio.

NICK DEAR

Plays One

The Art of Success
In the Ruins
Zenobia
The Turn of the Screw

Introduced by
the author

faber and faber

First published in this collection in 2000
by Faber and Faber Limited
3 Queen Square, London WC1N 3AU
Published in the United States by Faber and Faber Inc.
an affiliate of Farrar, Straus and Giroux, New York

Typeset by Country Setting, Kingsdown, Kent CT14 8ES
Printed in England by Mackays of Chatham plc, Chatham, Kent
All rights reserved

The Art of Success and *In the Ruins*
first published by Methuen in 1989, revised and reprinted in 1994
by Methuen Drama, an imprint of Reed Consumer Books.
Zenobia first published by Faber and Faber Ltd in 1995, revised in 2000.
The Turn of the Screw first published in 2000 by Faber and Faber Ltd.

The publishers are grateful to Meridian Broadcasting and
United Productions for their kind permission to reproduce
the screenplay *The Turn of the Screw*.

A CIP record for this book is available from the British Library

ISBN 0-571-20393-0

2 4 6 8 10 9 7 5 3 1

Contents

Introduction

The Art of Success began as a play about the political manipulation of art. Along the way it snowballed into a rather lurid comedy of sexual manners. At its core, though, is a debate about the nature of ambition, and the lengths to which one will go to succeed, and the degree of compromise one learns one will accept. Its historical setting is purely a matter of convenience.

Conversely, *In the Ruins* is very much *about* history, the experience of history, the knowledge that – from a certain perspective – history is what you do when you get up in the morning. At least, it is if you're a king presiding over an age of unparalleled innovation and expansion. Yet this king is a deranged lunatic, by dint of an ungovernable disease; the fact that he rules half the world lends the play its irony. Hereditary monarchy is a form of social insanity. *In the Ruins* attempts not only to solicit sympathy for a doddery old man; it also suggests that we look at the source of the affliction, which is the nature of royalty itself. George III is not just a figure of bathos and epigrammatic fun – he's the best argument for republicanism our history has given us.

Zenobia pits a tribal monarch against the mighty republic of Rome. A middle-eastern state takes on the global superpower in a battle for control of trade and commodities. Any similarity with the events of the early 1990s in that part of the world is entirely uncoincidental. On a more personal scale, it's another play about ambition and accommodation, about principles and their dismemberment, about survival. History, here, is something you've got to get through.

Henry James's *The Turn of the Screw* shows that, curiously, things do change for the better sometimes. The hundred years since it was written have loosened the stranglehold with which Christian zealotry once gripped our society. Arguments continue about whether the ghosts 'really exist' or not; that's an irrelevance. They exist for the person who sees them. End of story. What's more – much more – alarming is the degree of violence to which a Christian is prepared to go to preserve religious orthodoxy. The Governess's battle with the undead is an hysteria born of reading the Bible. The Victorian obsession with 'manners', on the one hand, and with the studied obscuration of sexual realities, on the other, results in catastrophe. I was delighted to see it shown on TV at Christmas.

It's been my great good fortune to have had these works served by a large number of highly talented directors, producers, actors, composers, designers and technicians. My thanks go to all of them, as well as to the audiences who have taken the trouble to come and watch, and the critics who have given me such a lot of laughs.

Nick Dear
December 1999

THE ART OF SUCCESS

The Art of Success was first performed by the Royal Shakespeare Company at The Other Place, Stratford upon Avon, on 2 July 1986. The play transferred to the Pit Theatre at the Barbican on 13 August 1987. The cast was as follows:

Jane Hogarth Niamh Cusack
William Hogarth Michael Kitchen
Harry Fielding Philip Franks
Frank David Killick
Oliver Simon Russell Beale
Mrs Needham Dilys Laye
Louisa Dinah Stabb
Sarah Sprackling Penny Downie
Robert Walpole Joe Melia
Queen Caroline Susan Porrett

Other parts were played by members of the company.

Director Adrian Noble
Designer Ultz
Music Paul Reade

Characters

Jane Hogarth
William Hogarth
Harry Fielding
Frank
Oliver
Mrs Needham
Louisa
Sarah Sprackling
Robert Walpole
Queen Caroline

Act One

*London in the 1730s. The Beefsteak Club. A group of
drunken men asleep at a table in the middle of the
afternoon. They have collapsed amongst the debris of
a huge meal. They snore contentedly.*

*A woman (Jane) enters stealthily. She circles the men
in quiet anger. She makes out the one she's looking for
(William). She raises a large pair of scissors, then puts
them between William's legs. There is a loud 'snip' and
William wakes in panic. Jane exits. He doesn't see her.*

William No! Jane! Don't!

*He jumps away from the table and examines himself,
but nothing has happened to him.*

Christ, what a bitch.

Harry (*waking*) What is it, Will?

William My wife, she –

William looks under the table for her. She's not there.

Nothing. A dream. My head is full of nightmares.

Harry It's the rich food and drink.

William It's the cuts of beef, the blood-red beef –

Harry The cheddar –

William The quantity of ale. The dreams get worse the
more you gorge. It's as if the brain, it fractures open, and
horrible creatures spew hot from its crack.

Harry I thought you said it was your wife.

William Well, yes, it was Janey, but she was – she had her dressmaking shears and she – well, let's just say it's not what I had hoped for from a marriage.

Harry You regret it already?

William Don't talk daft.

Frank (*stirs and mumbles*) Minutes of the Annual General Meeting of . . .

Harry Tell me your dreams, if they're upsetting you.

William They're not upsetting me, nothing's upsetting me, there's just some bastard forever chipping away in my bloody sleep, carving away at my sense of myself, and why? Why? Is it envy of my talent or what is it?

Harry It's all this boozing at lunchtime.

William I know, I know, and the pressure of work.

Harry And you have a lively imagination and you –

William Lively? It's running fucking riot, mate!

Frank (*stands, uncertainly, pissed*) Minutes of the Annual General Meeting of the Sublime Society of Beefsteaks, held in Mrs Needham's upstairs room this afternoon the –

Harry Meeting's adjourned, Frank.

Frank Normal agenda. Election of officers.

William Shut up, Frank.

Frank Officers re-elected without contest, as per last year. Minutes read and agreed with no dissent. Treasurer's report revealed a surplus in the bank and as per usual all new applications for membership of our estimable Club were unanimously rejected. Whereupon the Secretary volunteered the observation that the Society of Beefsteaks could well be said to mirror in little the happy torpor of our kingdom as a whole.

Harry Tell that to the poor of Dorset.

William Shut up, Harry.

Frank The membership thereupon with due and proper ceremony devoured the half-cooked rump of a bullock, sang several rather long songs of dubious tastefulness, burped a bit, farted a bit, and drank themselves into oblivion. (*Sits.*)

William A vote of thanks, to the Secretary.

Oliver (*his head on the table*) Seconded.

Frank (*rises*) Gratefully accepted. (*Sits.*)

William What about a small drink?

Frank (*rises*) We now proceed to Any Other Business, William.

Harry What's that, Frank?

William Oh no. Not me.

Oliver Hark at the newlywed.

William I don't want to catch nothing, do I.

Frank Wear your armour.

William I've chucked it away.

Frank They'll wash one out for you, I'm sure, they always have some spares.

Harry Spare what? What are you talking about?

Oliver The dried gut of a sheep.

Frank Cundums, boy. Are you telling us you've never worn one?

Harry No . . .

Frank Are you telling us you've never – had it off?

Harry No! But I've never been with a rented woman. Always gone with nice girls. When mother's back is turned. You don't fiddle about with a length of intestine in front of a girl from a genteel house. You discharge your obligations at once.

William Very gratifying.

Frank Dangerous, though.

William Not with your wife.

Frank Not with yours, perhaps. But my beloved . . . the sight of her unlaced would turn your thing to mush. (*imploring*) William . . .!

William No, I've got work to do before the daylight goes. And I said I'd meet Jane for a walk.

Frank A walk! The change in the man! Where once the fires of lust roared in his gut, now all is calm and sensible, a candle-flame of passion.

Harry I burn, though, Frank. I smoulder.

Frank You?

Harry Yes, I'm in the market. I believe a writer should sample every experience.

Frank Then I move: that this Annual General Meeting invite our good friend Mrs Needham to offer us a selection of her stock, the Meeting having a view to purchase, and the necessary funds being made available by the Society.

Oliver Seconded.

William It's not coming out of the kitty?

Harry Don't see why not. Treasurer's just seconded it.

William (*outraged*) Fuck off!

Frank William, this is a formally-constituted AGM, please speak through the chair if you have a point of order.

William Are you trying to tell me that you lot intend getting your collective leg over and paying for it out of my bleeding subs?

Oliver Yes, we are. Absolutely, yes.

William Are you fuck! That's never fair!

Oliver Yes it is.

William What, you mean I lose out just because I love my wife?

Harry Will –

William What, mate?

Harry You always drink more than your share. (*laughter*)

William (*beaten*) You tight-fisted shits . . .

Oliver Oh, stop complaining. Potter off home to the warmth of the bridal couch.

William He desired my wife himself, you know. He would come sniffing round her doorway like an over-eager pup. When I was already inside.

Oliver This kennel-talk is witty.

William Is it. Then why don't you sod off and play with your bone?

Oliver I'm only concerned for a fellow-member's welfare.

William He's jealous!

Oliver What is it, don't she come on heat quite as frequent as one might prefer? Or is it – dear Janey's a lovely tall bint, isn't she? – is it just too high for the mongrel to reach? I mean I've heard of marrying above oneself but this is –

Frank Oliver –

Oliver – fucking ridiculous.

William (*makes a run at Oliver*) Come here, I'll cripple you!

   William is restrained by Frank and Harry.

Oliver Oh, the upstart's frightfully drunk.

William Of course I'm drunk, what do you think I come here for, the company?

Oliver I am a peer of the realm – I could ruin your career!

William I'll pull your purple bollocks off, that'll fuck your pedigree!

Frank Gentlemen, please, behave like Beefsteaks! – Will, apologise to the Viscount.

Harry And Oliver, shake hands with a great artist.

Oliver A great artist? The runt with the inky fingers? A great artist? We talk a different language, Mr Fielding. Willy Hogarth, a great artist? Let us assess his curriculum vitae. What cathedrals has he done? What frescos of what battles? What mansion walls adorned with Roman heroes? What royal features stippled with immortal pigment?

William My portraits are widely reputed to be –

Oliver Oh, portraits, portraits, any hack can do titchy portraits to clutter up sideboards, but a great artist – Let me remind you one has toured the Continent and one has *seen* great art, I mean the originals, vast canvases in gold leaf frames, huge blocks of stone chipped up to holiness, Annunciation, Pietà, and in the damp palaces of Venice spent my inheritance, spent money like water building my collection of Madonnas –

William Dead Christs, Holy Families, flying fucking angels, and ship-loads no doubt of similar dismal, dark subjects.

Oliver Historical allegories, mainly, drawn from the well of antique myth.

William Which no one can understand.

Oliver Not open to the common herd, I grant you.

William Which *I* can't understand.

Oliver Lack of education is such a dreary thing.

William I didn't have time for an education, I had to earn a crust. I have no patron, no office, no inheritance, but what I do have is this body of work behind me, built from nothing. It's not great, not quite, but not inconsiderable, though I've flogged some shit I know, some rotten illustrations, but I do believe, I must allow myself to believe I have it in me – great work! Lasting work! I mean I am still learning, yes, I'm not exactly a prodigy, Christ, I hate prodigies, I've hated prodigies since I was about twenty-five years old, but fucking hell I'm making a fucking go of it, aren't I? (*He goes and sits in a corner and sulks.*)

Oliver . . . Something I said?

Harry You ought to see his latest work, it's bloody good.

Oliver Oh? What is the subject?

Harry A harlot.

Oliver A harlot? What, a tart? Oh, jolly well done, Will, a picture of a tart –

William Six pictures.

Oliver Six?

Harry He calls it a Progress.

Oliver Six pictures of a whore? Progress? That is utterly silly. What chap of any character or standing is going to want to be seen buying six pictures of a prostitute, for heaven's sake?

Harry Well, I've ordered a set of prints.

Frank Me too, the wife wants some.

Oliver Oh, prints, well, prints, absolutely, naturally one shall have a set of prints oneself, but one is talking about paintings, canvases, one is talking about art. Art rests in the original, not the copy.

Harry Does it?

Oliver Why certainly. Anyone can own a copy. Genius is not shared around like a bag of peppermints.

Frank Buy the originals, then. You've got the cash.

William They're not for sale. Not to him, who covets my wife.

Oliver See? He's petrified.

William (*returning*) Of what am I petrified?

Oliver That your work will not stand compare with the fruits of my Grand Tour. How can a man who has barely been south of the Thames seriously aspire to be a painter?

William What is art?

Oliver Now let's not split hairs.

William No, what is art – property? Or communication? Does it exist to be owned, or to be understood?

Oliver I think I'll just nip downstairs and have a word with Mrs Needham.

William Do you know what I'm talking about?

Oliver No, damn you, but I know what I like.

William And what do you like?

Oliver Well . . . As a rule, William . . . Something with a certain 'je ne sais quoi', that's what I usually go for.

Exit Oliver with a superior air.

Frank That is the great benefit of a Club such as ours. The interchange of ideas between men of civilisation and intelligence – A picture's a picture, I would have said.

William But what if every bloke in the street can own a masterpiece for sixpence? Then where are your connoisseurs? Your gentlemen collectors?

Frank I never imagined you as a champion of the heaving masses.

William Champion my arse. I want their sixpences. I reckon I can as well get a living by dealing with the public in general, as by hanging on the whims and fancies of the rich. In fact I could be very wealthy.

Frank Then why aren't you?

William Because of the pirates. The bastard pirates of print. Some geezer will come round my place posing as a buyer for the original painting, and the next thing you know there'll be a shoddy bloody copy of it in the shops before I've even got the acid off my etching, and then they'll knock down my payments because the market's flooded with imitations – it makes you weep!

Frank But surely you have copyright on your design?

Harry No, he doesn't, because it's very hard to legislate for the ownership of an idea. The thunder and lightning in your head. Writers were only granted protection of our ideas a few years ago. There's nothing that covers the specific problems of engravers.

Frank I'm only a simple merchant. The world of art is strange to me, all I know anything about is life. Now, in life, if I've a boat-load of sugar, say, or blacks, or molasses, I expect to have a document to prove I own the cargo, and I don't expect a soul to challenge it, or if they do that's stealing and they'll hang. We have greatly widened the scope of the capital offence under Mr Walpole. Can you identify your pirates?

William 'Course I can, they're all old mates.

Frank Then you must have redress.

William What, you mean like, take them round the back of the printshop and –

Frank No, man, in the courts! Go through the courts! Use the law, it's made for you. Whether you like it or not, you're a businessman now.

William (*thoughtful*) Art as business. Yes.

Harry But you'd have to get the law changed, Frank. You'd have to get a Bill through parliament.

Frank Then petition parliament. That's what it's for. It's made up of perfectly ordinary fellows, Harry, very like me if the truth be known, and very understanding of another fellow's needs.

Harry You mean it's a corrupt little clique whose sole reason for existence is to line its own pockets.

William Run by Robert Walpole . . .

Harry Precisely, that's why I ridicule him in every play I've ever written. In the new one I represent him as a –

Frank Don't tell me, don't spoil it, I'm coming to the show! Oliver and I are going to drum up some trade for you.

Harry What, tonight? Thanks very much.

Frank (*to William*) No doubt you've satirised the Great Man as well, have you? It being so much the fashion.

William No, not him personally, I haven't.

Harry Then now's your chance, Will! What a chance! 'The Harlot's Progress' is going to be a huge success. Why don't you follow it up with a political one? Why don't you do a 'Statesman's Progress' and drag our tyrant through the mud?

William No.

Harry Why not? Depicting how he bribed his way to power?

William No.

Harry It'll sell in tens of thousands!

William There are more important things in life than money, Henry!

Harry Yes, I'm talking about them!

William I said no, didn't I?

Harry But you never said why not.

William Look, I know you're my best mate and all –

Harry Well, I used to be.

William But if there's one thing I won't do it's peddle second-hand ideas, Harry, because I'm not interested in theories, I'm interested in people – you get bogged down in theory, you never reach into yourself –

Harry We're above it, are we? We're untouched by the world?

William Nobody tells me what to paint! – I'm bursting for a slash. (*Exits.*)

Frank Ah, the tactical widdle, veteran of many a board-room skirmish.

Harry (*bitter*) Interested in people . . .! I remember a time when no one was safe from the blade of his graving-tool. The rich and the mighty and the idiotic chiselled out in black and white. Simple monochrome of judgement.

Frank Attack, attack, attack, it's all attack with you. Some things are worth defending – stable government for one. Learn a little balance, or the Prime Minister will close you down.

Harry He can't, I'm far too popular.

William (*returning*) The bucket's gone – what shall I do?

Frank Into the street. I think I'll join you.

Harry Now you come to mention it –

All three piss out of the window with sighs of relief.

Frank Bet you a tanner you can't get it in that window.

Pause.

William You owe me a tanner.

They giggle. Unseen by them, Mrs Needham enters with Oliver. She peers at the men.

Mrs Needham You'll get another drop out of that if you wring it.

Frank Mrs Needham!

The pissers are embarrassed.

Mrs Needham We, too, live in the sight of God, remember. This is a respectable street! How would you like it if I came and urinated over your neighbours?

They all approve of the idea.

Cheeky devils. What is it you want, then? Don't be bashful, we must have a proper order. The goods are stored below, it only remains to make a requisition. (*She takes out a notebook and checks off a list.*) May God forgive me what I do. My constant prayer is that I might make enough from this commerce to leave off in good time to atone. You, young man, what sort of a slut is your heart's desire?

Harry gawps.

They're all quite clean and they go to church on Sundays. I've got Peggy free, she's a little fat one, she will rub you in her bosom till you come off in her face, she doesn't mind, she's used to it, what do you say to that?

Harry Er, I –

Mrs Needham Good, that's you sorted.

Frank Elizabeth – don't make it difficult for us.

Mrs Needham It's not me making it difficult, Frank, it's the Lord. And I hope you've lost your taste for stinging nettles. I had a rash for a week.

17

Frank You weren't holding them right. If you hold them right you don't get stung.

Mrs Needham That's if you hold them with your hands, Frank. Now then, you sir – what can I tempt you with? Birch twigs? Leather face-mask? Would you care to join a filthy masquerade?

William No, I don't think I would, thank you.

Mrs Needham Boys, is it? I've got boys if you want them.

William No, it isn't boys! It's – I – it's because I – oh, fuck.

The others laugh at him. Stumped for an explanation, he turns and leaves angrily.

Mrs Needham Some people shock very easy. But not my favourite Viscount. I have a treat for a regular customer. I have a little virgin, a real one mind, nothing sewn up or otherwise embroidered, an innocent young beauty I've been schooling in the sciences of lust, and for an extra guinea you may shag her infant brains out, if you wish . . .

Pause. Oliver takes out his purse and drops it on the table. Blackout.

SCENE TWO

A pleasure garden. Amongst the classical statuary and symmetrical borders stands Louisa, on the lookout for trade.

Louisa (*shivers*) Wind off the Thames blows down the avenues, round the rotunda, through the triumphal arches and directly up my skirt. I must have the coldest

legs in England. A sailor in a Bermondsey cellar said that
in China they tell of a wind disease, a cold, cold wind
blowing round the body, typhoon in your arms and legs,
whispering draughts at the back of your skull. I told him
I think I've got it, mate, it all sounds dead familiar. He
laughed and bit my nipple with splintering teeth. What
I would have loved, at that moment, what I longed for,
was that all the air would whoosh out of me like a burst
balloon, and I sink down to nothing at his feet, and
teach the disbelieving rat a lesson. Here I am out in all
weathers, all the entrances and exits in my body open to
the elements day and freezing night, what's to stop the
gale when it comes in and fills me? And blows round my
bones for ever? – Wait, is he walking this way? That
dragoon? He looks so sad . . . doesn't he look sad . . .
I don't know, they call this place a pleasure garden, I've
never seen such misery, I'd christen it the garden of wind
and disappointment, or cold and frosted cunt.

    Jane has entered, unseen. She listens.

Is he coming over here? Come along, then, miss, get all
your gusts and breezes together . . .
    Nice time with an old windbag, soldier? It's not
wearing any knickers.
    (*She promenades. She sees Jane.*) And what do you
want, may I ask?

Jane Aren't you cold? You look blue.

Louisa Well who's going to want to shaft a shiverer
wrapped from head to foot in rags? You have to show a
man a bit of skin.

Jane Why don't you wear some stockings, at least?

Louisa (*mimes being strangled*) That's why. And they
never see the goose-pimples. Lust is a great blinder, oh
isn't it just. – Oh farts, he's wandering off. That was you

done that. He must've thought we're only working doubles.

Jane I do beg your pardon. I couldn't help overhearing – I couldn't tear myself away. Please let me give you some money.

Louisa What have I got to do for it?

Jane Why, nothing. Take it. You have the most appalling life, don't you?

Louisa . . . Are you looking for an unusual experience?

Jane Um, I don't think so.

Louisa Because it makes me livid. Young ladies of quality coming down here, all for an hour of rough sex.

Jane Oh dear.

Louisa Taking the bread right out of our mouths!

Jane You have my sympathy.

Louisa Good. (*She hits Jane.*) Then perhaps you'll heed a gentle warning. Stay off my patch! You won't enjoy it. Soft skin bruise up like a peach. And what about the bite-marks and the blood?

Jane You misunderstand, I'm waiting for my –

Louisa hits her again.

Ow! – I suppose if you are forced to live like an animal you are going to start to behave like one.

Louisa Don't call me an animal. Animals don't do this for a living.

William enters.

William Janey, there you are.

Jane You're late. I've had to send the carriage away and I've had to wait here alone.

Louisa (*staring pointedly at William*) I don't know you from somewhere, do I, sir?

William (*rigid with panic*) I shouldn't think so, no.

Jane My husband is actually rather famous. It is possible you may have had him pointed out to you in town.

Louisa That must be it. I thought he looked familiar.

Jane He is an artist.

Louisa Well isn't that a nice thing to be? A profession as old as my own.

Jane William, this poor woman is a prostitute.

William Oh, is she?

Jane She is forced to solicit for custom even in this foul weather. Isn't that shaming? To you, I mean? A man? – What is your name?

Louisa Louisa, madam.

Jane Louisa, I hold nothing against you. But for the accident of birth I . . . Oh, the trade in flesh, isn't it pernicious.

William Yes, but there's nothing we can do about it today.

Jane Perhaps there is. Perhaps if we took this woman home and gave her a hot meal and a bath, she might regain her – self respect –

William You're joking!

Louisa (*shivers tragically*) The wind . . . The wind blows through the warmest men, and turns their hearts as cold as stone. There's a bloke over there by the Temple of Virtue, I think he's wanting business. Excuse me. (*Exits, flashing a leg at William.*)

Jane And where I wonder will she sleep tonight?

William Up Drury Lane by the Queen's Head, that's – oh – that's where they all live, Janey, isn't it? Up Drury Lane? Them back alleys?

Jane I brought your basket. With roast beef and beer – Will, you don't have anything to do with such women, do you? Not now we're together?

William No, never, never, I swear it. Temptation comes my way sometimes but I am strong and I resist it. Save myself for you. And your little cheeks red from the wind. (*Kisses her.*)

Jane Imagine them out here . . . brr! . . . having to . . .

William (*interested*) What?

Jane You know. Up against the trees, the rough bark in your hair, linen down in the leaf-mould . . .

William You find it – exciting?

Jane Not so much exciting as just –

William Dirty.

Jane A tightness at the back of the throat and I –

William Sordid.

Jane Well . . .

William But somewhere down in the dregs of your mind you –

Jane Yes – ?

William Jane, I love you, let's get on the floor.

Jane I beg your pardon!

William It's not very wet.

He tries to drag her down.

Jane William! Are you out of your mind!

William Yes, yes, I'm berserk for you, come on darling, you're my prize –

Jane This is a public place!

William – my reward for being good, give it to me Janey –

Jane I'm sorry but I can't!

William – open your lovely knees!

Jane breaks away. Pause.

Jane I thought we were going out for a walk . . .!

William Oh, fuck.

Jane What sort of woman . . . What sort of woman is it you want me to be? You seem to want to make me something I am not.

William I'm trying. I am trying! There aren't many men who understand women at all, you know.

Jane Understand women . . .?

William Yes, well, I'm making a bleeding effort, at least.

Jane An effort?

William Yes an effort! Do I force you? Do I ever? Hot with humiliation in the Vauxhall mud and do I complain? No, I try to understand.

Jane He thinks he understands. Hallelujah! Pass the paintpot! Pass the pedestal, let me get on! – God, the limitless arrogance of them.

William Thanks very much, Jane, that's just the gesture of support I was hoping for.

Jane I love you, I love you, idiot! But you take so much for granted! That I will need you when you need me. That I will be clean but dirty, ignorant but clever. That I will have a mind of my own that you can say you're proud of. Loving you is such a struggle . . . hand-to-hand every inch of the way . . . I am enmeshed in you, and I don't always like it. But it happens! It happens! I am a tangle of things not easily unravelled. So please, don't go round thinking you begin to understand me. Just love me. That's all. Just accept. Because I refuse to be understood.

William (*pause. He averts his eyes*) I'll see you tonight.

Exit William with basket. Jane takes a step after him, then stops with a gesture of anger and frustration. Fade to black.

SCENE THREE

A prison cell. Piles of dirt and straw. A high barred window and heavy door. A table and chair, and a stool. Sarah sits at the table, sunk in daydreams. There is a woman's cry, far away in the depths of the gaol. Sarah comes to, blinking. She pays no attention to the cry. She empties the contents of a jug of water into a bowl: about half a cupful. With a sigh of annoyance she rolls up her sleeves and prepares to wash herself. Then changes her mind, picks up the bowl and goes to drink. Then changes her mind again, puts it down, and washes her grimy arms and face. When finished she looks into the water with distaste. She arranges her filthy clothes as neatly as she can. She has a silver spoon concealed in a

pocket. She polishes it up and checks her reflection.
She smells her breath, pokes at a rotting tooth. She puts
the spoon away and looks at the water again. Then in
one swift movement she grabs the bowl, drinks the
water, and sets it back on the table again as if it hadn't
happened. She stares ahead with an innocent look.
The bolts on the far side of the door are drawn back.
A Gaoler shows William into the cell. He carries his
basket. He sniffs the air and recoils.

Sarah You came then. I weren't sure.

She extends her hand to him.

Gaoler Sir, the fever in a gaol . . . They say you feel it
dance beneath the skin . . . Like a fire in a turf-moor,
never put it out. If you're lucky you go mad before you
die.

William Cheers, I look forward to it. (*Shakes Sarah's*
hand.)

Gaoler I have to bolt the door, has this been explained?

William Yes, but do it quietly, I've got a miserable
headache and I'm not in a very good mood.

Gaoler You can still change your mind.

William I've been in a nick before. Grew up in the
shadow of the walls. Father a debtor, poor old bugger.
Done well for myself, though, haven't I? (*Shows off his*
clothes.)

Gaoler Yes, sir, you have.

William Obviously being terrorised at an impressionable
age by shits with whips and manacles provides a first-
rate training for the wider world.

Sarah laughs. The Gaoler turns nasty.

Gaoler I'm going to lock you in, now, sir, in the bowels of Newgate, all right?

The Gaoler leaves and locks the door.

Sarah It is an honour to meet you.

William The light in here is rubbish. Rubbish.

Sarah Your eyes soon get accustomed.

William But the smell – the excrement of fear – that takes me back.

Sarah I'm sorry about the pong but –

William Don't be.

Sarah – there's an open sewer –

William Dung does not disgust me. Quite the contrary. It reminds us what we are. I refuse to let myself be offended by any human functions.

Sarah Very nice it must be, having the choice.

William I see you have a flicker of wit. How would you like to be – preserved?

Sarah Don't care.

William 'Course you do.

Sarah No I don't.

William Are you going to mess me about?

Sarah I don't care!

William But your appearance – you've gone to some trouble – I'm amazed you can keep as clean as that in this fuck-awful place. The power of a woman's self-respect! – Or am I being condescending, sorry if I am.

Sarah I ain't gone to any bother.

William Sit you at the table I think.

She sits.

Background of barred window and bolted door. I'd like to do something with the stench. The way the air hangs heavy with disease, drip of plague like dew . . . But how do you show a smell, I wonder? How do you paint an aroma?

Sarah You can't, it's impossible.

William Not if you have any art. You might for example draw someone holding a scented handkerchief to their nose, standing nearby and, what could they be – glancing at the pisspot?

Sarah How do we know it is scented?

William What?

Sarah This hankie. This feller, he could be just blowing.

William Perfume bottle –

Sarah Oh, good.

William – peeping from the pocket of his coat.

William sits on the stool and prepares his sketching board.

Sarah You got a bit of a brain, too, haven't you?

William Ta, yes, as a nipper I was apprenticed to a silver engraver, my widowed mum being very poor, and since then I've developed this system of like visual language, this technical memory, which is unique in that it –

Sarah How do I know it is perfume?

William What?

Sarah In the bottle.

William Well of course it's perfume.

Sarah Could be water.

William Well it's not.

Sarah Could be gin.

William It's perfume!

Sarah But how do I know?

William Because it's written on the side! 'Perfume'!

Sarah No it's not.

William It is, it is!

Sarah (*bangs table*) Look, prick, it's bloody well not.

William (*wary of her*) . . . Why not?

Sarah 'Cause I can't bloody well read, that's why not. Is it so much, that I should understand?

  Pause. William begins to work.

William Sketching in chalk and pencil, Sarah. Won't take long. Sorry I was late, been rushing round town all day, I'm so bloody busy it's not real. On my way here I thought I would put in the Gaoler. With his keys and whip. But that would kind of prejudge the case, wouldn't it?

Sarah Good, I can live without him breathing down me neck.

William Does he pester you? I could have a word with the Governor or someone.

Sarah He daren't come near me. He's scared I cut his throat. (*Laughs.*) Would too. That brute. I seen him rub his self. He'll prob'ly wait till I'm done for, then he'll stick it in. Then he'll turn me over to the surgeons.

William Haven't you got no family to –

Sarah What, hang on me legs? They say it's a blessing if you can get someone to hang on your legs, don't they? Speeds things up considerable.

William I meant – to take the body. And bury you.

Sarah Not in this parish. Or if I have I've forgotten 'em. (*Pause.*) Another life. Like a dream now. (*Pause.*) They'll have me on the butcher's slab and set to with the chopper. I'll be splayed out there like a lump of meat, I'll have no defence, clamp me knees together they'll chop 'em off, slice my thighs to rashers, and there's my honour up for grabs. And off with her hands. And off with her noisy old head. And now I am dismembered by a dozen men, me giblets all over the floor, and they have their leathery fingers in me in the name of science, searching for the bit that went bad.

William (*aghast*) How can you talk like that?

Sarah How? Damn, if I got to think it, every other bugger will too.

William . . . I don't half pity you.

Sarah You after the bad bit, too? That what you come here to paint? The evil, the rot, and that?

William Well, I'm just doing a sketch.

Sarah I can throw a fit if you like.

William (*interested*) Oh? What sort of a fit?

Sarah I don't know, a mad fit. (*She rolls her eyes.*)

William And what's the effect of that?

Sarah Scares the shite out of magistrates, mainly. (*Laughs. Subsides.*) Something bubbles up inside me, I don't know.

William (*disapproving*) But we all have these urges, and we all have to contain them.

Sarah Why?

William Don't ask stupid questions, it's bleeding obvious, isn't it?

Sarah Why?

William Well – for fear of what the law will do to us otherwise!

Sarah But I am a law to myself. Now. The judges have run out of punishments.

William Oh, Christ, how can you argue against it? – You have to have respect for the law, Sarah.

Sarah You're not getting fucking hung in the morning. – How is it out, is it wet?

William It's windy, with the last of an autumn sun.

Sarah I bet it rains tomorrow then. Now, I shall sit like a proper lady so's you feel at your ease. I want you to do your best work. You can imagine for yourself the lapdog and the velvet and the little negro feller with the studded silver collar and you can put them in when you get back home. Just get the essence of me for now. (*Pause.*) I'll sit as still as still. (*Pause.*) Like I sat after I done the killings. Ever so peaceful. Not thinking no more. Calm as a duck on a pond. God there is such relief in murder . . .! (*Pause.*) The dogs stop baying in your head. – I ain't alarming you, am I, Mr Hogarth, you seem to have stopped . . .?

William Yes, you are, slightly.

Sarah Why, whatever sort of a person do you think I am?

William You're a murderess.

Sarah Oh, that. I have my better side. Jesus, I wasn't born killing.

Without warning, she gets up, hoists her skirts, and squats over a bucket.

William Oi!

Sarah What?

William What the fuck are you playing at? (*He looks closely.*)

Sarah Won't be a tic.

William That's indecent, a woman piddling in public.

Sarah I don't care.

William That's obscene.

Sarah All done now. (*She resumes her pose at the table.*)

William . . . Haven't you got no shame?

Sarah It's a blank, it's all a blank. Decency, dignity, pride. A sour piss in a rusty bucket. From the moment I picked up the razor. To the moment my feet swing through the air. A blank. Get drawing, then, it's getting dark.

William I hate despair, I really do.

Sarah I ain't despairing. It's just all one to me. This world, it don't change. I just don't fight against it no more. – Here, what you got in that basket?

William That's for later.

Sarah What's for later? Is it me food?

William Do you want your picture taken down or not?

Sarah I want to know why a famous high society painter wants to do a portrait of silly old me.

William Well, I'm recently married, I need the cash.

Sarah Why you bothering with me, then? I haven't got none.

William It's business, that's all. I'm a businessman.

Sarah And I thought you were an artist.

William I'm an artist who likes to eat.

Sarah What've you brung me? What?

William So you *can* be tempted . . . Something in you stirs . . .

Sarah It's me belly, it's going mad!

William Let's finish the sketch first, shall we? Then eat?

Sarah I'm destroyed with hunger, root and branch I wither, look at me droop, me neck'll be slipping out the noose at this rate and you'll be to blame, go on, give us a crust to chew on while you're working.

William No, you wouldn't keep still.

Sarah groans.

I haven't got for ever, have I? It's not as if I can come back next week and re-do your great chomping gob!

Sarah stands.

I'm sorry, I'm sorry –

Sarah goes to a dark corner of the cell.

Where exactly do you think you're off to?

Sarah I can get out of the light, at least.

William But you made your mark on a legal paper. Your consent.

Sarah Don't mean a thing to me. I can't read.

William Look, do you want your place in fucking history or don't you?

Sarah I am about to die, I think I am entitled to a bite to eat!

William (*considers the situation*) Miss . . . 'Sorry' is a remarkable word, isn't it? In the few months I've lived with my wife I've begun to see the value of it. Every little petty quarrel can be sorted. Jane tries to make me see the female point of view. I would have said to ask forgiveness was unmanly. My fists were permanently clenched. My jaw thrust in to any barney. But now I can be meek as a bleeding lamb when the need arises. Give me two more minutes. Please. You did make your cross!

Sarah (*suddenly returns*) Well! Who is this woman who can work such wonders?

William Her father is Sergeant-Painter to the King.

Sarah Oh, married the boss's daughter.

William Don't be so cheeky.

Sarah I see now how you got in with the nobs.

William I did not marry for reasons of commerce. I married for love. However I do have a new series of paintings on view at my house, inspired by some ideas of my wife's, which I've reason to believe may make me a fortune.

Sarah Why've you come here then?

William You are notorious. I think there may be a quick profit in it. I have a lot of debts.

Sarah (*smiles*) . . . As long as people see that I am bad.
I want to be bad. That's how I want to be remembered.
As an insult. A spit in the face. Do me like that.

William nods.

I could kill you for the food, I s'pose . . . But I can't be
bothered. Not after I just had a wash.

They both resume their seats.

William Christ, what a day. (*He draws.*)

Sarah A blunt razor I used to kill the old women. The
widow's memento of her long-dead man. I was that
ravenous, I had ceased to think, and that felt good, you
can think too much when you're starving. I knew that
my mistress's treasure was under her cot. So I bled the
bitch and her bedmate while they slept. (*Laughs.*) Two
stuck pigs in their petticoats. The rage, the urge to eat
crept over me, and I succumbed. The peacefulest
moment I ever have known . . . that second I abandoned
trying to be good. You throw off the wretched, useless
rags you've gone cold in all your life – the common
sense, the reason – throw it to the wind and go naked,
raw, free suddenly . . . Then Mary, the maid, with who
I shared the attic, appeared on the stair, so I had to kill
her too – aren't you done yet?

*William is sitting with his chalk held in mid-air. Then
he scrawls on the bottom of the paper, and is finished.*

William (*quiet*) The two old women, yes, I kind of
understand, I read that they mistreated you . . . but the
maid? Why the maid? Why on earth?

Sarah Shrieked at the blood, soppy cow. I knew that if
I was committing the perfect crime I could scarce afford
to leave a witness.

William . . . Why'd you get caught then?

Sarah Ah. Don't know. I can't explain things. Not in words. I never even managed to sell the damn silver. So hunger follows me down to the lime-pit.

William (*sickened*) Women killing women . . .

Sarah Don't men kill men? – Can I have a look, then?

Wearily, William puts his sketch in front of her. He takes a bottle of beer from the basket and drinks.

William Understand, it's not finished, it's only a rough –

Sarah Me?

William I'll work it up in the studio, oh sod, I hate it the first time they –

Sarah That – is me?

William That is a – preliminary version of you.

Sarah takes out her spoon, polishes it, stares at the picture, stares at her reflection, stares at the picture again.

Sarah It's warped.

William No, the spoon's warped, the spoon distorts –

Sarah That's a good silver spoon! Are you telling me I look like that?

William I'm not completely useless with a stick of chalk.

Sarah Liar!

William What's this, criticism?

Sarah Look at her with the little pout and the sparkle in the corner of her eye. The face is hard but. But! Do I ever sit like that with my damn knees apart? I do not. You give me desire. I have none!

William It's the best I could manage.

Sarah But the whole blasted reason I'm in here in the first place is that I would not whore! And you gone and made me one! Oh, there's plenty of room in the brothels for hungry farm-girls, plenty of quick shillings to be earned in cold and dingy courtyards, but would I descend to it? – no, I had my respect, dullwit I now see myself to be, I lived like a beast but I wouldn't sell *that*!

William My head is throbbing, will you pipe down? I must say in my defence it said in the newspapers that –

Sarah The newspapers are the main reason I have never bothered to learn to read.

William You are described as a laundress.

Sarah Possibly because I am one.

William But you can't make a living as a laundress, can you? Too many people are content to go dirty.

Sarah But I've a right to a reputation like anyone else!

William Look, I'm an artist, an artist must be free to view the world unhindered.

Sarah Why?

William Well, he can't let his subjects dictate to him!

Sarah Why not?

William Christ you're impossible.

Sarah You have made me some creation of your own. Warped what you see sitting here. You assumed. You are a prick. And what's this squiggle at the bottom?

William (*picks up sketch*) That? Oh, that's my signature. So people know it's authentic. (*Explains.*) By me.

Sarah . . . What people?

William The ones who'll come to look when I exhibit the finished painting.

Sarah Where?

William In my house in Covent Garden.

Sarah Never. I want it destroyed.

William Oh, please don't be difficult.

Sarah You got me mad now.

William It's just one bloody thing after another. (*He gathers his things up*.)

Sarah It's not how I want to go down! In the future! I told you, I want to look evil, I feel evil, I got demons in me and where are they in this balls-up? I want to be bad! Through and through! Not fallen angel! Not mildewed rose! Now give it back!

William I am truly sorry, Sarah, but it's mine, I own it, I hold a thing called the copyright you see. I must be going now. I have a pressing appointment. Why don't you help yourself to supper?

He hammers on the door. It's quite dark in the cell now.

Sarah It is my picture. *My* picture. Picture of *me*.

William (*calls*) William Hogarth! Open up!

Sarah (*calm*) Give me my likeness back, you are stealing it, you are taking my soul.

William Sarah . . . Believe me . . . I am so sorry for you.

A horrible wailing noise, the screaming of women, very loud. William clutches at his head. Sarah is still.

Oh . . .! What's that?

Suddenly, from the shadows in the corners of the cell, a number of nightmarish women prisoners emerge and run at William. They clutch at him. He tries to get away, yelling for the Gaoler. All the time this dreadful noise, half-pain, half-laughter. Sarah remains still. The cell door clangs open. The Gaoler stands brandishing his whip. The prisoners, except Sarah, disappear. William runs out with the picture. Sarah falls on the basket and stuffs food into her mouth. She bends over, retching. The Gaoler goes up to her.

Gaoler Here, love, you all right? What's the matter, can't your stomach take it?

Sarah comes up in a swift movement and gets her arm round the Gaoler's neck. Her other hand comes up from the basket with a small knife in it. She slits his throat. He falls and dies.

Sarah Mad I said. Good and mad.

She picks up the Gaoler's bunch of keys. Blackout.

SCENE FOUR

Louisa's lodging. William is asleep, sprawled in a chair, a glass of red wine clutched in his lap and tilting dangerously. Louisa enters, taking off her shawl. She sees him. She groans inwardly. She goes to him and removes his wig from his head. He mutters in his sleep.

William The faces . . . Those faces . . .

Louisa smoothes his cropped hair. She tries to take the glass out of his hand but he won't let go. She kneels in front of him and starts to prise his fingers open. He hangs on so tightly that he wakes up. Seeing Louisa kneeling between his legs, he fears the worst. He leaps away in panic.

What, again? Why can't you leave me alone?

Louisa You were spilling your drink.

William Lou . . .? Louisa? Is it you? Am I awake?

Louisa You were dreaming. Your eyes flicking back and forth beneath the lids. Like a lizard on a pebble.

William Had to come. Couldn't keep away no longer.

Louisa (*sighs*) I've only just knocked off work.

William I've had a pig of a day and all. I've been locked up in Newgate Gaol. I'm doing a print of Sarah Sprackling. (*He has it rolled up in his pocket.*) Plan to have an edition on sale straight after the poor woman's turned off. Get in while she's still fresh in the public imagination – all those crowds who will bay at the hanging – last portrait of the deceased – got to be an earner. So I went down to her dungeon to sketch a design for the engraving and I – I can't describe them, there were these females – they come at me and – their faces! The eyes of them!

Louisa Sit down, Will.

William Feels like the seams are splitting in my head, the skin tight on the skull . . .!

Louisa Let Louisa make it better. (*She cradles his head.*)

William The dreams are bad enough, but waking visions – Christ!

Louisa You can always come to me, you know that.

William I know I can, Lou, I haven't been since the wedding because I –

Louisa Don't have to explain. I understand.

William You do, I know you do.

Pause.

Louisa What's her father like? The Sergeant-Painter?

William Oh, you know who she is, then?

Louisa Well, today was the first time we'd been formally introduced, but I like to keep myself in the picture, yes.

William He's not a bad bloke. We have a natter up the scaffold in St Paul's – he's doing the inside of the dome. We get along all right, but I don't feel I'm in the presence of a fellow-genius, if you know what I mean.

Louisa I know what you mean.

William Not everyone does.

Louisa You're not very happy, dear, are you?

William No I'm not. I know I ought to be. That makes it worse.

Louisa Do you talk to anyone else about it?

William Who for example?

Louisa I don't know. Your friends?

William I haven't got any. I have allies, yes. I don't have friends.

Louisa Well, what about the wife? Can't you confide in her? I thought that's what they were for, baring of the soul and what have you. – No?

William Well, she's young, isn't she, she's a lot younger than you or me, mate, there are things I wouldn't want to burden her with, seeing she's –

Louisa You mean she doesn't know about –

William – a respectable girl from a good background who –

Louisa – how you like your lover to –

William – is deeply in love with me and –

Louisa – piss and shit in your –

William Well of course not, she's my wife! I stood up with her in a bleeding church, I can't ask her to do that! She's a decent, well-bred girl!

Louisa Then presumably she doesn't push her finger in your bottom when you –

William No she doesn't, of course she doesn't, she wouldn't know where to start!

Louisa So we're not completely satisfied with married life . . .?

William Not completely, no!

Louisa Husbands . . . Out there in the world you seem so capable, on top of things, the man in the saddle. But in my dingy bedroom . . . the dark, wild longings . . . stampede of forbidden desires . . . secret needs which you'll only admit –

William Oh, the sex in my dreams!

Louisa – to your whore.

William My erections in the dead of night, dear Christ, like wood, like stone!

Louisa Sometimes I think I understand men. What a mistake that is. A woman will talk to another woman about what gives her pleasure. In this trade, we have to work at it if we want anything for ourselves, so we swap

ideas, trying to . . . remember . . . – But the way you lot
carry on you'd think it was against the law to admit
you'd got your dick up. Probably is, come to think of it.

William Listen, I had this dream –

Louisa You are paying the going rate, are you, Will?

William What, after all these years?

Louisa Yes.

William Jesus. – A little old woman was sucking me off –

Louisa What?

William A little old woman was sucking me off –

Louisa Is this a dream or a nursery rhyme?

William A little old lady, yes, I thought it repulsive at
first but then I got to quite enjoy it. But then it turned –
my whatsit – turned into this kind of brittle, burnt-up
sausage effort, and it broke off in her mouth, all flaky
and crumbly, and she munched away at it until it was
gone. Completely gone! I looked down to see if another
one was growing. At first I had only a bit of a stump.
Fuck, I thought, that's the last time I'm unfaithful. But
then I saw I had a little winkle like a little boy's. It was
growing back. I was turning into some kind of reptile.

Louisa (*laughs*) Perhaps that means you've got a hidden
fear of –

William Don't try and interpret it! I'm not interested in
interpreting it! I'm interested in making it go away! –
Another time I was making love with a man. And I
enjoyed it. In the dream. How am I supposed to explain
all this to Jane? She thinks I'm a great painter. She thinks
I'm an idealist!

Louisa Someone ought to put her straight.

William Well, that's not very friendly.

Louisa And why should I be? Once, way back in the mists of time, you spoke love, whispered love . . .

William (*quiet*) Heat of the moment, darling.

Louisa Thought I was getting out of it . . . New life dawning and all that bunk.

A drum roll, off.

Drummer (*off*) Announcing, tonight at the Haymarket, at prices to suit every pocket –

William Oh God. Harry's play.

Drummer (*off*) A brand new farce by Mr Henry Fielding!

A parade enters and marches round the auditorium. It comprises a Woman Drummer, wearing a fancy bonnet and a flowing skirt, and beating a large drum which sways on her hip; Harry Fielding, separated from the main group; Oliver; Frank; Mrs Needham; and a Man in a comic mask from a masquerade. Louisa and William look out at the procession, but the marchers do not acknowledge them.

Harry A dozen years? Fifteen? How long has the bastard been in power? How long will you stand for it?

William Christ, he's pissed as a rat.

Harry Butterfly-like he flits from crown to crown, with his tongue in the nation's honey!

Louisa He'll get himself arrested.

William It's pathetic. Why can't he face up to reality? Oh, you can make a big noise, let all the world know how radical you are, but then down comes the polished boot of power – prevents you from doing your work!

Louisa You don't have to justify yourself to me.

Harry Listen to this catalogue of corruption: 'First Lord of the Treasury, Mr Walpole. First Lord of the Admiralty, Mr Walpole. Clerk of the Pells, Mr Walpole's son. Customs of London, second son of Mr Walpole.'

William But in my silence I am eloquent you see. I keep on turning it out.

Harry 'Secretary to the Treasury, Mr Walpole's brother. Postmaster General, Mr Walpole's other brother. Secretary to Ireland, another brother of Mr double-damned Walpole! Secretary to the Postmaster General, Mr shit-head Walpole's shag-wit brother-in-law!'

Louisa I told you, it doesn't matter, I'm just a worn-out old jade.

Harry It's disease at the heart of the state!

William No, Louisa, sweetheart, sweetheart, you're much more than that.

Harry He's like a man who poisons a fountain from which everyone must drink!

William Just ignore him, maybe he'll go away.

Harry Are you all deaf? Are you all blind? Or do you just choose not to look?

Louisa Will – is it true you put me in a set of drawings?

William (*defensive*) Everyone always thinks it's *them* I've used for a model.

Louisa I have no illusions. I only wondered. What could I do about it if you had?

William I want you to do what you know that I like.

Louisa I'm right at the bottom and on the way down.

William Fart for me. Go on, Lou. Fart in my face, Lou. Please.

Louisa Oh, Willy . . .

With a sigh Louisa lifts her skirt and William disappears underneath. He is completely hidden. The parade floods onto the stage. Louisa stares straight ahead, sad, unseeing.

Harry It's so dark . . . So bleak . . . How long till dawn?

Harry slumps. Oliver, with bottle in hand, approaches Louisa. He squeezes her breast. She does not respond.

Frank Look at him, he's on the go again already, the dog, and barely an hour since we left your house.

Mrs Needham I had to get him away, Frank. He was killing her. The Viscount's underclothes are caked with blood.

Oliver (*leaves Louisa*) Slack like a fish washed up on the beach. Not sure if one can be bothered.

Drummer Performance begins in fifteen minutes! Good seats still to be had!

They all prepare to move off. The Man in the mask beckons Frank aside, away from Harry.

Man Frank? 'Tis Frank, isn't it? – A word with you.

The Man lowers his mask. It is Walpole. Frank is stunned and frightened.

Frank Sir . . .! Christ.

Louisa senses something.

Louisa What's that?

45

A noise of howling wind. They all look around, uncertain.

Mrs Needham Where?

Suddenly Sarah passes through them at great speed, skipping, dancing across the stage, her knife flashing close to throats and wrists and genitals, a manic Samurai in rags. As quickly as she came, she is gone. A stunned pause. A blackout. Then Mrs Needham screams.

SCENE FIVE

The Hogarths' house. A large bed. Moonlight coming through a window. Flickering shadows from candles in corners. Jane is in her nightclothes, brushing her hair.

Jane Listen, my hair crackles with desire. Why don't you come home? William? I would do now what you wanted in the park. I just must be private, it is my nature. Under my sheets I will do anything, nothing's too dirty for my little man. He will come a million times. His heart will burst from coming.

She looks out of the window.

This is all assuming he gets home within the next five minutes, because otherwise, forget it, I'm not that devoted to the idea.

She gets into bed and blows out her candle.

His hands! I can't rid my thoughts of his hands. Stubby fingers exploring the bones in my back, grimy nails that rasp on silk, slipping, sliding, tumbling down my grassy slopes . . . We lie for hours, twined like rope, like vines, all licks and dribbles, tooth on grape, inner thigh –

Silent and unseen, Sarah enters, and listens.

– on inner thigh, he calls it the Line of Beauty, perpetual spiral of perfect art – we lose our limbs, begin to blend – we become snakes, we slither together – our flicking tongues – oh William –

Sarah knocks against something. Jane sits up.

Will? What are you –

Sarah leaps on to the bed and puts the knife to Jane's throat.

Sarah It's a cheese knife. Recognise it? I fancy it come from your kitchen. Not a murmur now or I take the rind off you. I gather from your whimpering that Willy is not home yet . . .? Then I shall have to wait, shan't I.

Jane What do you want? Money? I deal with the money in this house.

Sarah No, I don't want your money, what would I want with money? Unlike every other beggar in the world, I can not be purchased. My name is Sarah Sprackling.

Jane gasps.

Oh good, someone's heard of me. Your husband came to see me in my cell, down in the sump of human sewage, promising to do my picture.

Jane Didn't he do it?

Sarah Oh, he done it –

Jane He keeps his word.

Sarah – but I don't like it.

Jane Ah.

Sarah I want it back. And if he won't give it I'll kill him.

Jane Do you think that will be absolutely necessary?

A commotion outside in the hallway. The voices of Robert Walpole and a servant.

Servant (*off*) No, sir, you can't go in there, that's my lady's bedroom!

Walpole (*off*) I goes where I damn well wants.

Sarah (*knife*) Hide me.

Jane Under the blankets! There's nowhere else.

Walpole (*off*) Matter of state security, this is.

She hides in the bed next to Jane. Walpole blusters in. Jane pretends to be waking up.

Jane Oh, what a horrid dream . . .

Walpole Mrs Hogarth? Is that you?

Jane Who is it?

Walpole My name is Robert Walpole. Please forgive the indiscretion.

Jane Mr Walpole!

Walpole I must speak to your husband. Where is he?

Jane I don't know. Is he in trouble?

Walpole He will be if he's not careful. You know this prostitute thing? This 'Harlot's Progress'?

Jane Well what do you think? It is on easels in the drawing room.

Walpole There is a rumour, madam, there is a nasty little worm of a rumour wriggling through town. It slithered up to me only this evening, and whispered, through a mouth of slime, that William's planning a follow-up – based on me.

Jane 'Sir Robert Walpole's Progress'?

Walpole It doesn't have that ring, does it, that poetry, it lacks a certain something, do try and put him off. Mrs Hogarth, your husband is a genius. But he is no politician. He is like a child out there in the big world, away from his brush and palette. And I am very conscious of my somewhat battered public image. After all he is beholden to me, on account of the Salver.

Jane Salver? What Salver?

Walpole Hasn't he told you of the bond between us?

Jane He's always said he was an independent artist!

Walpole There is no such thing. Madam, a history lesson, very brief. Perhaps you know that on the demise of the monarch the Great Seal of England has to he redesigned, and it is the honour and duty of the Chancellor of the Exchequer, who by some accident, at the sad death of His Majesty George the First, happened to be me, to convert the old matrix into a memorial silver plate. Now Chancellors of the Exchequer do not as a rule survive the turmoil of an incoming reign, having usually made a fiscal bollocks of the preceding one, but by some fluke it chanced to be me who took delivery of His Majesty George the Second's spanking brand new Seal. Then I sets about getting an engraver for me plate.

Jane A silver engraver.

Walpole Oh, you've a sharp mind for a woman in her nightie. Some vicious satires he had done. The Royal Family scorned! You have no idea how the laughter of the illiterate rings in the halls of St James's. Put your satires in books, by all means, 'Gulliver's Travels', yes yes yes, the Queen enjoys a read – but pictures? Everyone will get it! Worse than bloody plays! Can you imagine –

a picture in every home? Your hubby-to-be was sailing into danger. I could hardly allow such influence to rest in the hands of an artist. I had to help him to the safe high ground of creative endeavour – the oil painting. But how to bung him up there without denting his pride? Blinding flash of inspiration, commissioned him to engrave the Walpole Salver. Lovely job he did, too, old Hercules putting the allegorical screws on Calumny and Envy. A charming introduction into the bosom of polite society, and with it the opportunity to make enough to marry. Always chuffed to help a genius earn a shilling. But he is my man now, and damned if I let him forget it.

> *There is a burst of angry laughter from beneath the bedclothes. Walpole pulls them back to discover Sarah.*

And now I am embarrassed. I thought it might have been the genius. In hiding. Wrath of the gods et cetera et cetera.

Jane My friend is keeping me company whilst my husband is out.

Walpole And devilishly pleasant company, too, if a wee bit of an urchin.

Jane The noise in the hallway . . . she snuggled down . . . I will give my husband your message, Mr Walpole. If that is all? We are very tired.

Walpole Yes. No. (*He drops a purse on the bed.*) Twenty guineas. If you – do it. Now. In front of me. I burn with curiosity, it is something I have always desired to watch. How exactly do you manage to –

Jane How dare you! Please leave at once.

Walpole Very well. Pity.

Walpole picks up his money and turns to leave. Sarah takes Jane's chin in her hand and plants a long, hard kiss on her mouth. Walpole gapes. He takes the money from his pocket again. But when he does so, Sarah abruptly breaks off the kiss and shouts at him.

Sarah What do you think we are?

Walpole A brace of bitches. (*He pockets his money and exits.*)

Sarah More money than I ever seen . . . But they would make bed just like gaol. Have you ever noticed how they love the thought of women having women, but hate to think of men seducing men?

Jane That was the Prime Minister that you just made a fool of.

Sarah Well? Who's he going to tell? The Queen?

They fall into a fit of giggles, unable to contain themselves, letting out their tension. Then Jane stops laughing.

Jane What do you want here? Why don't you just go away and leave us in peace?

A distant bell tolls midnight.

Sarah This is the start of my last day on earth. Why should I leave you in peace?

Her knife-blade glints in the moonlight. Slow fade.

Act Two

SCENE SIX

Drury Lane, the same night. A dog barks in the distance. William stands wrapped in a white sheet in the middle of the road.

William I don't feel powerful. Naked like this. I don't feel like a bloke who takes advantage. Look at me, I stand here in a state of droop. Authority has been sucked and squirted from me like the juice from a Spanish orange. How can I be a tyrant? I am a deliberate weakling. My little foot is on nobody's throat! Look!

Louisa appears at a window above, half-dressed.

Louisa You're a bastard, you're all bastards.

William Men will be bastards, granted, yes, the evidence is overwhelming, but I'm sorry I refuse to accept complicity in every bloody crime of the sex. I am trying hard to rise above it. I have the greatest respect for womankind. I simply happen to have come out without any bloody money.

Louisa You are an exploitative bastard, Will! Like all men you try and turn every defeat to your own advantage.

William Oh, do me a favour! It's you! You, wanting payment for a thing that should be free. Simple human loving, and you present me with a bill. Christ, the avarice of this city . . .

Louisa You can't accept your imperfection, so you unload it on to me. You foul and you defile me, then claim it's you that's abused. It's always the same.

William Do I have to stand here and listen to this shit?

Louisa Looks like it, doesn't it?

William Fucking cunt!

Louisa Then you turn violent. And out comes the language. It's always the same. Viciousness tempered with guilt.

William All I want is my clothes back, Louisa.

Louisa Then pay what you owe.

William Oh come on, darling, I thought we was friends.

Louisa Friends! Is this any way to treat your friends?

William I only asked if I could put it on the slate.

Louisa You can put it on the stove and boil it, chum, before you put it anywhere near me again. (*Exits.*)

William Lou! (*Pause.*) What a slag, honestly . . . A mercenary on the battlefields of desire. Wading through acres of red genitalia, breast bared, hips flying, and hand stretched out for her ruthless shilling. – O pity the poor debtors! They are the wretched of the earth.

Louisa reappears above. He doesn't see her.

All this for a moment's peace, in her, one second of perfection, one fleeting glimpse of beauty, when the universe drops its knickers and puts everything on view . . . simple, simple, it's all so simple . . . Then back comes chaos crashing in. Back to the body and the bartering for warmth. Thinking, does she see this apparition too – or is she, as seems highly likely, conning?

Louisa You are so self-important, William Hogarth, so puffed up, I don't know how you survive the sheer ordinariness of life, never mind draw it. 'One second of perfection'! Talk about seeing things from a male point of view! You have to learn not to piss on your mates. You can't just use people for your own purposes and then abandon them.

William I never abandoned no one. – I've come back, haven't I?

Louisa You drive me round the twist, you do! You drive me bloody barmy! I should have shopped you to your pure-arsed wife.

William Yeh, all right, but what about my clothes?

Louisa Might get a few bob for them, I suppose. I don't want you to freeze to death, however –

William You're right, it's bitter, open the door.

Louisa – so you can have this back, it's no fucking use to me.

She throws his wig out. It wafts to the ground.
William puts it on his head and strides about, huffing.

William Oh, thank you very much, my precious! Thank you very, very much! At least now I can walk the streets with dignity! At least I won't be taken for a twat!

Louisa Good night. (*Exits.*)

William seethes. Then he sniffs and wipes his nose on the sheet. Then he seethes again.

William I have a sword, you know. Gentleman of leisure I may not be but I have bought myself a blade – saved for it for bloody years and never used the fucker! Shall I try it on your flaccid skin for sharpness?

Unseen, Harry enters, drunk, with bottle. He watches William from a distance.

Yes, I like the thought! I shall chamfer my initials on your droopy old tits, and on your bum engrave the crosshatch of my vengeance! You have gone too bloody far my girl.

He turns to leave and sees Harry.

Wotcher, Harry.

Harry Hello, Will.

William Yes, well . . .

Harry You wouldn't, would you?

William What?

Harry All that carving and slashing.

William (*jaw thrust out*) I might.

Harry Seriously?

William I might!

Harry Why?

William She done me a mischief.

Harry I see. Well, we've all got it in us.

William She nicked my clothes!

Harry And for that, you want to cut her up?

William Fucking do, mate. Fucking make me feel a fucking lot better.

Pause. Harry watches him. He breaks.

Of course I don't, she's a friend of mine, what do you think I am, a maniac?

Harry Why'd you say it, then?

William I didn't bloody mean it, did I!

Harry It's easy to over-react. After you've hired a woman. One wrong word and you could kill. You've been turfed out, have you?

William All because I forgot to bring my money with me. I ask you.

Harry Will, you have never been known to forget your money. The precise whereabouts and condition of your purse is invariably the thought uppermost in your mind.

William Yes, well, thing is, I'm skint.

Harry Then why go to a tart? It's asking for trouble.

William . . . I'm in love.

Harry How does it feel?

William It hurts.

Harry The heart will ache, it is traditional.

William Not the heart. My balls.

Harry Have you tried explaining your feelings to the object of your affections? (*He indicates the house behind.*)

William What? – No, no, no, I'm not in love with her! She's a prostitute! Christ!

Harry Then who – ?

William Why, I'm in love with my wife, of course!

Harry Sorry, my mistake.

William I fucking worship her, Harry. She is my life. The blood in my veins.

Harry Forgive my abject stupidity, will you, it is the alcohol has paralysed my brains, but just tell me why in that case you come down Drury Lane of a midnight?

William I want my wife to respect me. I have these impulses, you see, and I – oh, fuck, what's it got to do with you? (*He turns away. He turns back.*) Jane has certain expectations of me, right? Naturally I want to live up to them.

Harry But you sometimes need a break from being perfect.

William Yes! Need relief. Any man would.

Harry And, er –

William Louisa, yes –

Harry Does a very good job I bet.

William Hmm. – Here, how did you get on at Mrs Needham's?

Harry I don't want to talk about it. Change the subject.

Pause. They sit drinking in the gutter. Suddenly Harry breaks down.

Oh, Will, the bad taste of this town . . .

William It's as old as the wind. The disappointment after.

Harry It's not disappointment, I was not disappointed! But how could I enjoy it? I, a man of letters? A poet, dipped in that pot of flesh? Oh I got so angry with myself! The things I made the creature do . . . The worst of it all was she took it all for normal. Peggy. My bollocks adrift in her oceans of fat . . . Her weak eyes blank like bedsheets . . .

William Don't get upset.

Harry Always been in love before. Always been passionate. Union of spirits. This was like coming in a corpse.

William Harry, it's not important.

Harry (*snuffles*) To me it is, I think it's important to admit, to recognise, what we are capable of. Because it's so alarming.

William Look, will you please not cry, I can't stand to see a man cry. It's a tough old life I know, but . . . (*gently*) Harry . . .

> *William tries to comfort Harry without actually touching him. He offers him the bottle.*

Harry We alter the world around us but we never change ourselves inside. We hear the first rumbles of industrial progress but what will it bring us? Will it make us happy? Or will we sink deeper and deeper into the web of our own stupidity? Look at the people we allow to govern us, for God's sake! Are they working for the common good?

William Well, nobody's perfect.

Harry But you can't just leave it at that!

William I love human beings for their failures. It's the only way I can live with myself.

Harry Why won't you listen to what I'm bloody saying?

William Because you go in so hard. Everything you do is an act of aggression. Art should also celebrate. Or it does not tell the truth.

Harry No, no, it should abuse, it should insult, the audience should be shocked, disturbed, and made to think again!

William Don't be a berk. They love to be shocked! They love it! They take it as proof of their own broadminded-ness! It doesn't alter a bleeding thing. You have to work gently, cleverly, bit by bit . . .

Harry No, it's just that I'm not good enough. Not hard enough. A truly oppositional ideal will outrage the most unshockable of palates.

William Oh fucking hell.

Harry I have not found it. I make too many jokes. This evening they laughed and laughed. The bastards.

William . . . Well, it was a comedy, wasn't it?

Harry England in the 1730s? A comedy?

William But Christ, if it's *funny* –

Harry Well of course it's funny, you've got to mock or you might as well curl up and die! But satire is too sugary, too easy to swallow. I dream of writing something where the laughs turn into tears. Where the wit is sharp like a mouthful of lemon. The truth is not a joke. It's dark. The only light is love, the only thing that redeems us, salvages us from the world we have made. And what do we do? We betray it.

William But what do you want? People to suddenly metamorphose overnight into some better kind of being?

Harry Less than a hundred years ago these same people executed the King! Never forget that. Nothing is impossible.

William But there's no point swimming against the tide! It's daft! What I'm gonna do is, I'm gonna do a set of prints that'll be dirt cheap to buy, right, I mean fuck, I don't care if you wrap your fish in them, but what I'm thinking of Harry is this: they'll infiltrate. My modern moral subjects. They'll sneak into peoples' homes – ordinary people – and creep up on to the walls and they'll hang over the bedsteads and they'll niggle. They'll take on the old prejudices and they'll worry them by the throat . . . they won't sicken, but they'll nag . . .

Harry In an amusing sort of way.

William In an amusing sort of way.

Harry You just want the loot.

William I've gone so long without it, I do have rather a lust for the stuff.

Harry As an artist, William, you're a coward. You will not point your finger.

William To point your finger, Henry, you must first remove it from your arse. I admire what you write but you talk like a turd. The simple truth is, Walpole exists. He is power. I believe in the reality of power. It is a tangible thing. If power chooses to censor, then censor it will. He'll have you by the nuts, mate. You want to keep an eye on the little shrinkers.

Harry Don't patronise me. I thought you were ambitious.

William I am ambitious.

Harry But not for change. For yourself, but not for others. Not to bring down Walpole.

William Bring down this Walpole, up pops another Walpole.

Harry It's almost as if the satirist needs a sick society . . . has a vested interest in preserving it . . . so you can feed off it . . . suck its blood . . .

William I just want to survive. That is my ambition. Have another drink.

Harry No. No more drinks.

A sedan chair with drawn curtains is carried on by two chairmen. They set it down and open it up. Walpole steps out.

Walpole Mr Fielding. Mr Hogarth. In fancy dress.
Shared bottle of gin. Jolly good.

William Servant sir.

Harry Sir.

Walpole So glad I've managed to find you at last,
William. I have just paid a courtesy call on your
charming wife. I didn't know she was a lesbian.

William She's not.

Walpole She's not, she's not, what am I saying, how
could she possibly be? Married to a chap like yourself.
She must just have been experimenting. We all do when
we are young. But when we grow up we find we want to
settle down. Oh, we do, Henry, we do. We discover that
what we want most, what gives us the greatest pleasure
and the greatest freedom to enjoy it, is stability. The ship
of state on an even keel. No danger to the cargo. Oh,
heaving and rolling with the natural swell, perhaps, but
the captain in full command. By some strange quirk of
fate I have ended up at the helm, lashed to the wheel of
this glorious boat. And I have steered her on to a course
of peace and prosperity. Because peace is the perfect
condition for trade, and trade will make us rich, and rich
is what we want to be, correct? Fifty thousand men slain
this year on the fields of Europe, and not one of them
English! How proud I am of that. (*Pause.*) Or would you
prefer a hunting metaphor? Gentlemen? I am a hunting
man. Across the stubbly fields of Norfolk, I hunt, foxes
or women, don't mind which. Backside raw in the
saddle, horse at a furious gallop, naked lady making for
the woods, my idea of heaven. However it would be
positively no trouble at all to me to set my hounds on
the scent of meddlesome artists. Wherever you go, into
what ditch, behind what copse, through what fields of

swaying barley I will hunt you down and dip my finger in your blood and smear it in triumph on the nearest child's face. (*to Harry*) Metaphorically speaking, of course, this is all part of the same extended conceit, as I'm sure you recognise. I have some literary aspirations myself, you see.

Harry I wouldn't count on overnight success if I were you.

Walpole Success may not be what I'm after, boy. – I believe it will one day become the mark of a cultured society, that its artistic members realise when they have gone too far, and voluntarily apply the curb. It is a struggle, self-restraint, dear me yes – but think of the rewards.

Harry What are they exactly?

Walpole Well, I shan't have to raid your theatre and charge all the actors under the vagrancy laws, as I did shortly after the final curtain this evening.

Harry Oh, not again! Why?

Walpole The play was offensive. Public sensibilities were offended.

Harry How do you know? You weren't even there!

Walpole I will pass over the unkind satirical jibes at myself, for the age cries out for satire, they say. Which must mean the age is pretty damn sure of itself. But I hear, sir, that you are preparing yet another scurrilous item.

Harry It's going to be called *The Historical Register* – a political calendar of the year – all four seasons of your mould and decay.

Walpole Don't proceed with it. Or I shall be forced to introduce a censor's office.

Harry You can't.

Walpole I was thinking of giving the job to the Lord Chamberlain.

Harry You can't!

William Don't push your luck, mate.

Harry Parliament will never approve it!

Walpole Shut up. (*to William*) You're toying with the idea of another 'Progress' series, are you?

William I think you must be misinformed.

Walpole Good, I don't like progress, I like things as they are.

Harry I should like to know your constitutional –

Walpole Will you be quiet.

Harry This is a free country, sir! I am a freeborn Englishman, and I have a right to speak!

Walpole Oh, do grow up, Henry.

Harry Go on, then! Do it! Do it, if you dare!

Walpole You've gone all red.

Harry I was just thinking, when you burn your boats, what a bloody good fire it makes! (*Exits, angrily.*)

William (*defending Harry*) He's had a bad day.

Walpole Why? The play was a triumph. Why are you chaps so perverse? (*Pause. He sits and drinks from the gin bottle.*) My houses are stuffed full of art, you know. It's such a damned good investment. I got a Titian last year for two pounds ten. It's already worth double that. I love art, I love it more than all my other property, they're so neat and compact, those rectangles of wealth.

But you have to win through to posterity, William, or you are worth nothing. You have to exist in the future, and for that you have to function in the present. I believe you have a yearning for an amendment to the Copyright Act. To apply it to the visual arts.

William . . . If I am to live.

Walpole See what I can do. Are you going home to Janey looking like that? – I'm not surprised she's bent.

Walpole gets back into his sedan chair and is carried off. William wraps the sheet tightly about him. He clutches at his head. Pause. The sedan chair returns. It is set down in front of him. Nothing happens.

William Was there something we forgot?

The chair opens and out steps Louisa. She is in tattered rags, and ravaged by an indescribably disgusting disease. The flesh hangs off her in strips. Her face is horribly disfigured. Her hands drip green slime.

Louisa Yes, Willy, we forgot about the pox, didn't we?

William (*in terror*) Louisa!

William tries to run but, as in a dream, his feet are like lead. Louisa reaches a slimy hand under his sheet and grabs his private parts.
 Blackout.

SCENE SEVEN

An apartment in a palace. A large, ornate bed. A woman lies in it. Walpole, half-dressed, sits at a nearby table, writing. He screws up a sheet of paper and throws it away.

Walpole It's not as easy as I thought. The costume changes are a bugger. I need the heroine half-naked for the climax, so I've got to find a reason to get her off-stage and then I've got to find another reason to get her on-stage again. Give me the House of Commons any day. (*He looks to the woman.*) I know it won't be a popular law. But hang me a booming economy seems to breed subversion more than an age of hardship. It is precisely the popularity of the playhouses that renders them such a threat. Oh, I long to bring in a sensible, modern system, in which it is simply made plain to these chaps that it's in their own interests to toe the Lord Chamberlain's line . . . A hint here . . . A whisper there . . . Get the Artistic Director in for a cup of tea, wave a small cheque in his face . . . Just nudge the idea in. Where did the thinking spring from, that art must necessarily equal trouble? I am pacific, it is my nature, I believe with all my heart that what we need for the growth of the nation is peace. I don't like trouble and nor do the people. We like a quiet life and a decent dinner and why can't these toe-rags accept it? – Ah! Good! (*He writes fast.*) Get your costume off, you difficult old bag.

The woman in the bed is Queen Caroline.

Queen (*German accent*) I do not remember saying you could get up and work.

Walpole Oh, I thought we had done.

Queen Undress.

Walpole It's a critical scene!

Queen Undress!

Walpole Yes, your Majesty.

Queen We don't approve of censoring the people's entertainment. It's not the kind of thing we're used to in this country. It seems not to accord with our sense of what is England.

Walpole It won't be censorship, not outright censorship, I'd never get anyone to vote for that – just a system of licensing, a regulating hand on the temperamental shoulder. The actual dirty work of censoring will be done by the artists themselves. That's the beauty of it.

Queen So every play must get a licence. Then can they be performed?

Walpole But of course! If they can get a licence.

Queen Might I suggest, Minister, that this proposal of yours contains an element of – malice?

Walpole History's built on the lowest of motives.

Queen And every man has his price. I know your pet remarks. You are taking an unconscionably long time with your trousers. When we give a royal command we expect you to perform. Quick!

Walpole Yes, your Majesty. I'm hurrying up.

Queen I want to gaze upon your flesh, your flabby, blotchy flesh, your sinews, the slack pink muscle of government.

Walpole It is not something I normally shows to the world, ma'am.

Queen It is not elegant. Not beautiful. Not art.

Walpole I can go if the mood has left you –

Queen I fully intend to take my pleasure. To see the user used.

Walpole Caroline . . .

Queen What your political opponents are saying, of course, is that the time is ripe for expansion, we have the wealth, we have the resources, the army and the navy, we could thrust across the globe in the search for brand-new markets. Our merchant class has aspirations, Robin. There is a spirit of adventure in the land, I smell it. It hints that you are finished. Unless someone protects you.

Walpole Your Majesty's nostril is ever acute. But what about the King?

Queen I am the reign. Through my husband I exercise power. Let him march up and down with his soldiers. That leaves me free to concentrate on more important matters, such as the religious life of the state. As you may have observed, the people are morally lax. We need some tough new bishops.

Walpole Oh, we do, we do.

Queen I wish to appoint one. Robertson.

Walpole What!

Queen An excellent man. High church but with rationalist tendencies.

Walpole I know a better bet for a mitre – a chaplain who's demonstrated that the plays of our times offend against fourteen hundred texts in the Bible.

Queen Don't try to manipulate me. I have discussed the calculus with Leibnitz and astronomy with Newton. I am concerned with serious theology, not the sad boasts of the village idiot.

Walpole But Robertson will vote against me in the Lords! The balance of power will be upset!

Queen (*a smile*) Dear me. That sounds a terribly tenuous system. How will you get your Licensing Act through?

Walpole I'm working on a scheme, don't worry. (*He indicates his writing.*)

Queen But then you will need your Royal Assent.

Walpole . . . The price of which is a Bishop, is it? This is going to cost me a fortune in the long run. For that, will you also consider a little bit of business regarding the laws of copyright, which I beg leave to introduce?

Queen All I wish you to introduce at this moment, Prime Minister, is your tongue, your big, fat, talkative tongue.

Walpole It seems only fair and logical to me that, as we legislate to clarify the ownership of all our other products, so we should do the same for art.

Queen All right, all right! But why have you still your woollens on? Did I not say naked? Naked and kneeling before your Queen?

Walpole Majesty. (*Reluctantly he continues undressing.*)

Queen Wait. I have changed my mind.

He groans.

The carnal urge has suddenly left me. I think I'd sooner talk to the Archbishop. You may go.

Walpole starts to dress.

Go! At once! Audience over!

Walpole (*bowing*) Your humble servant, madam.

Humiliated, Walpole scoops up his clothing and his papers and bows his way out. Pause. Then the Queen collapses in a fit of hysterical laughter.

SCENE EIGHT

A pillory. Still the same night. In the stocks stands Mrs Needham. Egg, rotten fruit, and blood drip from her face.

Mrs Needham God is good. (*Pause.*) God is just. (*Pause.*) He is, he is! Prostitution is a wicked trade, I knew he wouldn't like it. But this sinner will hang on her cross, O merciful Father, until she hears your voice call down from heaven in forgiveness, Needham, the Bawd, you have suffered enough, pucker your lips on the soles of my feet, we shall enter Jerusalem together. I wish to announce my retirement from business. I have some capital, Lord, not as much as I'd hoped for given my talents – oh, I was a goer in my time, I could take ten bob with my legs together – but that was when I free-lanced. Once you become an employer your overheads hit the roof . . . And the paperwork!

> *Behind her, William comes on out of the dark. He still wears only sheet and wig. He creeps on furtively, shaking with cold.*

But if I survive the night, Christ Jesus, I will give my life and my savings to your mission on earth. Let me be your handmaiden, let me be your scourge in the city of sin. For I know the guilty. I can name names. You will see some blushing faces I promise you! – Who's there?

> *William's behind her. She can't turn round.*

Who is it? Come where I can see you. I smell you! You reek of gin.

> *William just stands there.*

Don't hurt me, don't harm me, I haven't done anything awful, but a mob of screaming puritans got hold of me

69

tonight, priests and thin women, I don't mind, allow them their outrage, there was a wave of morality burst upon us after Mr Walpole's constables had raided that theatre. And they dragged me to the Justice and he slammed me in the stocks! And then the apprentice boys pushed stones in their rotten tomatoes, and pelted me half to death! If you would wipe my face . . .? Be kind to me . . .? I'm cut in a thousand places . . . by the fruit of the self-righteous . . .

William puts a hand on her.

Oh! Mister! Your hand on my rump . . . I have the hindquarters of a horse, haven't I? I once heard of a gentleman who said England was a paradise for women, and hell for horses. Well he can take me out for a canter any old time. Little dig in the flanks and I'm off, mate. Oh, don't abuse me, don't, I feel so vulnerable, I'm dripping blood and egg-yolk, I can see it on the ground, like a little kiddie's painting of the sun.

William, from behind, pulls off the woman's skirt and puts it round himself.

Don't please! I'm dry! I'll scrape! A whore can be raped, you know, just as a bankrupt can be swindled. Lord Jesus protect me . . .

William pulls off her blouse and puts that on.

Do I know you? Is that it? Are you someone I have had? Some complainer out of all the happy thousands, bent on getting it for nothing? Will you speak to me, you pervert!

William tries on her shoes. They fit.

I will die of freezing . . . I'll be gone by dawn . . . But God will punish you. God will burn your lecher's eyes out. He will tear at your heart with his fingernails. God's fingernails, matey, think of that! God's rasping scratching omnipresent nails!

William, now dressed, drapes the sheet over the woman's head, and leaves.

Wanker! Pass by on the other side, then! Go on! Pass by! I can hear you shuffling away . . . Devil!

He is gone. Pause. Slowly her head droops.

Lord have mercy on me. Christ have mercy on me. Lord have mercy on me. Christ have mercy on me.

Fade out.

SCENE NINE

William's studio. Canvases stacked against the walls. Easels. Clutter. Enter Jane, with Sarah, who is holding a knife to her back. Sarah motions Jane to stay still. She herself wanders round looking at pictures with a great curiosity.

Sarah Has he ever painted you?

Jane No.

Sarah Why not? It's very odd. You'd think he'd want to paint his wife. Specially if she looked as clean and nice as you do.

Jane Oh, I'm very plain.

Sarah You're prettier than me.

Jane You have more character.

Sarah But no money to pay.

Jane Well, he had a commission to do you, didn't he?

Sarah Oh? Who from?

Jane How should I know? I don't keep up with all his business dealings.

Sarah I thought you said you handled the money . . .?

Pause. Sarah finds William's sword, hanging in its scabbard over the corner of a painting. She takes it out. She puts the knife aside. She examines the gleaming sword with pleasure.

You gone very quiet. I kill with delight, lady. That's what I'm like. It's how I make my mark. (*Pause.*) I thought, do one intelligent thing before I die. Get my future back. I was surprised I could be moved like that. I thought I was rock, a wall of granite, I thought I was the cliff that the waves bash against but never get inside of. But suddenly I was awash with it. Indignation. Well, shite, the cheek of it, to take my face and – ! (*Pause.*) Once you've made the big decision all the others make themselves. Long time since I've seen the smoky London streets. The fug whirled and eddied round me as I ran, my feet asplash in rivulets of piss, my neck and buttocks clenched expecting knife or fist or hammer. I came the back way. Through the shadows to Covent Garden. Now tell me truly why he's never painted you.

Jane . . . I don't want to be painted.

Sarah You do.

Jane I don't! Time and again I refuse him permission. I won't let him put me in that role, the role of the subject. I am not his subject, I am his lover and his wife, and I will never let him do my portrait, I will never surrender up that kind of power.

Sarah God, I wish I had your brain.

Jane You could have, I'll tutor you, I'll discover you to yourself, only put the sword away, Sarah, will you?

Sarah You been tutoring your husband, too, from what he says.

Jane Oh? What does he say?

Sarah He says you've got him thinking like a woman now. It all went over my head, rather.

Jane I simply want to make him think about his side of the bargain. The contract of marriage.

Sarah Why?

Jane Because I want it to last, I suppose.

Sarah Why?

Jane Because I love him. For all his faults. Heaven knows why I'm telling this to you. You want to murder him.

Sarah Whatever gave you that idea? (*Pause.*) How does he expect to put the whole of me, all my doings, all my dreams and disappointments in a few small dollops of paint? He done me in a prison in a city full of smoke. That's not me. That's not how I think of me. I think of me out in the open. Flat on my back in a hayrick, beneath a mackerel sky, dreaming of all the treats I'll have when I comes up to town . . . Ambition is a curse!

Jane It's not.

Sarah A fucking bane, ambition! A noose around your neck, that constant, constant yearning for more. Look at me for an example. Product of impossible desires.

Jane Oh, don't say that. Think of what William's achieved!

Sarah . . . Tell us yours then.

Sarah is leafing through bundles of drawings.

Jane It's not my place to have ambition. What could I do with it if I had it? I want my husband to get on. He is my voice, through him I make my presence felt. He is the one with the power. But I can tug him in certain directions, I can tweak his pencil as it skims across the paper. I've made him think a lot harder about the way he portrays women, for example. You find me there in the pictures, my brain in his brushstrokes . . .

Sarah I couldn't do it.

Jane Why, are you too proud?

Sarah No, I ain't proud.

Jane Yes, you are, I think.

Sarah I cut and slashed my pride. I butchered it. (*Pause.*) The difference is, that you believe in a time to come. Because you love. I don't. I don't know what it's like.

Jane It's a mixture . . . of being amazed and appalled by someone. Some of his tender sentiments amaze me. Whereas some of his habits in the toilet can be truly upsetting. It's a fine balance. If you're more amazed than appalled, you're probably in love. You're also in trouble, because you can be –

Sarah Used.

Jane Yes. Luckily William's too naive to sense when he might have me under his thumb.

Sarah I've got a feeling you ought to have a look at these.

Sarah shows Jane a series of drawings.

Jane Ugh, disgusting!

Sarah Mucky, yes.

Jane That's pornographic!

Sarah That's you.

Jane What?

Sarah That's you, that's a drawing of you. With a man's knob in your mouth.

Jane And another in –

Sarah He's got an imagination, hasn't he?

Jane Oh God!

Sarah He's done your portrait a hundred times.

Jane (*for the first time her composure cracks*) Oh my God! I'm going to be sick. – No I'm not, I'm going to kill him. Is that what he would like me to do? Look, there is pain on my face! My lover dreams of me degraded! Ugh! Look at that! And that! And that! Horrible, horrible man!

> *She tears up the drawings, ripping at them in fury, stamping on them, flinging them round the room. Sarah watches calmly. Jane eventually quietens down.*

How sad his life must be.

SCENE TEN

William makes his way through London, dressed in skirt, blouse, high-heeled shoes and wig. From the shadows comes a low wolf-whistle. William stops, frightened. From another corner comes a man's laugh.
William picks up his skirts and runs.

SCENE ELEVEN

The studio. William enters.

William Made it. Christ what a night.

He gets a drink, sits in his favourite chair and shuts his eyes. Sarah emerges from hiding and stands in front of him, holding the sword. He sees her.

Oh, fuck! Don't you ever give up? And that's my sword! (*An explanation comes to him.*) I'm asleep. It's all right. (*He sits down again.*)

Sarah I broke out of prison.

William (*unimpressed*) Well done.

Sarah I come for my picture.

William Don't be a berk, I'm not handing over valuable pictures to a wisp of bleeding ectoplasm, am I.

Sarah pricks him with the sword.

Bitch! You're real! Christ!

Jane emerges from a hiding place.

Jane Yes, William, she is completely real.

William Jane!

Jane (*stares at him*) Why are you dressed like that?

William . . . I've suddenly gone very muzzy in the head, perhaps I better go and have a lie down.

Sarah (*sword*) Stay there!

William (*to Sarah*) You keep out of this, it's purely domestic, this. (*to Jane*) It's a practical joke.

Jane You rotten lying pig!

William Please, please don't be difficult, darling, I've had such a terrible day.

Jane Why not? Why not be difficult?

Sarah Chop his knackers off.

William Oh, leave it out.

Jane Where have you been, then?

William I was with the lads, I ran into some of the lads, and I'd forgotten it was the first night of Harry's play, and they dragged me along and I admit we had one or two beers, I'm not perfect, I have my weak points and the booze is one of them, yes, anyway it was a huge success you ask anybody and we all ended up in the actresses' dressing-room, Harry insisted we all went backstage, because there was a – bit of a party, and I was prevailed upon to do a comic turn in female attire, that's another thing I've not told you about, but Jane we haven't been married that long, I'm renowned for this number I do in a frock, and then do you know what? The theatre was raided by Walpole's men and you don't believe a bloody word of this do you?

Sarah We found your drawings.

William Drawings, what drawings, the place is full of drawings – ?

Jane Drawings of me.

William I've never done a drawing of you, you don't allow it! (*Pause.*) Ah. Those drawings.

Jane Well? What have you got to say about them?

William . . . I think I got the proportions of your legs all wrong, but then I was working from –

Jane I hate you!

Sarah Chop his nuts off, I say.

William No!

Jane But those pictures, Will!

William I'm sorry!

Jane Of me in the sexual act!

William God, I'm sorry, I don't know what got into me, I'm very very sorry.

Jane Not good enough!

William Jane . . .!

Jane Not good enough! Not nearly! I devote my life to you. And how do you repay me? With ridicule and filth. I had somehow got this cranky notion that you were a sensitive man. But you're not, are you, you're just ordinary, this is what saddens me, you're just like all the rest!

William Who says? What bum-hole smears my honour?

Jane Sir Robert Walpole. Told us a tale. About a silver plate.

William Ah . . . well . . . Have faith in me, Janey, I may have done some daft things, but sweetheart, it's the same old Will under all his baggage.

Jane That's what I'm worried about. Whatever possessed you to do those awful drawings?

William Look, it's the pressure, that's what it is . . . I sit at my table and I fiddle with my charcoal and my mind is off and away, I don't even realise I'm doing it, there are nightmare things that I have got caged up, hairy, growling, they scrabble at the skin of me, and sometimes

slither out. Have you noticed there is that quality of
horror in even my gentlest work? How did it get there?
What is there in me that I cannot seem to tame? I'm
quite a nice bloke really! I'm only trying to make my
way in the world. And I do it all for you. Everything,
for you.

Jane (*softly*) You silly little fool, why do you always
have to learn the hard way? Fail! For heaven's sake, fail!
Be a disaster! Be a pauper! I wouldn't love you any the
less.

> *They gaze into each others' eyes. Sarah, whose
> presence they have forgotten, slips the sword up under
> William's skirt. He stands on tiptoe.*

Sarah (*quietly*) Listen, you pair of lovebirds, I want my
pissing shitting picture back and by fuck I want it now.

William . . . I'm afraid I've got some rather bad news.

Sarah What?

William I ain't got it.

Jane Where is it?

William I dropped it off at the printer's.

Sarah We'll go and get it.

William He'll he closed.

Sarah We'll get the key.

William I don't know where he lives, I'm sorry!

Sarah Why did you take it to a printer's?

William Oh, I've got someone working on the plate.

Sarah What's the plate?

William To make the copies.

Sarah Copies . . .? One picture, I thought. One painting, to hang in a rich man's study, and stare down relentless with loathing and hate, a curse on every generation! But no, not good enough for Mr Up-to-the-minute, you'd have me printed on a thousand sheets of paper, clogging up the gutters, plugging cracks in tavern walls, eat and sleep and crapped on, by them that think they're good . . .? And I'll be on sale at me execution, will I, with me last words in print before I've said 'em?

William I am an artist. I exist to put the world in pictures.

Sarah Well you're not putting me. Come on, we're off to this printer's.

William We can't get in!

Sarah We'll kick down the door!

William One small problem. I never went to the printer's.

Jane You never went to the theatre, either, did you?

William No, I . . . We . . . We went to a gambling club.

Jane Oh, William!

William I gambled away my money, my clothes – and your picture.

Sarah Oh, shite! Who to?

William A man I didn't know – with a long hooked nose and a limp.

Sarah You are fucking lying, aren't you! Right!

William I think I'll be able to win it back tomorrow, I'm feeling very lucky!

Jane Don't hurt him, Sarah, please!

Sarah raises the sword to strike William. He dodges away. Jane tries to hold Sarah's arm. At that moment Louisa enters, with a crash.

William Lou! What do you want?

Louisa I changed my mind.

She throws his clothes down in the middle of the room.

Sarah Who are you?

Jane She's a common prostitute.

William – Who does a bit of laundry on the side!

Jane Is that where you've spent the evening? Up this woman's skirts?

William Wait! Give me a chance to think!

Sarah Why've you come here?

Louisa I was invited.

Jane No you weren't.

Louisa My turn, I thought, to paint a picture. A very private portrait. Of Willy and his ways.

William Oh, no.

Sarah What, has he done you too?

Louisa I can't be sure, I never seen them. – You robbing him, are you?

Sarah No, he's robbing me.

Louisa Up and up he goes. I watch from in the gutter. Daubing paint on canvas with his fingers like a kid smearing shit on walls. And they buy it! They pay money for it! In the salons and soirées of the West End, they dip into the hot-pot of his brains, and what do they find? Pictures of a prostitute. Dying of the clap.

Jane He's just a man. You have to make allowances.

Louisa Fine, in that case I can tell you how he likes to lie down on the floor and have me stand over him heaving and straining and –

Jane Stop it! Stop it! Why are you doing this?

Louisa Because I loved him. Once.

Jane (*shock*) You? Why?

Louisa Well – why do you?

William (*glum*) Why does anybody?

Sarah Belt up.

Jane Be quiet.

Louisa Shut your fucking trap.

William With a bit of luck I'm imagining all this.

Louisa But can you distinguish any more? Between pencil lines and people? You pin us like moths to your paper and you sit and watch us squirm.

Sarah That's right, he does, that's right.

Louisa I'm finished, Will. I'm all wore out. Unsellable. Just wanted you to see.

Sarah I know how you feel. He done one of me and all.

Jane (*to Louisa*) Please go. I think you've said enough.

Sarah Fucking shut up, you, we're talking about art.

Louisa (*to Jane*) How can you stick with him? Despite everything you know?

Jane He is my husband. He loves me.

Louisa What makes you think he won't betray you? To get another step up that bleeding ladder he's got lodged in his head?

Sarah (*to Louisa*) Tell me how he done you, the composition and that.

Louisa (*to Jane*) We drag ourselves down, do you know that, not him, not anyone, *us*. Love? I shit on love. Daily.

Sarah (*urgent*) Tell me how he done you!

Louisa (*weary*) What difference does it make?

Sarah He sat me at a table. In a beam of light from the window. The shadows falling on the filth and straw. He were going to put my gaoler in but then he said he wouldn't. Good job too 'cause I've killed him. (*Laughs.*) Wouldn't look too bright, would it? Picture of me in a prison cell I've just escaped from being guarded by a bloke I've just done up.

Louisa Oh my God . . . You're Sarah Sprackling, are you?

Sarah That's right.

Louisa Then – this is meant to be you?

Louisa produces the sketch of Sarah and unrolls it.

Sarah Me picture!

Louisa I've been staring and staring, thinking . . . how does she feel?

Sarah Give it!

William No!

Sarah I said give it!

William Don't, Lou, please!

Jane Look out!

Sarah lunges for the picture and spears it on the point of her sword.

Sarah Now I have you, I have you at last. My little darling. Now I have a hold of you. Tried to go off on your own, din't you? Tried to give me the slip. (*She holds the paper to a candle flame.*) Oh, doesn't that look pretty. That pretty blushing face. Burn you whore! And don't never desert me again.

The picture burns.

I got this fantastical feeling running up and down my backbone like a ball of lightning, whoosh. Quiver of sleeping flesh come suddenly to life. I set out to do a thing and I done it. What a fucking wonderful feeling.

The picture is gone. She lays down the sword.

All done now.

Jane Then please – go.

Sarah Yes. Be dawn soon. Be time soon.

Louisa What way are you walking?

Sarah East. Back to Newgate.

Louisa To the hangman?

Sarah Coming with me? Keep me company?

Louisa Why don't you run for it? Go on, run for it, run free, take off across Islington Fields and vanish . . . Sleep by day and run by night . . . Change your identity, become someone else . . .

Sarah I am just barely smart enough to be me, what chance have I got of becoming someone else?

Louisa But surely you don't want to die?

Sarah Yes, I do. Who wants to live like this?

Louisa I'm confused, I don't understand – why?

Sarah . . . Tooth of a hanged person supposed to be a love potion, ain't it. Some unloved woman will pluck my yellow stumps. Grind them in some farmboy's porridge. And I hope she gets some pleasure from it, too. Little snatch of warmth in the cold time, just now, aching for the sun after the chaos of the night . . . Will you do me a favour?

Louisa I might. What?

Sarah Come along the road and I'll tell you.

They go off together. William grabs a piece of paper and a pencil and begins to sketch fast.

Jane Thank God they've gone . . . Trembling like a leaf . . . What are you doing?

William Ssh! Sketching from memory, technical memory, got to concentrate –

Jane I beg your pardon?

William Get it down the printer's first thing in the morning.

Jane William! No! (*Snatches away his pencil.*) Let the poor woman die gracefully.

William Gracefully? You call that gracefully?

Jane She thinks it is.

William She's bonkers!

Jane William, I have to say it, I think this is immoral.

William I know that. I'm not thick.

Jane Think how she'd feel if you published her picture now!

William Christ, she'll never know!

Jane She is choosing when to die. What else has she ever chosen in her life? Perhaps that has a kind of grace. (*Pause.*) Abandon it. For me.

William (*concedes*) The world will never hear of Sarah Sprackling, she will never have existed, she will be a ghost, who stalks the landscape of my brain, how's that?

Jane Thank you. I am going back to bed now. We shall discuss all this tomorrow. (*Pause.*) The thought of you with that old whore . . .! Ugh! And Robert Walpole. You're in too deep! And oh, when I saw those vile drawings, I was livid! But then I stopped and calmed down and tried to think sensibly about it and – I began to look on you as, well, what shall we say? Cripple? Some sort of emotional cripple? Not got the use of all your bits. And all I can feel for one of those is pity. Goodnight. (*Exits.*)

William Night night, sweetheart.

Immediately, from another entrance, a Stage-hand enters, crosses the stage, gives William a Polaroid camera, and exits.

Oh. Thanks.

William examines the camera with great interest. Immediately Jane returns. William guiltily hides the camera behind his back.

Jane And don't have any more to drink tonight, William, or you will ruin your health. (*Exits.*)

Immediately Oliver appears from another entrance, looking thoroughly debauched. He advances on

William from behind, seeing only the costume. He grabs at William's bum.

Oliver My dear! I came.

William (*turns*) Oliver!

Oliver Oh, bother, it's you, is it? I thought I'd find Janey here alone.

William What?

Oliver I will not be hobbled by convention, it's so very dreary, don't you think? I spend my nights up a lot of loose streetgirls, but it's no good, I don't come off. I need a female of good breeding. Your wife will do. Is that all right?

William Er . . .

Oliver One has to do what gives one pleasure, William. The world may end tomorrow. Pop. Then what are you left with?

William That's not a bad argument. Here, do you know how to work one of these?

Oliver Yes, you look through here, push this, and –

A flash. Oliver takes a photo of William. The picture ejects itself. William takes the camera back and stares at the photograph. It's blank, of course.

William Hmm, well I don't think much of that.

Jane enters, seductively dressed.

Wait a minute!

The picture starts to come up. William stares at it. Jane embraces Oliver, and leads him aside. They make love. She calls out to her husband.

Jane William. William.

William sees them now, and starts to take photographs of them. Harry enters.

Harry Hello, Will.

William Wotcher, Harry.

Harry kisses William passionately on the mouth. William is surprised, but doesn't resist. Walpole enters.

Walpole (*stern*) William . . .

William I'm a bit involved at the moment. With my friend.

Walpole produces a knife and sticks it in Harry's back. Harry dies.
  William jumps away.

Now look what you've done!

Walpole It's all right, I'll get away with it.

Walpole goes towards Oliver and Jane. Harry sits up. William yelps. Walpole turns. Harry blows a raspberry at Walpole. Walpole blows a bigger raspberry at Harry. Walpole goes to Jane and joins in. Frank enters with a mouthful of money. He spits the money at William.

Frank My turn.

Frank goes to Jane and joins in.

Harry And mine.

Harry goes to Jane and joins in. William photographs the proceedings.

William Christ, this is good. Jane, I'm disgusted with you. What a slut. I'm appalled! Four at once! Bloody hell. – Here, lift your leg a fraction.

Photographs rain from the camera. Jane jumps up,
runs back and points at William.

Jane Now! Get him! Get him good!

The Drummer enters, playing a pounding beat. Jane
exits. The four men advance on William.

William Oh no . . .

They chase him and strip him of his clothes. He tries
to scrabble away but he is surrounded. The drumbeat
drives into his brain. Each of the men produces a
camera, all with flash.

Walpole Now! Take his picture! Take his picture! Put
him in the file! Put him in the file!

They all photograph a naked and terrified man
crouching on the floor.

William Jane! Janey! Janey! Janey! Janey! Jan-ey!

Jane enters, now restored to her normal demure self,
and dressed once again in her nightclothes, yawning.
Immediately all the dream figures exit. All Jane can
see is the sobbing William.

Jane Oh, Will . . . oh, darling. (*Takes him in her arms.*)

William Janey, it was nasty, it was you, you were doing
it with Oliver and you were – nasty pictures –

Jane Now come along. I don't think you're very well,
are you, darling?

She wraps him in a blanket and leads him to bed.

It's dawn. Come along with me to bed. Little boy needs a
proper rest. Let's get you tucked up.

She puts him into bed. He sobs.

It's all right, cry. Cry and cry. You can't keep it all
rammed down inside. You have to let people know of
your feelings for them. It's vital, Will, it really is.
Otherwise your work is a lie. Isn't it? (*Pause. She looks
out of the window.*) It's starting to snow. Winter. – I'll let
you paint me if you want. Do you want? I'd sooner we
had it all out in the open. Paint me, I can contain it.
Knowing what I know. I will not let go of you, for the
sake of a little pride. (*Laughs gently.*) You and your silly
dreams. Oliver and I indeed! He is such a dreadful rake.
(*Pause.*) Snow covering up everything now. All the birds
will fly away. Where do they go, Will? Some unmapped
land? Can you see it in your head? (*She gets into bed.*)
I will guard you. I will guard your reputation. Sleep now.
Deep down underground like a tulip bulb. Sleep now,
and come up later.

> *She lies down and pulls the covers over their heads.*
> *Immediately Sarah drops from above, dangling on the*
> *end of a rope. She swings at the foot of the bed.*
> *Louisa runs on, grabs Sarah's legs, and pulls*
> *downwards with all her weight. Sound of the crowd*
> *roaring at the hanging. Spot on Louisa, her eyes wide*
> *with horror, and fade.*

SCENE TWELVE

*Several months later, by the banks of the Thames. Low
tide at a 'stairs' or landing-place at Wapping. Steps
leading down from the wharf to the river. Ancient
wooden beams and posts. An old boat overturned on the
mudbank. Harry stands on the steps. He writes on a
scrap of paper. He stops writing. He is dejected. Frank
and Oliver enter above, along the wharf. Oliver has the*

black patches on his neck and face which signify a pox.
The scene starts slow and quiet.

Frank The ice is breaking up.

Pause.

Oliver I hate spring.

Pause.

Frank We need a boat to ferry us downriver.

Oliver I hate sunshine. I hate it when the daffodils come out.

Pause.

Frank There's Harry.

Harry (*turns*) It's happened. Walpole's closed me down.

Frank Yes, we passed the Act last night, late night sitting you know.

Oliver You didn't vote for it, did you?

Frank I gave my maiden speech, against the motion.

Oliver Brave man.

Frank Then I voted for it.

Oliver Quite. So did I in the Upper House.

Harry I now have to apply to the office of the Lord Chamberlain for a licence to perform any new interlude, tragedy, comedy, opera, play, farce, prologue or epilogue. Or I shall be deemed a rogue and a vagabond and punished accordingly.

Oliver That is what you wanted, is it not?

Harry But how am I supposed to make a living?

Frank Get along and apply for the blessed licence. We all have to abide by the law.

William enters, looking affluent in a new coat.

Oliver The genius himself has come along. This is indeed an honour.

William Hullo, lads. Aren't I just a Beefsteak like the rest of you?

Frank Long time since we've seen you at a meeting.

William . . . And where are we going today?

Oliver Down the Thames to Kent. (*with distaste*) The green fields of Kent.

Frank We have undertaken to provide the aesthetic education of an English artist. This will be your Grand Tour. The fruity air of Kent will lend you inspiration.

William What for?

Harry The art of the dung-heap.

William . . . Thought you were a bit quiet.

Harry I've seen your advertisements. In the press.

Oliver Oh, yes, bravo! Astonishment in the coffee-shops! The general view is, with this new Copyright Act, you'll become the first English painter to succeed without patronage.

Harry 'The Rake's Progress'.

William Yes?

Harry 'The Rake's Progress'.

William You don't like the title.

Harry It's just sex. You're obsessed with sex.

William Am I fuck. It's a serious work. Me and Jane spent the whole winter on it. What I'm obsessed with is beauty. The truth about beauty.

Harry There is no truth about beauty. Beauty disguises truth. It is impossible to write a beautiful play.

Frank Ignore him, Will. The Prime Minister's just shut his theatre.

Oliver He read out a play in Parliament. It's called *The Golden Rump*.

Frank It's filthy. Mr Walpole says he got if off a theatre manager, who hinted Henry Fielding was the author.

Harry Which is quite impossible, I couldn't plot a play that amateurishly if I tried.

   Beat.

Oliver There's a boat.

Frank Hey, Waterman! – There's some old biddy in it.

   They go down towards the river.

William You coming?

Harry No. I've no business in Kent. I've met a very nice girl, I think I'd sooner be with her.

William Look, what's the matter with you?

Harry Nothing, absolutely nothing.

William You have to try, Harry. You have to make an effort.

Harry Why?

William God, what is the world coming to, when you can't even talk to your mates.

Harry You've done a deal, haven't you? They're calling it Hogarth's Act, do you know that? What do you have to do, Will, to get your name on the statute books? What do you have to sell?

William Well if you're going to be like that you can stick it up your arse.

William goes to Frank and Oliver.

Harry Oh, fuck . . .

William Harry ain't coming.

Oliver Oh, leave him to sulk.

William That our boat?

William exits to the river.

Harry Will, we're supposed to be friends, everyone thinks we're friends . . .!

But he's gone. Mrs Needham enters from the river. She wears black, and carries a crucifix and a bible.

Frank Welcome to London, madam. Christ alive, it's her.

Oliver Mrs Needham. Bonjour.

Mrs Needham Good morning, boys. Off to church?

Frank We are going on a peregrination.

Mrs Needham I see. Was that Mr Hogarth I just passed, whose 'Harlot's Progress' has turned so many maidens off the downward path to hell?

Frank Yes.

Mrs Needham Thought so. Here, boatman, here's a ha'penny tip.

*She lobs a coin towards the boat. But she throws
badly and it falls into the mud below. She gives Frank
another coin.*

Oh, silly me, Lord forgive my wastefulness. My spell in
the stocks, it withered my arms. Please, Frank, give the
man this and tell him I will pray for his safety upon the
foaming waters. Is there any act of sacrifice I can
perform for either of you? Any good deed? No? (*low
voice*) I've got a black girl in. Yes, a hottentot, a darkie,
dark as your deepest thoughts. Like to try, Viscount? An
extra half crown will secure it.

Oliver I've never had a black before.

Mrs Needham (*fingers his pox-marks*) Or double for the
blighted.

Frank Oliver, come on.

Oliver Perhaps when I get back . . .

Frank Cast off, Will!

*Exit Frank and Oliver. Mrs Needham goes up the
steps to Harry.*

Mrs Needham Young fellow? We're back to business as
usual. Except on Sundays, I don't hold with trading on
the Sabbath.

*Harry shakes his head. Mrs Needham shrugs and
exits. Harry sobs. A figure emerges from under the
upturned boat. It is Louisa. She is utterly filthy and
decrepit. She slithers across the mud, making for the
coin dropped by Mrs Needham.*

Harry My God.

Louisa (*gets the coin*) What do you want?

Harry Do you live under there?

Louisa Gives shelter from the wind, doesn't it?

Harry But how do you survive?

Louisa The wind blows particles of clever stuff all round me.

Harry I see. Are you alone?

Louisa Yes.

Harry What's it like?

Louisa It's sad.

Harry I'm sad too.

Louisa Don't come near me, I got a disease!

Harry Can I help?

Louisa No one can help. It just blows and blows and blows. And blows and blows and blows and blows and blows.

Harry I run a theatre. And I write the plays. They've just closed it down. That's why I'm sad.

Louisa My my. Dear dear. What a pity. – Look! (*She leaps across the mud.*) Lugworm! (*She scrabbles with her hands.*) Gone. Bugger! Not quick enough.

Harry I'm not allowed to work!

Louisa Very juicy, lugworms. I like a lugworm as a starter.

Harry What am I going to do? To hang on to my dignity?

Louisa I haven't got the faintest idea. I'm far too busy to go to the theatre. – Look! Out on the river! Oh look!

Harry Oh yes!

From the direction of the river, the sound of Handel's
'Water Music'. Coloured lights play on the mudbank
as a boat glides slowly past. The sound of voices
comes indistinctly from midstream.

I've never seen it before. And it is – despite everything,
isn't it – amazingly beautiful . . .

Louisa Yes! Yes! – What is it?

Harry Why, it's the royal barge! And that one coming
along behind is the barge for the musicians, do you see?
That's an orchestra! Floating down the middle of the
river! And look – there on the foredeck – that's the
Queen!

Louisa The Queen?

Harry Yes, and there's bloody Walpole talking to her,
kissing her hand! Oh, the bastard! You're an arsehole,
Walpole! You're a shit!

Louisa Will you be quiet! That's the Queen, for
goodness' sake! She doesn't want to hear that kind of
language! (*She goes down on her knees in the mud.*)
The Queen of England. All my life I've wanted to see
the Queen, and now I have, it is complete. On my river!
In front of my eyes! Your Majesty! Your Majesty!

Harry You're right. What point in yelling? Must find
another way. Some system harder to control.

Louisa It's a royal wedding, is it? Oh, I love a wedding!
I love to see the happy bride! These people, they're so
pretty, so clever! And the colours! And the music! And
the flags!

Harry I'm thinking of writing a novel.

Louisa A what? What's one of them?

Harry Hard to explain. They're new.

*Blast of 'Water Music'. Slow fade on Harry and
Louisa. The lights of the Royal Barge. The sounds of
a party: laughter, conversation, glasses being smashed.
Blackout.*

IN THE RUINS

In the Ruins was first broadcast by BBC Radio 3 on 3 June 1984. The part of King George III was played by Nigel Stock. The play was directed by Richard Wortley, with music by Ilona Sekacz.

The revised edition, with the additional role of the Page, received its first performance at the Bristol New Vic Studio in May 1989.

The play was revived at the Bristol Old Vic, on 3 April 1990 and transferred to the Royal Court Theatre, London, on 10 May 1990. The cast was as follows:

King George III Patrick Malahide
The Page Marcus Powell

Director Paul Unwin
Designer Anabel Temple
Music Gary Yershon
Lighting Tim Streader/Lorraine Laybourne
Sound Christopher Johns

Characters

King George III
The Page aged twelve

The time 1817
The place Windsor Castle

The play is published here
in the revised 1990 version

*The King's apartment on the north terrace of Windsor
Castle, circa 1817. A large, wood-panelled, wooden-
floored room. George III is a very old man indeed.
He has long white hair and beard, and wears a violet
dressing gown.*

*He sits at a harpsichord playing a slow section of
Handel's 'Water Music' suite. He plays at first correctly,
but in a rather ponderous, child-like manner.*

*In the room are a decanter of water, glasses, many
papers and scrolls, quill-pen and inkpot, and a naval-
style flute.*

*Soon the King's playing starts to degenerate. Before
long it is barely recognisable as Handel. It becomes
demented, yet played with the utmost decorum.
Suddenly he decides it is finished.*

King Aaah. Used to enjoy that when I was alive. Ah yes.
Podgy old Herr Handel. A man of most prodigious –
noise. He wrote that tune for my great-grandfather. No?
Yes. Doubtless he's dead now, been dead for years. As
indeed have I. Years and happy years before the flood
Handel waddled round London with my great-grandpa
but we're all three dead now and something died along
with us too.

Dear old plinkety-plonkety Handel; at least he's
buried; thank God, they have had the decency to stitch
up his eyelids and inter him into the earth. Me, no. Me,
no. Me, never. Oh, say a prayer for poor old George, a
good and pious man who loved his God and some of his
people and yes yes yes loved God and they forsake me.

The inferior sort. They leave me . . . to continue. Hah!
I here determine I shall live to be an hundred from sheer
damned spite! – forsaken and forsook and damn it all
abandoned dressed in my purple shroud. Ah. Ah. Ah. Ah.
Mr Secretary make a fair copy of that Pronouncement
and post it at the entrance to this cold castle, that the
freezing-folk of Windsor may read. Now. Let the audience
begin. (*He claps his hands and greets an imaginary
court.*) Hullo, hullo. How do, good day. Come in, come
in. (*furiously*) Come in! Ah yes. And you are the
Ambassador for – where? What? What? No I've never
been there. But was my playing good? or poor? or was
it poor? Good? Bravo! You may rise. I did perceive it
as good, within the narrow confines of my daily-blooded
skull. I must frankly admit, sir, with no boasting, 'twas
good.

For I will not boast. I will not brag. I do not pretend
to any superior abilities. But I will give place to no one
in meaning to preserve the freedom, happiness and glory
of my dominions and all their inhabitants, though I am
not an accomplished musician, and not one of those
puking babies who crawl round the royal courts of
Europe with their spindly hands out viz that Mozart I saw
years and years and happy years ago before I passed away
and didn't go to heaven. He was eight. The blubbing boy
was eight years old and could play anything on sight.
Bah! I loathed him. Eight! Unpardonable brilliance! Bah.
Stretch the fabric of your imagination and picture my
humble paltry self, fidgeting with embarrassment in the
presence of Wolfgang Mozart, pooh and pooh again. But
on no occasion do I perform Mozart's trivia when alone
as I am most of the time or with my wife who does strum
on the guitar with a most palatable mediocrity or indeed
even with pleasant abstemious company like yourself, sir.
I am glad now I recognise you as the Ambassador for –
the what? That's a long way away. Report that I play

Handel but never Mozart. They are both dead which is a point in their favour but I own I thought Handel died ever so much more graciously than that boastful boy and I hope if God wills it to do the same when my time comes which I heartily wish it would.

I thought I played my keyboard piece jolly well. No? Pretty fair? Not genius. Not Mozart-pozart. But fairly fair, between the ears, under the periwig, wouldn't you say? Hey? Hey? For sadly . . . for tragically . . . I cannot see, my estimable friends, to read the music. Or yet find the music. (*Laughs.*) Or yet look in the glass to see the sores where they put leeches to my temples. Or yet point at the harpsichord itself – which is not very old, it belonged to Queen Anne – if you turned me around and around and around and around. Doctors tried that oh yes long ago before the flood.

The Willises. Terrible men.

I'll tell you. The blackest of hearts. And to a man who is blind! Sightless. Blind. As a bat. As a bat. As a bat. As a bat. Fruit bat. Only luxury at the royal table. Favourite fruit of King: cherries. Favourite fruit of Queen: stewed pear. Favourite fruit of Prince of Darkness – (*sudden change of tone*) when normal we eat mutton chops and plum pudding. Yum yum. Won't get fat on that. Good English grub. And they say – the subjects, they say – the loving subjects – God preserve us from subjects – they calls us misers. Do! Yes they do. Fruit bat. Bite you. Yah! – Sirs, madams, I crave forgiveness. Thrift is a gift from God and it ill becomes the fiftieth King of England to behave like a fruit bat. But I cannot see to bite the music, though I play well and the blood drips down my chin, middling well, don't I? Know it by heart, d'you see, luckily, learnt it by heart, smart, hey? 'Water Music' off by heart. Clever fellow, hey? Hey? Clever old Nobs. Not mad at all. Smart in every particular. Plays very very well . . .

I think.

I don't *hear* terribly clearly, d'you see. Not any more.

Makes playing music rather – but lucky I learnt those tunes, hey? What? Lucky, what? What?

Yes.

Poor old fool gone mad thinks he's King of a time gone by.

Yes, King! *Avant le déluge*, at the very beginning of the reign, damn near sixty year ago, with sight and hearing and in constant communication with the Lord . . . issued a Proclamation. Yes. Did. (*He blows a fanfare on an imaginary horn.*) 'A Proclamation for the Encouragement of Piety and Virtue, and for the Preventing and Punishing of Vice, Profaneness and Immorality. We do hereby declare our royal purpose and resolution to discountenance and punish all manner of vice, profaneness and immorality, particularly in such as are employed near our royal person' – poor old beggar – 'And we do hereby enjoin and prohibit all our loving subjects, of what degree or quality soever, from playing on the Lord's day at dice, cards, or any other game whatsoever; and we do hereby command and require them decently and reverently to attend the Worship of God on every Lord's day on pain of our highest displeasure and our Biting out their Eyes.' (*He snaps his teeth.*) What? What? What? Vice? What? Send 'em home without any supper. Oh, don't turn your face away, please madam, dear madam, your pretty face, your perfect face with but a hint of blood at the corners of the mouth, madam you have over-eaten again, no please madam don't turn your face away, please madam the King is talking to you! In the presence of a prince of the blood you will stand next the wall and still your tongue! And God looked upon the earth, and behold, it was corrupt!

(*Fatigued.*) The audience is over. You people may go. (*He plays a few peculiar, wistful chords.*) I wonder, does the Queen still live . . .?

Wait! Don't go! I'm not finished.

I'm never finished.

Tell me, madam. Does the old croc live?

What? Say louder. Say louder. I cannot hear. Madam say louder!

It's hopeless and God said unto Noah the end of all flesh is come before me for the earth is filled with violence through them and behold I will destroy them with the earth. Charlotte . . .? Alive . . .? Or croaked . . .? I last saw the Queen for a quarter of an hour in 1812 I remember quite distinctly she smiled at me but with a tear in her bulbous bloodshot piglike eye and she so dreadfully reduced that her stays would wrap twice over I am damned I am damned I am if I know what's the matter with the old girl who was always used to eat her greens and I recall her then saying I had eyes like blackcurrant jelly yes blackcurrant jelly pinpoints of hell in shadowy sockets and would she kiss me? no the scoundrels pinioned my arms when I tried to kiss my Queen but she did smile at me – she did! – with her blotchy old face and this would be – let me see – this would be – let me see – this would be – I'll reckon it up now – this'd be about – (*He bangs five times on the harpsichord case.*) – five year ago. Well done. Five years. Good boy. Go to the top of the family tree. Five happy years ago. Five vacuous, desolate years. Since last I saw Charlotte my wife. And even then I was blind from my ages of crying and could but just feel the tremble of her little little wrinkled hand in my little little wrinkled hand only for a moment as we sat quiet and remembered . . .

And then of course I began talking again blasted fool. And she wept. (*Laughs gently.*) Crocodile tears. For with all the rest the Queen thinks the King's lost his head when in point of irredeemable fact he's the only monarch in Europe with a head left to stand his blasted crown upon, isn't he? (*He cries.*) Isn't he?

Never never never on any account leave me alone with the mad-doctors again I beg you Charlotte my dear love never never never never.

They tie me to my Coronation chair. (*He laughs.*)

It is not funny! My mind is ulcered by the treatment that it meets from all around. They tie me down they tie me up I bite me tongue. They leech my head. They blister me feet with squashed beetles and mustard immerse me in boiling blood. I cut my face. They snatch my razor. They take my mirror. Lest I lick the blackcurrant jelly d'you see Lord Malmesbury. But I am blind I remind them I am blind I scream! – but these scoundrels in the mad-business are so jolly ignorant of anything at all, even gardening's a thing they know naught of, even I know a bit about veg, blockheads, the King is blind I say and nearly nearly deaf. So the page tilts my chair slightly at night to signify time for beddie-bye but no sweet dream or woolly blanket because first they do drag me through hideous hot baths ho! horrid hot waters and they manage me with great violence and want of due respect and then they strap me in my cot where I may not presume to sleep lest the waters creep by me in the night-time and I drown and all the affairs of state get sopping wet . . .

Ahem. The cause to which they all agree to ascribe the unfortunate calamity that is me is the force of a humour which was beginning to show itself in my legs some thirty odd years past when, so they say, my imprudence – imprudence? phaw! I've always hunted in the rain – drove it from thence into my bowels which are an item I have long had cause to complain of as for example the streams of purplish water issuing therefrom and now d'you follow the medicines they were obliged to use for the preservation of my royal life viz the camphor the calomel the quinine the digitalis the tartarised antimony and so forth have repelled this malignant humour up

upon the royal brainbox at which juncture – can I speak
to you man to man my Lord? – the Willises and Sir
George Baker who's waiting outside are strongly inclined
to think the disorder permanent. This is despite the
frequent application of the baths and the bloodings to
divert these morbid humours from my anointed brow.
Permanent. Hah!

(*Calls.*) Sir George Baker come in here at once! Stand
still stop fumbling and say hullo to Lord Malmesbury.
He is my friend. Ah. Ah. Hand me that paper. (*He finds
a paper.*) 'His Majesty suffers an entire alienation of
mind. Opinion of the Five Physicians.' Bah! Pooh! What
cod is this? Sir Doctor George did you write this report?
It is feeble, sir, feeble. My mind has never functioned
better than it does this day. Were it not for the disabling
fact that I am deceased, who can say what further glory
might be Britain's?

D'you see you are I fear, or rather rejoice, quite
mistaken in your diagnosis of my condition Sir George.
It's only nervousness. I have always been a nervous sort
as you know. Really you're nothing but an old hen. We
shall deck you out in feathers. (*Laughs.*) Cackle cackle.
Come along. Cackle. (*He impersonates a hen.*) Come
along, now, cackle with the King! Cack cack cack and
(*Checks himself.*) Hold. Hold! I am calm. But I am
nervous. I am not ill, but I am nervous. If you would
know what is the matter with me, I am nervous. Sir
George you have said the shade by which soundness of
mind is to be distinguished from some degree of insanity
is often faint, and in many cases hardly perceptible. Now
there is an enormous burden of truth in that and it is an
exceptionally fortunate thing for the British Empire and
Dominions that it is only my slight attacks of nerves that
you have mistaken for lunacy in the space between my
ears and it's a confusion that could happen to anyone
even dimwit physicians now if you would have the good

grace to send for my naval uniform and have them unlock the door – (*He goes to a bolted door and rattles it violently.*) – we'll go a walk in Windsor without any attendants, shall we? You could not possibly hope to meet a more rational monarch than George the Third in the whole of history, man. Pray do not forget you are merely a Knight of the Bedchamber and entirely dependent on me for advancement.

As I say it is but a minor attack of nerves similar to that which struck me down in 1765 and again in 1788 and again in 1801 and again in 1804 – look I recall the dates well – and the reason I have by this last onslaught been mildly incapacitated for six and a half years is entirely due to there being a terrible lot to be nervous about. I own I incline too much to our John Bull, and am apt to despise what I am not accustomed to, and with this despising comes a sort of fear. I am utterly blind and almost deaf and the balance of my mind has proved inaccurate – but yet I am Your Majesty and I will not be held prisoner in my own castle in this obscene fashion. I have taken a solemn determination that unless I am this day allowed to go over to the house where the Queen and my family are, no earthly consideration shall induce me to sign my name to any paper or to do one act of government whatever! Then let's see how the nation gets along! What? What? What? . . . Any further talk of a Regency, Sir traitor George, sir, and I shall consign you to a certain inferno of my acquaintance.

Oh my dear Lord Bute of Long Ago, come forward, my loved one, you will put in a good word for me I feel certain. I do talk perfectly coherent as you see. I am now much weaker than I was, yes, yes, but as an example of my clearheadedness I have prayed to God all night that I might die, or that he would spare my reason. And as you see both of these things have gloriously come to pass. I am swimming for the Lord in the waters of night.

I am trying to talk as slowly as possible for one with a
devil of a lot going back and forth around the skull.
Stay with me and hold my hand a moment for I cannot
stop shaking and my pulse gallops like the winner at
Newmarket. Oh, I have the most profound consciousness
of terror, my dear, dear love, for I cannot find the Queen
of my Heart and I shan't be allowed on the Ark without
her. My footsies are swollen and I've a lingering pain in
the gut. In the translation of this pestilential flying
disorder from one part to another, the horrid thing
appears to have become locally fixed on the brain which
is the most appalling tragedy for a fellow who was used
to take clocks and chronometers apart and what is more
put them back together again with the aid of only three
of four servants. I insist upon walking on the Terrace
on occasion, that members of the public might know
without question I am still at work despite having died.
But it is so hard dearest Bute to explain to folk what it is
like internally to be this nervous when one is regularly
put bawling in the straight-waistcoat by those vile men
and left trussed like a breast of lamb and this is why I'm
telling you that the King is *not* alienated in the head and
not dangerous and *not* hungry for his bone and doesn't
require *any more* hot baths thank you for I will not
throw my Kingdom into confusion by pretending to be
alive when I ain't and this is why you'd better let me out
on the terrace where I can keep a blind eye on my
empire for I've the flying gout they say it flew from my
paws to my silly old head – and I've to think of my
crocodile wife with gargantuan mouth and my lovely
darling daughters who read to me in my darkness and
hold my jelly hand and this is why I've been saved from
the slavering jaws of death with the aid of Master Noah
and his splendid rowing boat and this is why I am
perfectly fit for the office of King except alas that my
water gushes the colour of port wine and stains my

breeches and this is why they wrap me legs in flannel which I don't think seemly for the most magnificent majesty walking on the oceans but please big sirs and bloated madams don't you know I am not ill but I am nervous so nervous I cannot keep still no I cannot keep static still incontinents to conquer and my men are on the job second sons of adventure all covered in gore but God it's a nerve-wracking business this ruling the world and I own I am prone to jump at the sound of my own voice wohah! for I don't . . . d'you see I don't hear it very often and when I do it is always talking such bosh always have the suspicion I am talking talking talking talking far too speedily Malmesbury and far too much and rattling away and heaven knows what and I know this and I know that and I can hear it I can hear it I can hear it now – my God what say I in my delirium! respecting this or that or Lady Pembroke's smelly fanny way way down in the hairy valley of perfect peace – I can hear it again! what torture! what pain! to hear what is said by means of words this fellow is *mad* and shouldn't be followed with the royal diadem of purple piss upon his head the sceptre in his skinny hand 'Rex Insanit' say the Seven Physicians! Damn I can still touch! Damn I can still smell! Lord it is too much take me and drown me in rivers of blood where we win all the battles and never lose colonies or ever outlive our allotted span or glug! or silence! or glug! or silence! silence in the vale of tears!

> *The King raves. The heavy bolts on the outside of the door are drawn back and a Page enters. He is an angelic-looking boy of about twelve in livery. He runs to the King and forces a large handkerchief into his mouth. Then he steps back. The King thrashes around a little more but then subsides. Pause. The Page steps forward and removes the gag from the King's mouth.*

He helps the King up and steers him to his harpsichord stool. The King sits and plays a phrase rather badly. He sings in a hoarse, cracked voice (Recitative No. 17 from Handel's 'Messiah'):

'Then the eyes of the blind shall be openèd, and the ears of the deaf unstoppèd: then shall the lame man leap as an hart, and the tongue of the dumb shall sing.'

He finishes playing. The Page pours a large glass of water and hands it to him. The King drinks it fast and scrabbles around for a piece of paper.

Here comes the latest bulletin. 'Opinion of the Eleven Physicians: The King is dead long live the King.' Oh – jolly good. That's more like it. I am coming, Master Noah, pipe me aboard, up the gangplank, two by two. Ah. Ah. Excellent. Excellent. But you have want of a fruit bat I notice. 'Of fowls after their kind, and of cattle after their kind, of every creeping thing of the earth after his kind,' sayeth the Holy Book. That includes bats. Have you a cabin for my Charlotte and I, Noah? With a porthole that faces north? We don't like the sun. For, sir, a most dreadful flooding of purple water has submerged London city of the gallows and everything that is in the earth has died. And I would be happy on the Ark where on the land I sorrowed.

Page. Give me a pen.

The Page gives him a quill-pen and ink. The King scratches furiously.

Now go away – I've a composition to do. 'Reflections on the Present State of the Navy and the Reasons why the Fleet is not in Greater Forwardness than it is.' (*He suddenly stops writing.*) Why? Why? Why me? Why do these imbecilic chores always fall to me? Because I am Rex Insanit I suppose. 'His Majesty is

multifarious in his questions, but thank God he answers
them all himself.' Thus Samuel Johnson, damned
scoundrel. Calls himself a doctor couldn't bleed the
cholic off a cow. Come come Johnson, speak up. By
what authority words in the dictionary may I consider
my naked corpse better than that of some miserable
petty . . . baronet, say? (*Laughs.*) I jest of course. Get
out of my library, Johnson. Oh, and collect up those
documents, in case they get wet.

He throws bundles of official papers everywhere,
laughing. The Page collects up the papers and exits.

What? What? Wet? Go sink in the salty sea three times
but only come up twice. If my work on the Navy's got
wet . . .! Oh I despair! This is the wickedest age that ever
was seen. An honest man must wish himself out of it.
Yes. Yes. Yes. Yes. I begin to be heartily sick of the
things I daily see – for ingratitude, avarice and ambition
are the principles men act by nowadays, nothing
whatever to do with our what? our what? our God-given
time-honoured national order of magnitude which holds
that I and I alone am fit to rule, that Lord Bute is to sit
beside me and hold my jelly, that Parliament's to do
what it's told, that a Duke comes first before a Marquis,
that there is an extremely sensible distinction to be made
between an Earl and a Viscount, and damn it all a
mighty profitable reward to be had from making it! All
of which is prior to even proposing for consideration the
middling sort, the stock-jobbers, moneylenders, seekers
of improvement and oh the mob. Peers and commoners
alike, may I remind you sirs that a King does not solicit
advice, he gives orders! I will have no innovation in my
time despite the drivel and dross of those whatyoume-
callem hell-begotten Jacobins across the foaming sea . . .
signing Declarations of this, that and the other . . .
Independence . . . Rights of stupid Man . . . bah! look

what's befallen them savages now . . . away across the
sea . . . cruel wretches who have possessed themselves
of power God gouge their eyes . . . over there . . . across
the slimy sea . . . (*Pause. Then a memory which delights
him.*) I saw a bridge.

I saw an iron bridge!

Marvellous thing in every particular, my dearest Lady
Pembroke. Bridge made of iron. Aye! My lady you
possess everything a hungry bat could want beneath the
foldings of your silks and velvets. Oh me oh my. And let
me tell you of my manufactures, the length and breadth
of the land! Such progress! Great strides leaps bounds
and forward march! Clever men, very clever men, bless
my soul, monstrously clever men whom we admire
without limit. The coming men. The new order. The
things they make for me! Beautiful machines! Pretty
pretty! Clockses oh watches oh barometers hygrometers
chronometers microscopes telescopes . . . Mr Herschel
built me a giant telescope for purposes of looking at
Uranus, my Lady. My new planet. And with my telescope
I can see Hanover. Look! Dry land, Noah! I can see
Germany! For the first time ever by God! Here's I
plodding along ploughboy-fashion at the sharp end of
the Hanoverian dynasty and I'm the only beggar never
to have seen the place! Damn me! I can see Hanover. But
not America. Oh blast. Was hoping to avoid (*change*)
now a hygrometer d'you see is a useful device bless me
yes, applicable to the management of the moisture and
temperature of the hot and green houses of our botanical
establishment at Kew for I grow turnips d'you see.
Exotic plants. Slimy green fingers of the King. What?
Yes. King George Three. Lives in England, likes it.
Ordinary man. Pleasant chap. Farmer George. With his
sheep corn spuds turnips. Much loved. Talks to the
people. And at Worcester, my Lady, we gave three cheers
for the new bridge built of iron and for three good

fellows all called George for a hundred years for a new
era wrought of iron and a million machines for spinning
and weaving and ploughing and seeding and coal and
canals and banging and blasting and bridges and boats
and buying and selling and sailing the seas!

. . . Ever hear of a noisy item called a Steam Engine?
Hey?

I've one. I've many. Oh-ho yes, two chaps called
Boulton and Watt build 'em. Not here, no. Not in
Windsor or London or Kew, spoil the view. Away to the
north in the wastelands of my Kingdom. I don't like the
barren ugly scarcely populated northern shires, my Lady,
I prefer Windsor Forest which is immeasurably more
perfect than anywhere else d'you see, and also much
nearer to hand. I have no taste for what are called the
fine wild beauties of nature, I do not like mountains and
other such romantic scenes, of which I sometimes hear
much. Never seen 'em, of course. Never been norther of
Worcester or souther of Weymouth. What's the point?

What my Lady?

(*furious*) I know there are insurrections and tumults in
every far-flung corner of the farmyard! This King still has
his head stuck on, madam, and still his black eyes see –
there is no government, no law! What's that my little
squirrel? Aye I do know why! For when religion and
public spirit are quite absorbed by vice and dissipation,
this sort of havoc is the natural consequence. Even,
'twould seem, at court. For, if we squint through our
cataract of tears, do we perceive you squatting on your
fat seditious hams? We do! I am standing on my two
hind legs why are not you? Get up! Have I not said I will
have no republics in *my* pigsty? And are the rest of you
all with this rutting Pembroke bitch who's in disgrace?
Get up I say! Here, Mr Secretary, I'll make my mark
on her death warrant. We will restore some dignity to
the method of proceeding with these audiences. Who

said they could sit? Here we are. (*Scratches with pen.*)
'George'. . . jolly good . . . and 'R' . . . damn my watery
joints . . . and 'R' . . . there! What? Pretty well for a man
who is mad. Hang the whore tomorrow.

. . . I love my subjects but why do they plague me so?
I know what it is. What? I know what it is. What?
Do I? Yes. It's because I lost America. That's the ticket.
It's because I lost America that's what it is. Had the
blasted thing a second ago and now where is it? Where?
Where is it? Where's Amerikey? Over the sea? Devil
take the place. Not a simple task, I will allow, to lose
something as apparently substantial as half a continent,
but I your King have done it. Abject failure. Pleasant
chap but consigned to the small print. Poor old Nobs,
the loving subjects despise me for losing America. Bad
for trade. Slaves in particular. And left us with nowhere
to dump our convicts. Hah! Discovered Australia, didn't
we? Ever resourceful. Captain Cook. Good fellow I've
shook his Yorkshire hand. Botany Bay. Long way. But
we had of course worked out arithmetically that there
must be a huge southern land-mass to counterbalance
Europe, or God's great world would have toppled over
years ago. We are ever mindful of the contribution of
science to our illustrious reign.

(*sadly*) But I that am born a gentleman shall never rest
me head on me last pillow in peace as long as I remember
the loss of my American colonies. For this squander of a
cornered market, I beg forgiveness, Oh my Lord, oh my
people. (*He prays a little.*) I've never been over the sea.
I've been in the sea. Go bathing in the briny good for
the pores. When I disappear beneath the waves the
band plays the national anthem which do demonstrate
how popular I be. At Portsmouth. Or Weymouth. Or
Bournemouth. Or Plymouth. May I say, one cannot
move in this country without meeting a myriad mouths,
there's a snapping of teeth a slapping of lips there's a

grasping snatching idle pauper person concealed in every fold of the hills and crying out for bread! bread! when we are desperately trying to sleep . . . there is hunger in the land, I know, but I am frugal, it is not my fault . . . I simply cannot sleep curse it . . . They surround my carriage, d'you see, wantonly breaking the windows with musket shot and pebbles and crying out for food, but the critical thing sirs and madams is that we do not show fear no matter how sticky it be in your britches. At the last counting I can recall precisely two verifiable attempts on my royal life, not including the deeds of doctors specially engaged in the department of insanity, nor the time I was attacked as I drove to the state opening of Parliament, let me see let me figure say five or six years after the fall of the Bonbons in Paris. On that occasion the mob, no doubt aggravated by all that French fol-de-rol and spurred on by bloody Voltaire and double-bloody Thomas Paine I fully expect, crushed against the gilded carriage yelling 'Peace and bread! No war with the French Republic!' Bah. 'No war! No King! Down with George!'

The Page enters.

This is precisely what I have this last half hour been attempting to warn you about, gentlemen of the House, from the vantage of my loftier position. I appeal to your nicer instincts. Think! King Mob on the loose . . . stocks and shares in decline . . . the Crown in peril. I appeal to you! What we are now placing under investigation, viz, the developments in France with respect to monarchs – head and shoulders, continued union of – is as far removed from the peace and serenity of our good old English ways as are all we decent law-abiding citizens from the dirt and heat and smells of damned Australia! God preserve us the scruffiest urchin of the street may now be heard belching the foul garlic-breath of

republicanism and God bless us demanding a vote in the
constitution of this House! Undoubtedly, if that sort of
ballyhoo holds good it is diametrically opposite to what
I have known all my life. The Crown rests.

*He sits, pleased with himself. The Page pours him
some more water which he gulps down. The Page
pours him the rest, then exits with the empty jug.*

Water is held to be unhealthy in these parts but the King
drinks gallons of the stuff and pray remark the excellent
condition of his coat. Spa water for preference, barley
water for a special occasion, and no need for recourse to
the rhubarb pills.

Where was I? Indeed where am I? Oh.

Once upon a time a domestic called Margaret
Nicholson sought with the aid of a kitchen knife to
slice us into cutlets on the very steps of our palace at
St James's. The heaving cheering crowd, good English
peasants all, some having walked for days to see us in
our splendour, made to rip her limbs from their sockets
exactly as one pulls the wings off a chicken. No! we cry.
Hold! The poor creature is inevitably mad. Do not hurt
her! The poor creature is mad! Who but a simpleton
would have motive to murder *me*?

The girl was spared and led to Bedlam it is my happy
duty to report.

As for the other fellow's cowardly attack, in the year
of 1800, well, bless me, his brain had been damaged by
sabre-wounds in my son the Duke of York's campaign
against Bonaparte. Not only was this witless assassin not
in his right mind but alas and alack his mind had been
perfunctorily divided into segments like an orange and
knowing which portion to reside his thoughts in would
have put to the test many a better thinker than he. The
royal party was at Drury Lane theatre where we often
went when I was alive to see a nice genteel sort of

comedies with no profanity and Charlotte the Queen
held my little pink blancmange. I put my opera-glass to
my still-seeing eye and look about the house for pretty
young squirrels as is my wont when on an instant boom!
boom! two shots whip past my still-hearing ear and as
I later learn one kills the lion and the unicorn is mortally
splintered. The Queen, dear heart, is preoccupied with
feeding sweetmeats to her lapdogs and fails to note the
piercing choral shriek of our assembled Princesses.
I stand perfectly still. I look about regally as before.
Subsequently I am complimented on my composure I will
have you know. Hah! Composure! I thought it was part
of the play . . . (*He laughs sourly at the memory.*) Hmm.
I am sensible of having been much out of order, Sir
George, but I am at present lucid d'you notice. When
I am composed I talk sense and take a paternal interest
in the running of things, but when nervous I am prone
to babble and speaking in tongues. For so long as I am
agitated by nobody in this chill castle, I am perfectly
easy to get along with. I trust you will mark my words,
Baker, and (*Whispers.*) defend me from mine enemies.
My singular enemy is Doctor blasted Willis God rot
his danglies. This is a man gave up the Church, an
honourable profession, for medicine, one I heartily
despise. The weasel defends this perfidy with the
probably blasphemous claim that Our Saviour himself
went about healing the sick. Well I have had a word
or two with the Archbishop on this exceeding nice point
of theology, Sir Knight of the Bedpan, and the upshot is
yes, yes, yes, we concede he *did,* but he did not get seven
hundred a year for it, did he! But the hateful Willises
father and son will not accept the superiority of my
logic, and they stitch me in the restraining-chair for the
making of the slightest sound and if I am bad they bind
me to my Coronation oath! Oh my dear dead Amelia,
why won't you save your father? These scoundrels have

the blackest hearts in the history of colour. I hate all physicians. But most I hate the Willises. Send 'em home without any grub.

He cries a little. The Page re-enters with fresh water. He sees the King crying and goes to comfort him. He holds the King's hand tenderly.

Oh, thank you. I feel quite tired now. I once had a hankering for a frisky Irish filly who thought me a bore but the Privy Council settled me unseen on a German, my beloved Charlotte of the sharp snapping teeth, and I was obliged to contract quick as the market in eligible, royal, protestant cunts was at that juncture quite impoverished. But since my Charlotte came to England I have loved her as a leech loves blood. Aah, yes. But now the subjects say I kept my young wife a virtual prisoner when first she came to this gruesome peasant land. Well, um, I did, yes. I wished to shield my blushing croc from the poisons and oh the corruptions of the age. I have already talked I think of the wholesale vice and dissipation here and the moves that were going forward on our part against it. I must declare our every effort a pitiful failure. Every single decree unheeded. Every act unheard. Every proclamation announced to an empty market square. The subjects blind and deaf to my will and as sinful as ever they were, possibly more so since the advent of this Freethinking la-de-da. Drat! One can try devilish hard to be good, and still be held a sinner.

And there is another reason why my Queen was rarely seen abroad in your poxed and reeking London society. Before she was forty years of age she had at my behoof presented you ungrateful dogs with fifteen little Princes and Princesses. Fifteen! I know them all by name. Even the bloody boys. – But my lovely darling daughters have stayed with me in my infirmity and never married no husband good enough and though rather old now they are terribly terribly content and would simply not dream of going away – not that I'd allow it of course I've enough troubles as I've made quite clear. Amelia is my favourite because she's dead and will hold my hand in heaven.

I was a good father. I mean, I was good at fathering. Unless you are good at *something*, you cannot be of utility to your country, nor credit to your family. I am a family man living the clean life of a country squire with my sheep and my turnips and enjoying my nuptial rights almost without limit. Aaah yes. (*Yawns.*) That's surely no bad thing for a King, to live a simple life, and take simple pleasures . . . oh . . . I strive to recall the tremor in my loins when she first (*change*) I take great joy in my patriotic duty and so I believe does my endearingly rigid partner, and I offer as proof that between us we have produced not only a lawful heir to the throne damn his profligate eyes but also a full team of quite legitimate reserves. I do sometimes wonder whether I be at all different in these respects, and in my method of going about it, from any malodorous farm-boy up a milkmaid in the hay but the answer is a foregone conclusion so I don't waste my clockwork upon it. Bless my soul I am getting tired. Been King for nearly sixty year. And with all my heart I wish my wife would unbolt that door and come and kiss me now on my watery eyes . . . for how else will I know she is alive?

Charlotte . . .?

Dear friends, I must sleep as I have great want of that refreshment. This levee is adjourned. (*Prays.*) Almighty God and Admiral Noah, settled in the joys of death I shut my eyes, amen.

Behold the unplumbed sea of dreams.

His eyes wide open, staring.

Drat. Wide awake. Ships of the line at Portsmouth, that usually helps. An hundred guns: HMS Victory,

HMS Britannia, HMS Royal Sovereign. Ninety-eight guns: HMS Neptune, HMS Temeraire, HMS Dreadnought, HMS Prince. Seventy-four guns: HMS Leviathan, HMS Conqueror, HMS Ajax, HMS Orion, HMS Minotaur, HMS Swiftsure, HMS Mars, HMS Colossus, HMS Bellerophon, HMS Revenge, HMS . . . Belleisle . . . HMS . . . and all the rest . . . sail on to glory at Trafalgar . . . aar . . .

With a sigh, he falls asleep. The Page waits for a moment and then disengages himself from the King. The King breathes peacefully. He snores once, twice. The Page exits, bolting the door behind him. As soon as he is gone the King wakes in a fury and leaps around the room.

GNNNNNNAAAAAAAAAARGH! Ireland! Bad dream! Bloody dream! Ireland!

Blast and smite and roast the papists for intruding on my private dreams! I am a tolerant man but these pisspot Catholics go too damn far!

Ireland, pah! Not another mention of the bog-ridden place! Am I fully understood? . . . Ssssh. It's somewhere we've never heard of, children, a wretched dark land full of witches and leper-corns and wafer-munching monsignors. But we have a lovely big army and a lovely big navy and we shall bring light and contentment to those desert shores. Now hush! boys and girls, not a word more. I wave my arms and away it goes – voila! (*He plays a merry tune to take his mind off it.*) I once, my dear Bute, dreamt I was making a speech at the Lord Mayor's banquet, and when I woke up I found I was. Ho ho ho ho ho ho ho. Broke bread that day with a Quaker fellow name of Barclay, David Barclay. The King likes Quakers simple people no ostentation. Brother Barclay's doing pretty well started up a bank I do believe. I like a man with the sniff of success about him but not flaunting

it under one's nose like the dull Mozart of ancient
memory and we have I am told created the perfect
climate for bankers, what with the investments in India
and the price of blacks and so forth. Yes yes. You mark
my words.

Yes. But I must beg pardon for I don't understand
money. I try but I don't understand. Look here for an
example. I sell my sheep at Smithfield Market sheep fed
on turnips I understand *that* I know my Rural Economy
madam, turnip-fed sheeps give dung and dung giveth
forth turnips hip! hip! huzza! God's mighty circulations,
and my sheep sell at fourpence ha'penny a pound in
Smithfield Market, all to the good so far, but now d'you
see the cooks at the Queen's House – Buckingham House
where my Lady keeps her pet elephants – say they are
paying a shilling for mutton. We are seriously confused.
The butcher fellow at the Queen's House is a slippery
fish with a rollmop tongue so I sent for him I was
nervous so I sent for him hey butcher! stand up man you
have legs not fins and butcher! explain! I sell my turnip-
fed sheep to your man at market for fourpence ha'penny,
and what do you sell 'em back to the Queen's kitchen
for? A shilling! Damn me damn you and damn the
animals, a shilling a pound for the exact same sheep only
deader and cut into chops! Bless us and save us! That's
a whatyoumecallit of sevenpence-ha'penny! Now what
pray is the ultimate fate of those extraneous monies?
Master butcher, will you please account! Tell me what
I want to know and I'll give you a glass of barley water.
There is something going forward here that we cannot
precisely put our finger on. But as I have said I don't
follow money matters too dogmatically. I've no spare
cash for I've spent all me money on bribes. Are you at all
aware that the vote of a prominent landowner or East
Indiaman may cost as much as a brand new barometric
clock? And by Jesus he may not even be titled nowadays

never mind ticking or chiming or pointing to Squalls!
Is it any wonder I am nervous, pretty madam? Damn
my boots, in a country where we permit a full quarter
million men to vote you'd expect a handful to poll freely
in my favour! Well, well, well, my ministers assure me
I need not worry, as no up-to-date government would be
so incompetent as to lose an election. But yet it is *my*
pockets being dipped and delved into, and *tradesmens'*
pockets being lined! What? Yes! What? Preposterous.
And now this brine-soaked butcher has told me a lie.
A white lie, he says, but I hate a white lie. If you will tell
me a lie, then let it be a black lie. Black is the shade I am
seasoned to. Black is the sheep for me.

Oh me flock have all gone astray, all run off to market
at a knockdown price and because I am me I can't haggle.
Come back! Back!

*He whistles like a shepherd, herding his flock. The
Page enters and tries to settle him.*

Here boy! Back into the fold! Here my bonny lass! Bah.
Hey! Farmer George is speaking! You listen to your
squire! . . . Oh, what point is there my sitting on the
five-bar gate and giving you bumpkins advice? You will
not act upon it. Yet I that am born for the happiness or
misery of a great nation, a tower of Babel, a silly old
fool with a strong constitution, am given to speak the
remains of my mind . . . (*softly*) and the awful dawning
between the royal ears is that all these spinning mules
and rolling locomotives and suchlike industrial whatdo-
youcallems do more or less presage a turnabout in the
wondrous God-given pattern of English life and I am
agin turnabouts as I have repeatedly said. I have the
fullest confidence in Divine Providence of course but can
our smoking pulsating new cities be ruled by the village
idiot? Oh 'tis most perplexing. The very thing that makes
us great I fear brings on our ending. No! Surely! Tell me,

Mr Ambassador, sir, what does the future hold? Oh I
don't know if I can endure it!

He cries in bewilderment. The Page is bored.

Well will you look at this French Turnabout for an
example? Bonaparte and the hounds of hell? The swish
of the murderous guillotine? – which is a triumph of
precision engineering and invented in Halifax, Yorkshire.
I will not pretend I was not at first heartened, to see
peacock Louis Bonbon a-sinking in the mire – but God
preserve us to chop him up like firewood! 'Tis inhuman!
and quite against the law! Yet we should not be surprised
at anything these trouserless savages might do. All Europe
is in flames! . . . except, um, Windsor. Hmm. But there is
at large in our land a species of thing called a Reforming
Society if you ever heard so much codswallop. Legacy
of that devil Wilkes. Blasted commoner spews sedition! –
and every time my men expel him from Parliament, the
double-damned voters elect him back in again. I am
afraid I have been forced to declare the loser the winner
and sling Wilkes in the Tower. Cost an absolute mint!
And now a thing called a Society for Constitutional
Information so help me God! The Constitutional
Information is, that *I am here*! Decked out in me purple
splendour! Now go home and be quiet. Oh, play us a
tune.

*The Page has found the flute. He plays a few tentative
notes on it. They permeate the King's consciousness;
he listens intently. The Page plays a sea-shanty. The
King tries to dance a hornpipe, which exhausts him
very quickly.*

Nelson.
Where's Nelson.
Where's half-pint? Is he among ye? I'll tell you
something. He's dead too. Lord Nelson. One gets along

best with corpses. I'll tell you something else. Died at
Battle of Trafalgar. Great hero. Dying wish: to be buried
in English soil. Good fellow. Problem: length of voyage,
Trafalgar to here, three months. Now in three months a
devil of a lot of decay can occur to a chap who's deceased.
Solution, courtesy brain of ship's doctor: embalm him in
a cask of rum. Jolly good. Duly carried out. Small chap,
perfect fit. Subsequent dreadful realisation on part of
officers in wardroom: rum is not nor never shall be a
gentleman's drink. Whip him out. Duly done. Put him in
a cask of *brandy*. Same effect overall, and without any
lowering of fit and proper standards. Officers go three
months without a drink but Nelson arrives home to our
ultimate accolade I shake his pickled hand and give him
a hero's funeral. All true.

Ah there you are. Lord Nelson of the Nile. You did
not mind our creating you a peer of 'the Nile', did you,
my short friend? Only we know you have unfortunately
no estate, d'you see, and although we aren't a skinflint,
setting you up with a few hundred choice acres in Dorset
was more than the royal budget would permit . . . But
you don't object? Splendid! The Nile is yours, then!
Plant whatever you like! Spuds are a damn good bet.
Now come here kneel down let me give you your next
command.

Have you ever stopped to consider, Admiral, how if
our manufacturing fellows had not mastered the casting
of iron frames, no one could have invented the piano
forte and the world would have been spared the horrors
of Beethoven? However, without our iron foundries we
should not have been able to build such splendid big
cannon, should we? Hmm . . . which to choose . . . good
music, or total domination of the map? – Ahem. This is
quite simply a war for the preservation of society. We
must vanquish the republican dragon and restore the
natural order. As to yourself, I will never doubt that,

whenever it shall please the Almighty to permit an English fleet fairly to engage any other, a most comfortable issue will arise. Ah indeed. For I am a man of the sea. The sea is in my blood. Whereas, Admiral, your blood is in my sea. Hmm.

Yes the ocean's a perilous place. I'm the old captain so I'll stay at home. You Jack Tar defend me. For I've stood on the sea wall at Portsmouth and watched the chain be hung across the harbour mouth to keep at bay the Frenchies, and the waves roll in hard and black the colour of iron, and the huge chain's of iron, and the sky's an industrial grey, and a molten lead rain blanks out the Island, and forty days and forty nights, and the chain and the sea and the sky and the rain and it's too vast and too wet for me and I'm back in me greenhouse at Kew where I've a few experiments going off. His botanic Majesty. Head down here look there's two turnips rutting in a bucket of manure – marvellous sight in every particular – and very quiet too. I hope you can run the railway of my thought, dear old Bute, for in fact I love the deep sea dearly. I go boating at Weymouth, row the wife and the little ones in ten-oar cutters. Go swimming in the deep blue blood. At Weymouth they have cut my picture in their chalky hill. Hooray! I like my subjects. But why will they never settle? Give thanks to God they're British and form up in order of precedence? But no. But no. I've seen such confusion and distraction in this too much divided land. I've seen the twitching drooling gob guzzle guzzle gobble gobble coast to coast and grinning like a valet when the Queen breaks wind, ever eating, loving subjects, ever stuffing, devouring with their champing chomping teeth, boiled beef roast beef roast pike pig's face pork's neck sheep's heart gooseberry sauce lamb chop yum yum hams and mint and fishies veal and onion meat and eat tart jelly and syllabub pears plums cream and butter eat and eat and eat your meat

fat English, look at 'em, staggering around with a belly-
ful of puke. Ooh they get fat! The subjects. Do. They do!
I am not fat I drink water.

*The Page pours another glass and hands it to him, but
the King does not drink.*

Take Handel for an example. Greatest composer in the
history of noise, but fat as a Christmas goose. Yuk! Hope
I never for if I'm too gross the great ship of state will
turn turtle damn my dung and I'm captain I'd drown last
of all I'd be lonely in the freezing cold flood! Captain
Cook, d'you see, has told me of the icebergs. My very
worstest dream. The sea cluttered with icebergs . . . (*He
drops his glass in terror. It shatters on the floor.*) Like the
wreck of a shattered world.

I am the King of Icebergs. And the Ark has passed me
by.

*A bell sounds, off. The Page manhandles the King
roughly into a special chair with straps at wrists and
ankles. The King is secured. The Page exits.*

Oh oh oh oh I am like sad Lear but thank God I have no
Regan, no Goneril, only a clutch of Cordelias and the
Prince of bloody Wales . . . and my Amelia, my Amelia,
who's now a nest of worms, lucky old thing . . .

*The Page returns with a series of pills and evil-looking
medicines which he proceeds to administer to the
King, who shrieks his annoyance. He continues to
speak during pauses in this 'treatment'.*

Sad stuff, Shakespeare, sorry stuff, he's missed the mark –
for the thing about a King is that a King can do no
wrong, he can't be judged naughty or guilty or bad nor
prosecuted criminally in tort or in contract in any court
in the land or the dominions beyond the blasted seas!
Aaaargh!

Oh my dear babies, do not forsake me because the pendulum of my mind has come to rest. I am good. I am a good King. I've never even seen Hanover, that horrid Electorate which has always lived upon the very vitals of this poor country. I born *here*! I glory in the name of Briton! Heart of oak! Head of ash! Never wanted to rule without Parliament – just wanted to rule Parliament, damn and blast the disobedient dogs!

The 'treatment' ends. The Page releases the King.

Phew. Be calm. I have lived on the active theatre of this world some six hundred years a man of sorrow and acquainted with grief and if I am not wise enough to consider every event which happens quietly and with acquiescence I must have lived very negligently. Shut your eyes I will play for you. Hush now. I will play for those boneheads among ye, of whom we sometimes hear much, saying there be sick and rotten stuff at the root of this our happy nation. Those who I am told would tear down God, would set sail for a mighty turnabout dear oh dear. Would ye have a bloody republic here? And make all men equal? And women too? Ye would see the crowned heads of Europe fall from their scented necks and tumble in the gutters, hey? Would play kick-ball with the Lord's anointed brains? Damn me, sirs, madams, your republic comes damned close to my personal vision of hell. What? No God? No King? No lords? No servants? One ruthless law for all? We have never heard such ferocious stuff. We refute it, we confound it, we deny it from deep in the ruins of our being. Hang it all, I am the living proof the shattered relic survivor of the flood and bless us underwater hero of the nation's great advance. I continue to continue and here's my song.

*He plays a great crashing discord on the harpsichord,
and stops. The Page stands next to him and sings
directly into his ear, very beautifully indeed. It's 'See
the Conquering Hero Comes' from Handel's 'Judas
Maccabeus':*

Page
'See the conquering hero comes,
Sound the trumpets, beat the drums.
See the conquering hero comes,
Sound the trumpets, beat the drums.'

The King is transfixed with delight.

King There! There! Hear it! Conquering hero. That's me!
England's glory! Pax Brittannicus! Me!
I know what I'll do. I know what I'll damn well do.
I'll escape that's what I'll damn well do. I'll escape, and
sit once more on my burnished throne! Find my Queen
and my babies and rule the land again! Escape! Escape!
Away flies the bat!

*He runs round the room flapping his wings and biting
the furniture, quite demented. He crashes into things,
rips and tears at fabrics, cries and yelps. The Page
runs after him, trying to restrain him, but the King is
possessed of great energy, and breaks away. At length
the Page just trips him up. The King collapses on the
floor and suffers a brief convulsive fit. The Page
stands by, watching.*

(*through chattering teeth*) Ugh ugh . . . oh oh . . . fetch
the leech . . . fetch the Royal Leech . . . quick! Ugh . . .
ugh . . . fire in the blood . . . water on the brain . . .
Haargh! (*He chokes.*) Fetch the five million physicians!
Quick! I don't want . . . to die . . .

*Slowly he subsides. Long pause. He lays still on the
floor.*

Oh I've wet meself.
   Please help us up.

   *The Page helps him get to his feet. He stands with as
   much dignity as he can muster.*

Our business is concluded I think Mr Ambassador and
please let me be the first to apologise for the smell. You
have read this Declaration of Impudence to me and
although I hold that all men are not created equal and
that they are not endowed by their Creator with any
inalienable rights whatsoever still I have listened
tolerantly with my inner ear, and have noted something
brazen in your manner, which I suspect to be the herald
of some brutish barren future. I harbour no doubts that
when you return to your own country there will be some
debate as to whether I am like I am due to some horrid
disorder of the blood our dull physicians cannot
diagnose, or whether I am like I am due to the cares of
state having at some juncture become too heavy for my
lightweight mind. I say does it matter, sir? I am still King
of all I can see, Regency or no. And my descendants will
themselves be in that happy position when next the
question is put. Aye, 'tis a grand thing for a family man
to think on, who has so many times sewn his oats in the
royal fertiliser, and who can now rest assured that if he
is like he is due to some foul humour in the blood, then
by God all his offspring and all their offspring down all
the leafy branches of the tree may suffer it as well which
should give you something to consider on your way
home. Hey, ho. Look to your Princesses. Their dark and
gloomy side. And stand up straight when I'm talking to
you. In my bleaker moments I do admit a doubt that this
tainted line can survive down the centuries. Subjects'll
never stand for it, I conclude. Dice of history roll against
us. But damn my dingle will you look at the hullabaloo I
have lived through? Eh? All the world in flames, but still

the crumbly blood-pudding of our privilege bonds
together, and we like the phoenix arise from the ashes of
Old England! Hip hip! Huzza! Hip hip! Huzza!

*He sits, exhausted. The Page steps forward and tilts
his chair slightly from behind.*

Now I must go to bed. And so this audience is hereby
terminated. But I remain, Mr Ambassador, my Lords,
Ladies, Gentlemen, and Others, His Majesty George the
Third, by the grace of God, of Great Britain, Ireland,
and the Dominions beyond the Seas, King, Defender of
the Faith, nor your nor anybody's servant, and thoroughly
deserving of blissful extinction. Proclamation for this
day, eighteen hundred and something or other. Now I will
let you go.

God save Me.

*Very gently, the Page takes the King's hand and leads
him off.*

ZENOBIA

Author's Note

In their essentials the historical events described are true.

The quotations from 'On the Sublime' are taken from *Classical Literary Criticism*, translated by T. S. Dorsch (with kind permission of Penguin Books); and I must acknowledge my debt to Richard Stoneman's book *Palmyra and its Empire*, published by the University of Michigan Press.

Zenobia was first performed at the Young Vic on 2 August 1995, in a co-production by the Royal Shakespeare Company and the Young Vic. The cast, in order of appearance, was as follows:

Odainat Colin Farrell
Hairan James Barriscale
Moqimu Stephen Clyde
Worod Gregor Singleton
Longinus Robert Gillespie
Wahballat James Frain
Timagenes David Beames
Yedibel Colin Starkey
Zenobia Penny Downie
Malik Clive Rowe
Zabdas Conrad Asquith
Porphyry Emily Raymond
Quintinius Gwynn Beech
Gratus Arthur Cox
Aurelian Trevor Cooper
Probus Sean O'Callaghan
Pertinax David Hounslow
Bedouin Scout Quill Roberts
Roman Prefect Colin Farrell
Cato James Barriscale
Antoninus Gregor Singleton
Philip Gwynn Beech
Syrus Darren Roberts
Dawkins Quill Roberts
Wood Darren Roberts

**Roman Soldiers, Generals, Palmyrene Soldiers
and Courtiers** played by members of the cast and
Joanne Howarth

Director Mike Ockrent
Designer Tim Goodchild
Lighting Bob Bryan
Music Jonathan Dove

Characters

Odainat King of Palmyra
Hairan his son
Moqimu a waiter
Worod a general
Longinus a philosopher
Wahballat son of Zenobia
Timagenes a statesman
Yedibel a clerk
Zenobia Queen of Palmyra
Malik a eunuch
Zabdas Commander of the Palmyrene Army
Porphyry a student of philosophy
Quintinius a Roman senator
Gratus a Roman senator
Aurelian Emperor of Rome
Probus his tribune
Pertinax a Roman general
Bedouin Scout
Roman Prefect
Cato Roman soldier
Antoninus Roman soldier
Philip Roman soldier
Syrus Roman soldier
Dawkins an explorer
Wood an explorer

Roman Soldiers, Generals, Palmyrene Soldiers
and Courtiers

The play begins in Syria, AD 267

Act One

SCENE ONE

A camp in the Syrian desert, AD 267. The tent of the King, Odainat. He is with his son, Hairan, a soldier. They are coming to the end of a feast. Odainat pats his stomach.

Odainat Food tastes different when war is won. Every flavour is a blessing – every crumb an answered prayer.

Odainat's hands fall on a cochlis brooch that he wears. He removes it and gives it to Hairan.

This is one of our finest royal jewels.

Hairan Thank you, father.

Odainat It was given to me by my wife.

Hairan Then you should –

Odainat No, keep it. You fought well. You deserve it. – Four days march, and we're home. I have sent Zabdas ahead to announce our victories.

Hairan You will enter the city in triumph.

Odainat I left it Odainat, a son of the desert. I return Odenathus, friend of Rome, Protector of the East. I am satisfied.

Servants enter and clear away the dishes. A valet, Moqimu, brings a large jug of wine, and glasses.

What is that, Moqimu?

Moqimu Wine, Majesty.

Odainat We have no wine.

Moqimu A gift, Majesty, from the Roman Commander at Emesa.

Odainat The Romans send us wine? We *have* done well today! (*laughing*) Drink with me, Hairan. Drink a toast: to home!

Moqimu pours wine and exits with the other servants, leaving the jug behind.

Hairan To Palmyra!

They drink. Odainat toasts again.

Odainat To the Queen!

Odainat drinks. Hairan hesitates.

She will never replace your mother, I know that. But have the courtesy to show respect where it is due.

Hairan (*drinks grudgingly*) To your wife.

Odainat My wife . . . like a glittering star, lighting up the night of my old age. Her eyes as dark as a raven's wing; her teeth so white, they seem inlaid with pearls. How I cherish her.

Hairan The soldiers say she never lets you in her bed, father.

Odainat I have with her five children.

Hairan Five visits only, they say.

Odainat Envy breeds malice in a body of men.

Hairan I would be ashamed, to have such a reputation.

Odainat You are sour tonight.

Hairan Forgive me. I miss the war. Peace brings a dreadful silence. I miss the clatter of swords . . . the whisper of arrows . . .

Odainat Then drink: to the noise of battle.

Hairan To Persian blood in the dust!

They drink, and laugh. Worod, a general, enters escorting Longinus, who carries a travelling bag. He kneels before the King.

Who is this?

Worod A scholar. Says he got lost.

Longinus I am Cassius Longinus, Majesty, of Athens. I travel to Palmyra.

Odainat Palmyra? On what business?

Longinus Philosophy, my Lord. With some Greek, a little rhetoric, a parcel of mathematics. Sophistry, disputation, the Emanation of the Universal Mind. And I can read and write.

Worod (*laughs*) A joker.

Hairan Kick him out.

Longinus No no, I have a letter! A formal invitation to attend the court of Queen Zenobia, and tutor her son!

Odainat (*reads the letter*) It is my wife's hand. (*Smiles.*) Wahballat wants to take up philosophy.

Hairan Wahballat is a girl. He should take up knitting.

Odainat (*to Longinus*) My sons . . . are as alike as wormwood and syrup.

Longinus It is rare indeed to find all the great qualities conjoined in one man's form, Majesty. Perhaps your soul is too capacious for your seed, and must, therefore, subdivide itself?

Odainat (*laughs*) No. They had different mothers. – Sit with us.

Longinus and Worod sit down. Longinus won't accept the proffered glass of wine.

Longinus I regret I cannot take wine.

Odainat No wine?

Hairan Why not?

Longinus It impedes the trajectory of logic. To launch a thought, to see it fly, to watch it arc gracefully and land with a thud in another man's brain – that is my one pleasure. Fill me up with wine, and all my best ideas buzz hither and yon like a nest of hornets, impressively voluble but in the end quite devoid of purpose. I'll have a cup of milk if you've got one.

Worod The ass wants milk.

The soldiers laugh, and drain their glasses. Longinus watches.

Longinus (*cautiously*) May I enquire – the bodies strewn across the landscape – whose they are?

Hairan Persians.

Longinus . . . And is that good or bad?

Worod You are new to the East?

Longinus Fresh off the boat.

Worod But you do know who the Emperor of Rome is?

Longinus looks puzzled for a moment, then rummages in his bag for a coin.

Longinus Unless something terrible has happened, it's – (*He peers at the head on the coin.*) – Valerian. But they come and go at such a lick, don't they?

Worod Something terrible has happened.

Longinus Ah.

Worod Valerian was taken prisoner by the Persians, who rose against him. Their leader used him as a footstool for his horse, then cut the flesh off the Emperor, and had him tanned and stuffed.

Hairan gives a little involuntary grunt, and puts his hand to his stomach, grimacing.

Odainat What is it?

Hairan Rich food.

Worod The Empire itself was in danger. My Lord Odainat, an illustrious King of Syria, and loyal subject of the new Emperor, Gallienus, answered the call with seventy thousand tribesmen. Those Persian corpses are the outcome. We have restored the Empire in the East. We are the heroes of Palmyra! (*to Odainat*) And you are made a Roman Consul, so I hear?

Longinus A Consul? From a small city-state in the desert? It would seem to me, in my ignorance of matters political, that that is some achievement.

Odainat Palmyra is no mud-hut enclave round a stagnant pool, Longinus. It is a union of tribes. We rule from the Great Sea to the Parthian border. And thus control the trade routes, east to west. We are rich beyond imagination.

Hairan Yet you can't buy a kiss from your wife.

Odainat raises his arm – from nowhere a dagger has appeared in his hand. Worod catches his arm. Stools are overturned.

Odainat You dare insult the Queen once more – !

Hairan You prefer her to me! I am the first in blood, yet you prefer her and her litter!

Odainat You will show respect!

Hairan Respect? When I am King of Palmyra – your widow will show respect!

Hairan throws to the floor the brooch that Odainat gave him, and leaves the tent. Worod pours more drinks.

Worod He will learn to be a statesman.

The King is morose. He drinks hard.

Odainat (*to Longinus*) Have you sons?

Longinus No. But I have a pupil. He is just as bad.

Odainat gives an involuntary burp, and clutches at his stomach.

Odainat What did we eat?

Worod Ostrich.

Odainat That'll be it. (*to Longinus*) Don't judge Hairan too harshly. Can't be easy for the boy. His mother died in childbirth. A year later I found a girl of noble blood, but wild and wilful – radiant, but difficult. I tamed her. Taught her dignity. The Queen she has become surpasses every wonder of the world, ancient or modern, take your pick. But nothing I can do will make her love my son and heir. Her own boy she dotes on and pampers.

Longinus Oh, that is quite natural.

Odainat Is it?

Longinus I have little experience of women – well, none, to be perfectly frank – but they surely all promote their offspring, and resent another's claim?

148

Odainat Yes, petty jealousies they nibble at like nuts,
to dull their appetite for power. I bear no grudge –
Wahballat is our son – but how do I content her?

Longinus Flatter her. Indulge her. Lay siege to her with
presents.

Odainat Good, Longinus. The fortune I won in the war,
I will lavish on her! She will live in luxury, the wife of a
Consul –

Longinus I'm sure that's all she's ever wanted.

Odainat – and Wahballat shall have his philosophy.
I may even dabble myself.

> *Odainat and Longinus laugh. Worod falls off his seat
> and has convulsions on the floor.*

Worod!

Worod Where did you get the wine?

Longinus What is it?

Odainat The wine?

Worod Poison!

> *Odainat is stunned. He remains very still, hands on
> his stomach.*

Odainat Not the ostrich . . .?

Worod I didn't eat it!

> *Hairan crashes into the tent, reeling and vomiting.*

Hairan What's wrong with me?

Odainat Poison.

Hairan I am poisoned?

Odainat (*to Longinus*) You?

Longinus I'm afraid I feel quite all right.

Worod The wine! Where did you get it?

Hairan Sent by the Romans!

Worod Treason!

Hairan Father, I am dying! (*He groans.*)

Worod We saved them! And this is how they thank us . . . (*He dies.*)

Longinus Majesty . . .?

Odainat Yes, I can feel it. The trickle of eternity. Good subject for an ode, Longinus. Disillusion of a King at the hour of his death.

Hairan Father – forgive me. (*He dies.*)

Odainat Hairan . . .? (*He sinks to his knees and crawls to his son's body.*) At least he thought it was the work of Rome.

Longinus I'm sorry?

Odainat This wine came from my wife.

Longinus (*shocked*) How do you – ?

Odainat Sweetened with honey. Only she knows my taste. – Now it is racing, racing through my veins. My guts like a blizzard of broken glass, kicked up by horses' hooves. A bear's claw lodged in my heart. (*He collapses.*) Now she has got what she must have desired. Her son on Palmyra's throne. (*He has convulsions.*) Where am I going, philosopher?

Longinus To join with the one-ness of all matter –

Odainat Zenobia . . .! (*He dies.*)

Longinus – I think. (*He takes stock.*) A king, a prince, and a general, dead at one's feet. No amount of rhetoric can avert a catastrophe, no erudition shield my innocence from angry spears and swords. My training affords a clear grasp of the available options. One could ruminate at some length on the false grandeur of kingship and the levelling blade of time. Or one could run.

> *Longinus grabs his bag and goes to leave. He passes the jewelled brooch that Hairan threw to the floor. He picks it up and hides it in his cloak. He runs out. A pause. Moqimu enters and sees the bodies. He puts his hand to Odainat's heart. Nothing. He bangs his jug loudly against his tray.*

SCENE TWO

Palmyra. A palace. A procession enters, in funeral attire. At its head is Wahballat, a teenage boy, followed by a statesman, Timagenes, and Yedibel, his clerk. Behind them come more statesmen and courtiers. Wahballat slumps wearily on the throne and shuts his eyes. Cautiously, Timagenes and Yedibel approach him, with documents.

Timagenes The tariffs, Majesty?

Wahballat So soon?

Timagenes We need the Royal Assent.

Wahballat I have just buried my father . . .!

Timagenes We should be expeditious. It is the height of the season, and four separate caravans are approaching the city. Any delay means a massive loss of revenue.

Wahballat If you put the tariffs up, won't the traders simply go another way?

Timagenes There is no other way. Every oasis between the Euphrates and the sea is under our dominion.

Wahballat You can do what you jolly well like, then, can't you, Timagenes?

Timagenes You must approve it. Please let my clerk read the proposals.

Yedibel (*reads from a papyrus scroll*) Aromatic oils in alabaster, per camel load, from 25 to 30 denarii; aromatic oils in goatskin, per camel load, from 13 to 15 denarii; bales of silk, per donkey load, from 40 to 50 denarii; bales –

Wahballat All right, all right!

> *He takes the official seal which Timagenes offers him, and stamps the document. In the background Zenobia, wearing a headscarf and ceremonial robes, emerges from the procession with her escort, the eunuch Malik. He fans her with a palm frond as she watches her son.*

Seems an awful lot of money just to pass through the city.

Timagenes We have water, Majesty. Water commands high prices. Now, as to the matter of the new pediment upon the Temple of Baalshamin –

> *Yedibel unrolls another scroll. Wahballat leaps from his throne in frustration.*

Wahballat Look here, I don't care about your pediments! My mother is in charge of public works! Why can't you leave me in peace?

Timagenes Because you are King, Wahballat.

Wahballat I never asked to be King! Hairan should be King!

Timagenes Hairan is dead.

Zenobia Hairan is – regrettably – dead.

Zenobia comes forward. The statesmen bow.

Wahballat Speak to the Queen. Leave me to my books.

Wahballat finds his book in a corner and sits down to read. Zenobia advances. Malik fans her.

Zenobia You have attended to the tariffs?

They show her the scroll. She glances over it, checking figures.

Not enough. Not enough. Not enough.

Yedibel Not enough, Majesty?

Zenobia Raise them further.

Timagenes We are in surplus already. Any more, and the Romans will take steps.

Zenobia Steps, Timagenes? Steps? I don't know where you have been this afternoon but I have been in the Valley of the Tombs, mourning my dear husband. I designed the vaults of his funeral tower. I did not think to see them used so soon. Who did this? Who stocked these rooms of death?

Timagenes The Romans, Majesty.

Yedibel The Romans.

Zenobia Yes. Odainat went to war on the westerners' behalf – and they killed him. Their meek client-king.

Timagenes We understand your bitterness. The nation shares your grief.

Yedibel The troops are enraged. They sing songs of revenge in their barracks.

Zenobia Then let us show our anger. Are we taxing our own people here? No, we are simply raising the price of saffron on the Via Piperatica. The Romans are addicted to their silks and scents and spices; life without black pepper would be simply inconceivable; so let them pay. Death duties.

Timagenes King Wahballat has already sealed the warrant.

Zenobia My son is a minor.

She rips up the document.

Re-draft it. – Malik, show them out.

Timagenes and Yedibel leave with Malik. The courtiers disperse. Zenobia goes to Wahballat and runs her hand through his hair.

You miss him, don't you?

Wahballat Why, don't you?

Zenobia I am saving my tears for my pillow. (*Pause.*) There is a gap, a void, in the nation. A space that must be filled.

Wahballat I don't have the qualifications!

Zenobia No. But are you not ambitious?

Wahballat Not awfully, no.

Zenobia Look. Money drops into our purses like sweat off a merchant's chin. This place we have built is unique. We could fill it with people of genius! Create the greatest society the desert's ever known!

Wahballat But what if the trade-routes shift? Or the Romans go off pepper?

Zenobia (*thoughtfully*) That, we must prepare for.

Wahballat But how?

Zenobia . . . It intrigues me, the living muscle of power.

Wahballat It gives me a headache.

Zenobia (*smiles*) One day you will govern with wisdom and strength. Your glories will make five hundred years of Roman civilization look like footprints in the sand. But for now, devote yourself to study. I will act for you.

Wahballat . . . Did you love my father?

Zenobia (*smiles*) Love him?

Wahballat Love him . . . as a man?

Zenobia You mean did I sleep with him? I bore him children. So I must have done. It is not a very interesting subject. But you I presume are obsessed, seventeen and obsessed, with the secrets of slippery bodies. (*laughing*) Have you thought of wrestling?

> *She grapples with him, but Wahballat is unwilling to play, and pulls away.*

Wahballat No, mother!

Zenobia Oh, my darling . . . I hate this adulthood. Once I could do anything with you: hurl you in the air, or lay you down and suck your toes. Be my little boy again . . . kiss me like you used to.

Wahballat (*kissing her dutifully*) I don't like fighting.

Zenobia Nor did your father. But he did what he had to do.

Wahballat Yes, and look where it got him!

Zenobia Your father saved Rome from the Persians.

Wahballat Is that why they killed him? He was a threat?

Zenobia Well, he defeated an army they could not defeat –

Wahballat So if the Persians beat the Romans –

Zenobia And he beat the Persians –

Wahballat . . . So he was assassinated.

Zenobia These creatures are not fit to rule the world! They kill for pleasure! They are savages in well-cut clothes, drunk on barbaric spectacle and hollow victory parades – for they win no victories! Their Empire is weak!

Wahballat It is nursed by centuries of power.

Zenobia It is a dream, conjured out of sleep, and the toil of slaves; its leadership corrupt; its army committed to holding the North, where the Goths are streaming through the mountains like goose-fat through your fingers. And look – the East lies undefended.

Wahballat What are you suggesting we do?

Zenobia I am not sure exactly. But perhaps we could – prod them a little.

Wahballat Don't be hasty, mother.

Zenobia These murders are an insult. And we must respond.

Malik enters with a guard leading Longinus, who looks the worse for wear. Longinus prostrates himself before Zenobia.

Longinus Great Regent of Palmyra!

Malik He was found by a patrol, wandering the camel-trails. They would have brained him as a spy, but he produced a letter.

Malik hands Longinus' letter to Zenobia.

Zenobia The philosopher . . .! What happened to you? We have been waiting months.

Longinus I landed safely at Laodicea. I set out with a caravan, and was half way here, when I witnessed a – moment of inspiration. I took my pen and ink, and ran, far away, into the wilderness, among the rocks and crags. (*He hands her a tattered manuscript.*) Here is the fruit of my labours. I call it 'On the Sublime'. I humbly dedicate it to you, Zenobia, super-eminent Queen.

Zenobia That is gracious.

Longinus One could hardly arrive empty-handed.

Zenobia What does the manuscript contain?

Longinus It is the repository of all my best ideas on beauty.

Wahballat May I? (*He glances through the text.*)

Zenobia My son, Wahballat.

Longinus (*bowing*) Cassius Longinus, of Athens.

Wahballat You left Athens? For this place?

Longinus I am told the climate is good.

Wahballat For years I have longed to see Athens.

Longinus The German tribes are banging on the gates. It's not a good time for a visit.

Wahballat (*reading*) I say, this is very intriguing . . . All my books are out of date.

Longinus All mine I left behind. To be wiped on Gothic arses. Ah, books, books . . .

Wahballat Send for them.

Longinus All of them?

Wahballat We shall start a library.

Longinus It will be a pleasure to induct a seat of learning. Especially in such a magnificent setting. One would never have expected to find so glittering a metropolis in the desolate heart of Arabia.

Zenobia (*to Malik*) Give him wine.

Longinus (*hastily*) Thank you, no. (*to Wahballat*) You have before you a treatise on the art of excellence in literary composition. That is the highest achievement of the mortal mind, you know.

Wahballat Is it?

Zenobia (*aside to Malik*) What do you think?

Malik Harmless.

Zenobia Then he can stay. My son is happy, look at him. Is Zabdas at the palace?

Malik He's outside, buffing up his armour.

Zenobia Send him in.

Malik and the guard exit.

Longinus, what is your attitude to Rome?

Longinus Rome is the sea. We are the waves.

Zenobia . . . You answer cautiously.

Longinus This is a Roman province, I believe?

Zenobia Can the sum of the waves ever be greater than the sea itself?

Longinus One has not studied the ocean, Majesty, or examined the virtues of its constituent parts.

Zenobia But is it possible the sea could split in two?

Longinus The Jews would have us believe so.

Zenobia Then you say it is possible.

Longinus I say there is textual evidence in the history of Moses . . . but historians, you know . . . notoriously unreliable. It is a hypothesis.

Zenobia Might the sea wage war on itself? Hypothetically speaking?

Longinus Experience, which is not a thing I am particularly fond of, would suggest that the sea is constantly at war with itself. There are whirlpools, currents, racing tides . . . the thunder of surf on the rocks . . . the dead calm of illusory peace. I have no doubt, Majesty, that the ocean is a natural battle-zone. Indeed, on my way here I was sick as a pig.

Zenobia Thank you. One thing more. If this sea had drowned your lover, how would you take revenge?

Longinus (*laughs*) I would take ten million buckets, and sling it off the edge of the world.

> *Zenobia and Wahballat laugh. Zabdas, the Commander-in-Chief, enters escorted by Malik. Malik resumes fanning the Queen.*

Zenobia Commander. I am sorry to have kept you waiting.

Zabdas I have infinite patience, Majesty. My condolences, on this hateful day.

Zenobia We are finished with sorrow. We are forging ahead. I would like to know the precise disposition of our armies.

Zabdas May I ask the purpose?

Zenobia . . . My husband called you the Good Soldier. 'When I need my orders obeyed,' he told me, 'I send Zabdas.' I hope I can count on your loyalty.

Zabdas Aye, you can.

Zenobia Come what may?

Zabdas I will serve the wife of Odainat to my final breath.

Zenobia You serve not his wife but his blood. The line of Odainat rests in this boy, and in his descendants, and his descendants' descendants. For them we must take action. Casual slaughter on our own soil must not go unpunished! We are fortunate to have with us a wise man, Longinus of Greece. I have sought his advice, and he counsels quick reprisals.

Longinus (*worried*) I don't think I actually –

Zenobia Our forces stand ready, and hot for revenge. The only decision remaining to be taken is – where? North into Persia, east into Parthia, south into Palestine? – Prepare your report.

Zabdas We have just made peace, Majesty.

Zenobia And no doubt we shall do so again, Commander. When the gains made by my husband have been consolidated. The time is auspicious. We *must* expand. For our country and this boy!

> *Wahballat is engrossed in the manuscript, and is not listening.*

Zabdas (*bowing*) It will be an honour to lead to victory the armies of Palmyra.

Zenobia An honour, yes. But *mine*.

Zabdas Naturally yours. All glory is yours. I simply mean that when we fight it will be me commanding.

Zenobia You miss the point. I will command. And not from some hilltop, either.

Zabdas With respect, you cannot lead the troops. You are a woman.

Zenobia I will become a warrior.

Zabdas No, the men will not accept you.

Zenobia I will inspire them.

Zabdas Look, it isn't –

Zenobia My sex is immaterial! There is nothing manly in the field of battle that I cannot equal! Or do you challenge me?

Zabdas I? Fight you? (*He laughs lightly.*) No.

Zenobia You're beginning to annoy me, Zabdas.

Zabdas Nothing could be further from my wishes.

Zenobia (*angrily*) I was born to this. I am descended from Ptolemy of Egypt. The dynasty of Cleopatra! And you tell me a female cannot do great things! (*to Malik*) Stop fanning. Never fan me again. Never let it seem that I am weak. Let the sun burn me and the wind chill me; I will harden myself.

> *She rips off her headscarf.*

This is how I will face the enemy. I will put shame in their hearts. They will be beaten by a woman.

> *She turns to leave, then turns back.*

I know where to strike. Egypt!

Zabdas Egypt? But Majesty, the Romans have a standing army there!

Zenobia And is this just? Have they the right? Have they legitimate title to the lush lands of the Nile? – Or should we not reclaim the kingdom of my ancestors, for Wahballat and his sons?

Zenobia exits with Malik. Pause.

Longinus Egypt supplies one-third of the grain that Rome needs to feed itself. The Emperor Gallienus will take it as an act of sedition.

Zabdas Scared, Greek?

Longinus A nice quiet place to retire, I thought. A little light research in the morning, a rest in the afternoon. (*He sighs.*)

Zabdas exits angrily.

Wahballat (*looking up*) This is jolly interesting, Longinus. (*Reads.*) 'The greatest of all blessings is good fortune, and next to it comes good counsel, which, however, is no less important, since its absence leads to the complete destruction of what good fortune brings.' I'd never thought of that.

SCENE THREE

Palmyra. Three helmeted soldiers enter, fighting with swords, one against two. The First Soldier defends well, until with a swirling slash the Third Soldier wounds the First Soldier, cutting him behind his knee. The First Soldier goes down in pain, blood flowing. They stop fighting immediately. The Third Soldier is Zenobia, dressed in full armour as a man. She throws down her sword, pulls off her helmet and turns to the Second Soldier.

Zenobia Fetch help!

The Second Soldier leaves at a run. Zenobia kneels by the wounded First Soldier and pulls off his helmet. It is Zabdas.

Zabdas, forgive me.

Zabdas I do.

Zenobia I was wild! I did not mean to hurt you!

Zabdas You have not hurt me.

Zenobia But – your leg –

Zabdas This meat is yours, to do with as you will. I bleed, but there is no pain.

Zenobia I tried to parry, but I was wild!

Zabdas A soldier must learn to control his passion.

Zenobia I will learn.

Zabdas Turn it on the enemy. Never on your friends.

Zenobia (*taking his head in her hands*) Never again, I swear to you!

Zabdas (*twisting his head away, as if in pain*) Majesty, you cannot be seen here. The people are not ready – a woman in armour – there will be uproar. Go inside.

Zenobia And leave you wounded in the road?

Zabdas They will come for me. Go, I beg you.

Porphyry, a student from Athens, enters and watches from a distance.

Zenobia When may I be seen?

Zabdas What, as a man?

Zenobia No, simply as I wish to be.

Zabdas How is that?

Zenobia Simply free to act as I choose. Free not to be gentle, or kind. Free to fight. *When?*

Zabdas In the chaos of war, when all formality's abandoned, and the only law is the strength of your arm. Then you may cut hamstrings to your heart's content, but now, please – go!

Zenobia exits.

Aagh! The pain! Where she touched my face! Delicious pain! Her fingers, like snowflakes on my skin! She could slice every cord in my body, for one more touch of those hands!

Porphyry approaches Zabdas, who doesn't see him at first.

Porphyry Can I help you?

Zabdas How can you help me? You, a boy? You do not know the vicious thrust of love!

Porphyry (*kneeling*) Let me see.

Zabdas It is nothing. A scratch. A pleasure!

Porphyry You will bleed to death from this pleasure.

Porphyry takes the rope belt from around his waist and applies a tourniquet to Zabdas' thigh.

I have read that the flow of blood can be obstructed, if this is tight enough – there! I think we have staunched it. How did it happen?

Zabdas I dropped my guard. For a second, I dropped my guard. And the bright sharp blade drove in.

Soldiers run on, with a litter.

Soldier Over here!

Porphyry (*taking herbs from his shoulder-bag*) Apply these herbs to the wound, with balsam, if you can get it.

Zabdas . . . You are a capable lad. Where do you live? I'll send a reward.

Porphyry I don't know, sir. It's my first day in Palmyra. I've got to find my master.

The soldiers lift Zabdas on to the litter.

Soldier Easy now, Commander.

Zabdas You heard me cry out, didn't you?

Porphyry nods.

Just pain, that's all, just agony . . .

Porphyry That's all I heard.

Zabdas Good boy. I'll remember you.

The soldiers carry off Zabdas.

Porphyry What kind of place is this? The architecture of your dreams, and generals cut down in the streets? There are marble columns on every house, triumphal arches, treasure vaults, masonry wrought like filigree rings . . . And everywhere soldiers. Marching, drilling, racing dusty chariots through crowded alleys . . . The city smells of war.

Wahballat enters, reading as he walks.

Excuse me, I'm a stranger here. Can you tell me – the military activity? Is there going to be a battle?

Wahballat (*looks up from his page gloomily*) Several, I expect. (*He turns back to his manuscript and walks on.*)

Porphyry And what is the cause?

Wahballat My mother.

Porphyry laughs.

Oh, you think it's a joke? Perhaps you haven't got a
mother?

Porphyry Believe me, I've got a mother.

Wahballat They always know what's best for us, don't
they?

Porphyry Oh, the lectures, the arguments, the shutting
yourself in your room . . .

Wahballat (*laughing*) Yes! You try saying, 'Mother,
I don't want to be what you want me to be, I'm quite
content as I am,' but all you get is a withering look and
a smart new uniform to wear.

Porphyry I never got the uniform. I had to buy my own.

Wahballat What are you, a lawyer?

Porphyry A philosopher.

Wahballat Gosh, that's what I want to be!

Porphyry (*abashed*) Well, I'm training.

Wahballat Ethics?

Porphyry Natural science.

Wahballat It's a long, hard road, isn't it? (*Sighs, indicating
his manuscript.*) Been on the same page for a week.

Porphyry What's the text?

Wahballat It's new stuff. Pretty dense.

Porphyry May I? – Hmm. (*Reads.*) 'No-one would
dispute that periphrasis contributes to the sublime. For

as in music the sweetness of the dominant melody is enhanced by what are known as decorative additions, so periphrasis often harmonises with the direct expression of a thought, and greatly embellishes it.' The style is familiar . . .

Wahballat Elegant speech is a terrible struggle.

Porphyry Personally I think it's over-rated, this fanatical obsession with oratory.

Wahballat Do you?

Porphyry Who needs to string fourteen sub-clauses and a pluperfect together, just to conduct an experiment? I incline to observation as the basis of all discovery.

Wahballat That's curious. My tutor says observation is the long holiday of the lazy thinker.

Porphyry Was he lying down when he said it?

Wahballat Come to think of it, he is fond of a snooze.

Porphyry Your tutor is – ?

Wahballat Cassius Longinus, of Athens.

Porphyry (*suddenly worried*) So you are – ?

Wahballat Me? Oh, I'm the King.

> *Porphyry throws himself to the ground in front of Wahballat.*

Porphyry Majesty! I did not know.

Wahballat Perfectly all right. Don't get much conversation around here. It's a muscle-builder's paradise. A javelin-thrower's dream.

Porphyry I have brought the books.

Wahballat The books?

Porphyry My master's library, from Athens.

Wahballat You are Longinus' pupil? Oh, stand up, please. I'm so very happy to meet you. My name is Wahballat. You are called – ?

Porphyry Porphyry.

Wahballat And you are a scientist?

Porphyry Chemistry, mainly. My master disapproves. But it's the future, you see? It's the future!

Wahballat (*overjoyed*) Two schools of thought! Two! In Palmyra! Where before there was barely a glimmer! – You are welcome.

Porphyry It's a magnificent city.

Wahballat Yes, a magnificent city, somewhere on the outer rim of the cosmos. Tell me about the West. Is it true that you can buy –

Porphyry Majesty, I should find Longinus, and unload the books from the donkeys.

Wahballat Of course.

Porphyry You won't mention what I said . . .? About the sub-clauses and so on?

Wahballat I heard nothing but enthusiasm. Come, I will take you to the palace. (*He starts to lead Porphyry off.*) Would you do something for me?

Porphyry (*smiles*) Anything you ask.

Wahballat Teach me, in secret. The rudiments of chemistry.

Porphyry It's a bit hit-and-miss –

Wahballat It's got to be better than playing at soldiers.

They laugh. As they exit, the sounds of a marching troop of infantry are heard off, growing ever louder until they merge into the noise of a great battle, from which emerges:

SCENE FOUR

Egypt. Zenobia alone on the battlefield, clad in a man's armour, but without a helmet. She carries a sword, literally dripping blood.

Zenobia It took all day. Hours and hours of killing. Pyramids of death. Now I know why they like it so much: the sheer exhilaration of being left alive at the end. Ankle-deep in offal, lips blistered from the sun, and a strange new taste in your mouth – (*She puts the bloody sword to her lips.*) – but still alive. There's no great mystery: you throw your weight through your shoulder, and swing. Sparks decorate your shield. A shudder rocks your arm as you strike the bone. A man's eyes glitter in your face, then fade. You step over his corpse, and go on. Always forward. Never back. Never look down at the face in the sand. The screams of the dead are like music.

My first battle. Now I am blooded. Now I know why they like it so much.

SCENE FIVE

Rome. Two Senators, Gratus and Quintinius, holding garlands of flowers.

Quintinius They say she gives no quarter, but flails about like a dervish, her hair matted with blood, her sweating thighs quite naked; and hardened veterans of our Egyptian legions, facing this vision of unfeminine destruction, took to their heels and ran. They say she cut the beating heart from a man, and held it to her lips.

Gratus I once saw a Gaul do that in the arena. The audience were so impressed they yelled for more. So a Greek cut the heart from the Gaul.

Quintinius But they were men!

Gratus Absolutely, yes, I grant there is a difference. – Do you see him yet?

Quintinius No.

Gratus He must pass this way to enter the Senate.

Quintinius With Egypt fallen, we will go short of bread. If the people lack bread, they will riot. Rome itself will resemble a battlefield.

Gratus And will subsequently need to be rebuilt, providing thereby a welcome fillip for the construction trade.

Quintinius (*grins*) I didn't get where I am today by not taking my opportunities.

Gratus Neatly put. No more did I. But it grieves me, this abysmal deterioration of civic pride. In the golden days of the Republic, people would have begged to go hungry, and reached for their swords. Now we live in an age of baseness and dishonour.

Quintinius Do you suppose the new Emperor will have any noticeable effect?

Gratus In the immortal words of Tacitus, 'I hope for good Emperors, but I take them as they come.'

They laugh quietly. This conversation is discreet.

Yet another soldier, I gather?

Quintinius Cavalry man. Risen from the ranks. Son of a Pannonian peasant.

Gratus My point exactly. Standards have declined. We are ruled by the dregs of the Danube.

Quintinius Already I miss Gallienus.

Gratus Yes, he may have had the shortest reign in history, but he knew how to put on a show.

Quintinius He certainly did. And the spectacles you staged for him were beyond compare. The naval battle on the artificial lake . . . I'll never forget that . . .

Gratus Four thousand drowned. Went like a dream.

Quintinius Good old Gallienus.

Gratus He spent public money with a vengeance, the fat bastard.

Quintinius And what did it get him?

Gratus A knife in the guts.

They laugh quietly.

Quintinius . . . Here comes his successor. A crate of oysters says he doesn't live five years.

Gratus Done.

The Emperor Aurelian enters with his Tribune, Probus, and a squad of soldiers guarding him closely. The Senators bow and offer their garlands.

A warm welcome to Rome, stern victor of the North. The Senate salutes you. Jupiter, Juno and Minerva smile down on you. And honest citizens sleep safely in their beds, now the German menace has been checked.

Aurelian stays tight behind his bodyguard. He nods to Probus, who takes the garlands.

Probus I accept them on the Emperor's behalf. Your name?

Gratus Septimus Gratus.

Quintinius Lollius Quintinius.

Probus Thank you, Senators.

Aurelian nods to the Senators, and the squad begins to march on.

Quintinius Emperor . . . the revolt in the East?

Aurelian stops.

Gratus The woman who fights like a man . . .?

Quintinius What measures have you taken?

Gratus When will you be marching out again?

Aurelian nods to Probus.

Probus We do not perceive the threat to be sufficiently volatile to justify an armed response.

Quintinius But she has taken Egypt!

Probus And she will hand it back. We have sued for peace.

Quintinius Peace!

Probus The Palmyrenes are merchants. They will deal. The wheatfields of Egypt are a bargaining tool. There is no direct challenge to Imperial rule.

Gratus With the greatest respect, Emperor, the Senate will never permit you to negotiate with barbarians.

Probus It is done already. Envoys have been sent.

Gratus But this is an outrage! Held to ransom? By a woman?

Aurelian (*losing patience*) Look. I fuck women. I don't fight them. My men would laugh at me.

Quintinius But we have not debated it! We have protocols, traditions . . .

Aurelian Good for you.

Aurelian walks on. Gratus goes after him.

Gratus Emperor, I feel sure we can come rapidly to a consensus on foreign policy, but there is also the outstanding matter of the Roman Mint – which you have closed down –

Aurelian ignores him and exits with the soldiers.

Probus The coinage is debased. Tin passing for silver. Chicanery and deceit. We are initiating a raft of currency reforms. Meanwhile the Mint remains closed.

Gratus Tribune, would you be so good as to invite the Emperor to come to dinner, at my villa in Tivoli? For an off-the-record chat?

Probus The Emperor doesn't eat dinner. (*He exits.*)

Gratus Pannonian arsehole! What did we do to deserve him?

Quintinius We sold our souls to the army. To keep the wild wolf from the door.

Gratus And now they think they can govern by themselves!

Quintinius (*sighs*) Bring back the old days.

Gratus Yes, absolutely, bring back Gallienus! At least he liked his food.

SCENE SIX

Palmyra. A private room in the palace. Zenobia enters in full armour, dusty and exhausted. Malik follows. Piece by piece he removes her armour.

Malik You should have ridden back from Egypt. In a chariot. Or on a horse.

Zenobia I wanted to walk with my men. We sang songs of victory, all the way home. At night we drank by camp-fires, and compared our looted treasure. Never have I felt more alive.

Malik I'm delighted for you, Majesty. Sadly your shoulders somehow failed to get the message. They are crabbed like an old, stunted vine.

Zenobia I carried my sword and my pack.

Malik (*groans*) But you are Queen!

Zenobia They must never see me weaken. One slip, and I am gone.

Malik laughs to himself.

Are you laughing at me, Malik?

Malik No, at us. At the irony of it. I almost a woman. You almost a man.

Zenobia Would you like to be a woman?

Malik Ooh, yes please. Do you know a magic spell?

Zenobia What is it that appeals?

Malik You have things done to you. You do not have to *do* them.

Zenobia But I like to do things.

Malik You will tire of it, Majesty. Women are allowed to change their minds. And are wonderfully good at it, I believe.

Zenobia I hate women –

Malik No –

Zenobia – their flabby arms, their make-up, their smell of cooking oil –

Malik This is why you sent away your daughters?

Zenobia Girls are a distraction in a war.

Malik Yes, they were pretty.

Zenobia No they weren't. They were just weak. Do something to my back, please.

Zenobia lies down and Malik massages her back.

The Romans have offered us peace.

Malik Sweet of them.

Zenobia In return for abandoning Egypt, they will give us the right to crown Wahballat, Emperor of the East – or, as the document puts it, 'Imperator Caesar Julius Aurelius Septimius Vaballathus, Persicus Maximus, Arabicus Maximus, the Devout, the Fortunate, the Unconquered, Augustus.'

Malik Some scribe with a sense of history, killing the hours till teatime . . . And yourself, Majesty?

Zenobia Me? I am nothing. Me they do not recognise.

Malik I have never met a Roman who was not a ghastly snob. They go somewhere foreign, and want to make it just like home. They want the same food, the same entertainment, the same over-heated rooms – see them cruising the bazaars in their ghastly clothes, haggling for trinkets that look 'typically ethnic' . . . Total world domination is a hideous thing. And their sense of geography! A Roman once asked if I had relatives in India! He thought it was just down the road!

Zenobia Malik, I don't know what to do! The troops are exultant. They would fight for a field of stones. I have only to say 'advance'. We could take Mesopotamia, Persia – we could blaze to the shores of Byzantium, and have Europe at our feet!

Malik So what's stopping you?

Zenobia There is a new Emperor.

Malik They do like a change, don't they?

Zenobia He is called Aurelian. My intelligence says he is not like the others. He can fight. He rules his army with a fist of iron. He has secured the northern border, leaving villages burning in the forests, men impaled on trees. He is not the kind of soft fruit we are used to. He is hard. (*Pause.*) I dream of him, Malik. I conjure his face. I try to guess how he will act. I can lead us to the brink of all-out war – push at the skin of the Empire, and see if it will split – but how will he respond? Will he retaliate in numbers, or leave the East to us?

Malik What I know about military strategy you could write on a grain of salt.

Zenobia I must know what he's thinking . . .!

Malik Well, take advice.

Zenobia From?

Malik Your advisors. All those clever fellows you employ.

Zenobia The only one I trust is you.

Malik But I'm the stupidest.

Zenobia You're my friend.

Malik Majesty, you have no friends. (*Beat.*) I am your eunuch. I love you as a slave. (*She looks sad.*) Do you remember, when first you were married, how I would entertain you?

Zenobia nods.

Relax. Clear your mind of everything.

Malik signals to some musicians, who begin to play. Then he dances – a sensuous, erotic dance – and sings:

A bed of flowers
A bed of straw
A bed of feathers
From African birds
A bath of milk
A scented garden
Or rolling, tumbling by
The waterside . . .

I will lie with you
I will lie with you
I will lie with you
Anywhere you choose.

When he is finished:

Now – say quickly – what do you *want*?

Zenobia (*with fierce determination*) Rome.

SCENE SEVEN

Wahballat's library. Longinus lies asleep on a couch, a book open on his chest. Nearby, Wahballat and Porphyry work on a secret chemical experiment with a makeshift apparatus. A glass alembic is heated over glowing embers from the fire. They speak softly, surrounded by huge, dusty books, and phials of powder.

Porphyry Does he still sleep?

Wahballat (*looking at Longinus*) Like a baby.

Porphyry Good. Now we can work. I am today attempting to distill the essence of nitre. Do you understand what nitre is, Majesty?

Wahballat (*sighs*) No, I don't. And please call me Wahballat.

Porphyry shows him some nitre.

Pooh! It stinks.

Porphyry I get it from the camel stables. Some mystical reaction in the soil.

Wahballat It's camel shit?

Porphyry It was camel shit. Now it's a chemical called salt of potassium.

Wahballat I say, this is jolly good fun!

Porphyry The earth reveals its secrets to the wise. You know the pigment they call 'imperial purple'? That dyes the Emperor's cloak?

Wahballat I know it costs a fortune.

Porphyry But where does it come from?

Wahballat shakes his head.

Shellfish.

Wahballat Shellfish?

Porphyry You farm it, a few drops at a time, from a gland in a species of mollusc found only in Phoenicia. (*with a glance at Longinus*) Try gleaning that from a well-turned peroration. – But let us proceed with the experiment. This nitre is the agent. Blue vitriol – here – the reagent. I am adding some charcoal, for its combustible properties are well known. Gently heat. What forms in the collecting glass should be the essence. If people know what we were doing, they would think us mad. The world is unaware of what is possible.

Wahballat What can you do with this essence?

Porphyry It can separate silver from gold.

Wahballat Why would you wish to do that?

Porphyry Purity.

Wahballat You want pure gold?

Porphyry I want purity.

Wahballat You disappoint me. You are doing this just to get rich! I can make you rich, if that is your desire. But wealth alone is nothing. Knowledge is supreme. I thought you were an explorer, probing the recesses of nature.

Porphyry I am!

Wahballat I thought this was an odyssey of learning!

Porphyry It is!

Longinus stirs. They quieten.

I am trying to make *medicine*. The properties of minerals are central to that pursuit. I am trying to find the drug that will cure all pain.

Wahballat Is there such a thing?

Porphyry The ancient masters thought so. There exists a universal spirit, I am sure of it. And all matter can be reduced to this chief agent, given skill and dedication. One day someone will discover the essential power that will heal wounds, retard decay, prolong your days indefinitely.

Wahballat Eternal youth?

Porphyry Why not?

Wahballat Tantalising!

Porphyry Why must we age, and decline, and die? Once we understand the driving force of life, what benefits will follow?

Wahballat And you will do this! And I will be your apprentice!

Porphyry (*smiles*) Perhaps. There's the small problem of our acid of nitre, though, which as yet we have not solved. And it looks like the fire's going out.

Wahballat takes a bellows to the fire.

Wahballat Awfully sorry I spoke so harshly. I jump to conclusions – forgive me. I would like to be your friend. There are so few people I can talk to.

Porphyry You are not like the others.

Wahballat Nor are you.

Porphyry How strange, that I should find my way to Syria, and you and I should meet.

Wahballat When we are together I –

Porphyry (*suddenly businesslike*) No activity in the alembic. I think sulphur should be added.

> *Porphyry tips a phial of sulphur into the apparatus. The retort explodes with a loud bang. The apparatus is shattered, but no-one is hurt. The noise wakes Longinus.*

Longinus The five sources of sublimity!

> *As Longinus sits up, he drops to the floor the cochlis brooch he has hidden under his robe. Nobody notices this. Porphyry and Wahballat hastily hide their alchemical textbooks and the ruined apparatus, and pick up the work they ought to have been studying.*

As I was saying, the five sources of sublimity *are* – ?

Porphyry The ability to form grand conceptions, master.

Wahballat The stimulus of powerful emotion –

Longinus – though some emotions are mean, and not in the least sublime –

Wahballat The . . . the . . .

Porphyry The proper formation of the two types of figure, namely, figures of thought and figures of speech –

Wahballat – coupled with the choice of words, the use of imagery, and the elaboration of style.

Longinus The fifth source of grandeur embraces all those already mentioned, and it is the total effect resulting from dignity and elevation. What was that ghastly noise?

Wahballat (*to Porphyry*) Did you hear a noise?

Porphyry I was intent on my studies.

Wahballat I too. Perhaps you were dreaming, Longinus?

Longinus Dreaming, Majesty? (*It occurs to him that perhaps he was.*) An old affliction, nothing more. Wounds won in the cause of art. The crash of split infinitives, the hoot of rude tumidity, the bombast of the third-rate panegyrist – this clamour fills my head from time to time.

Wahballat I expect that was it, then.

Longinus (*to Porphyry*) What is the text for today?

Porphyry Book Sixteen of the *Iliad*, master.

Longinus Well fetch it down, man, fetch it – this is no *experiment*, to sit and watch for hours – this is literature, literature fit for a King!

    Porphyry climbs a ladder to reach the book.

Wahballat Let me help you. (*aside to Porphyry*) Well, that was jolly interesting, wasn't it?

Porphyry (*aside to Wahballat*) What on earth happened?

Longinus (*to himself*) Could have sworn I heard a bang . . .

    Yedibel enters.

Yedibel Philosopher.

Longinus We are at our books, sir.

Yedibel Then you must put them away, Longinus. The Queen is coming.

Longinus (*jumps up*) The Queen? I am barely awake!

Yedibel The Queen has consulted the oracle of Aphrodite Aphacitis, as to whether the war should be prolonged. You are required to interpret the signs.

*Yedibel exits. Wahballat and Porphyry come to
Longinus with the* Iliad.

Longinus Runes, entrails, chicken's blood – what signs?
Interpret – advise – oh, heaven! The Queen – courtiers –
any minute!

Wahballat Asyndeton, or the omission of conjunctions?

Longinus Quite correct. To give the impression of
agitation. – Porphyry, bring everything we've got on
prediction. Quick! Never done oracles before. Witness
the final humiliation of logic, in a welter of omens and
spells!

*Porphyry runs to fetch the books. Zenobia enters
with Zabdas, dragging his bad leg, Timagenes,
Yedibel, Malik, and other courtiers. Zenobia wears
a customised version of her army uniform: a short
tunic, with gems dangling from its lower edge. Her
arms and legs are bare, and a short sword hangs at
her side.*

Most illustrious exarch of the Palmyrenes, welcome to
our cave of mental labour. The great Library is complete.

Wahballat Absolutely first-class tuition, mother, without
a doubt.

Zenobia You would not have thanked me had I brought
you a charlatan. Longinus, we need your help. Some
of us believe we should reject the Romans' overtures
of peace, and challenge their authority throughout the
whole of Asia. Some others of us feel differently, asserting
that peace will benefit trade, that we have all the wealth
we need, and that the terms from Rome are in fact quite
favourable.

Zabdas Favourable? We beat them!

Timagenes But why waste more life? It will all end in destruction.

Zenobia As you see we are divided. So I made a pilgrimage to Heliopolis. I sacrificed at the shrine of Aphrodite, and offered my gifts to the sacred pool. As I did so I asked for advice.

> *Porphyry places open volumes before Longinus, and indicates sections of text.*

Porphyry Here, here, and here.

Zenobia Into the pool I placed gold, silver, linen and silk, consecrated by the Priestess of the temple, and blessed by every church.

Longinus (*reading fast*) They sank to the bottom?

Zenobia Yes.

Longinus Good.

Zenobia Then they rose back to the top.

Longinus Ah.

Zenobia What are we to make of this?

Timagenes A bad augury, is it not, philosopher? A sign that further war will court disaster?

Zenobia Or a miracle, perhaps? A thing of joy?

Longinus If I might have a moment or two for consultation – ?

Zabdas Get on with it, Greek. Thirty thousand archers stand at arms.

Longinus (*aside to Porphyry*) I think we could call this a conundrum.

Porphyry (*aside to Longinus*) She likes to fight.

Longinus (*aside*) What?

Porphyry (*aside*) Be careful, master.

Longinus . . . Majesty, albeit the weapons of divination and clairvoyance have no true rank in the rhetorician's arsenal, I will venture a gloss on the preternatural wonders you have seen. Gold, silver, linen and silk are representative of all your prosperity on earth. By casting them into the sacred pool, you demonstrate your willingness to renounce them. What is the official state religion?

Zenobia We have none. All faiths are accommodated, from Jews to votaries of the Sun.

Yedibel We even have a Christian, Paul of Samosata.

Longinus An enlightened policy. And you are right. It is all one. All roads lead to the centre. We serve a Great Unknown, a Demiurge, creator of the Universal Mind.

Zabdas Cut the riddles. Speak to the point.

Longinus The point? We are dealing with a celestial allegory, Commander. The divine riddle of the future. One is not convinced there is a *point*.

Longinus turns to Porphyry, who whispers in his ear.

The gifts rose back to the surface. Did they float?

Zenobia Yes.

Longinus Defiant of physical laws! Then what happened?

Zenobia The Priestess made us take them away. Now we don't know what to do with them.

Longinus Treasure them! Encase them in your deepest vaults! They have been sanctioned by heaven! The Gods have viewed your worldly goods, and sent them back to you, imbued with esoteric properties. They approve your actions.

Zenobia In taking Egypt?

Longinus In taking Egypt, Majesty, and, I think, in defying Rome. The connotation is clear. If you risk your most precious assets, they shall return to you, with even greater value than before. Whatever you choose is for the best.

Timagenes Bah! Longinus, you preposterous sycophant!

Longinus You doubt the omniscience of the oracle?

Timagenes The gifts are meant to vanish in the depths of the pool – any fool knows that! I cannot believe you are taken in like this, Majesty!

Zenobia Timagenes suggests my judgement is unsound.

Timagenes No, but you fight out of pride!

Zenobia Pride? Yes. That's why I fight. And have you none? No feeling for your country?

Timagenes I am First Minister. Head of all the Tribes. I care for the land, for the people. Of course I am proud; but proud of our intelligence, our statesmanship, our will to survive!

Zenobia Like fleas in the fur of our oppressors. Is how we survive.

Wahballat I say, that's a bit rich –

Zenobia Be quiet. – I have a vision of the future. We are making Palmyra an oasis not of wells and springs, but of culture, of science, of tolerance and achievement. Longinus has spoken well; and Timagenes has strengthened my resolve, with his fears and his appeasements, like a rat scuttling for cover when the sandstorm blows up.

Timagenes May I remind you of my position –

Zenobia You have no position! Kneel!

Reluctantly, Timagenes kneels. Zenobia draws her sword and holds it to his neck. The courtiers pull back.

I swing my arm. That's all. What can you say to save your life?

Timagenes No – no –

Zenobia Is he eloquent in his plea, Longinus? You judge.

Longinus Me?

Wahballat (*to Zenobia*) You are making yourself look ridiculous!

Zenobia Ruthlessness is not thought ridiculous in a man. (*to Timagenes*) You oppose me. Why should I not cut your head off?

Timagenes I don't want to die!

Longinus A line of high poetry, Majesty, in my opinion . . .

Zenobia I have read Homer. That was not poetry.

Longinus It had a sincerity – a naïve charm –

Zenobia Metre? Assonance?

Longinus But the sentiments expressed – a universal truth –

Zenobia But so unoriginal!

Zenobia swings her arm.

Wahballat Mother! I thought we were going to be tolerant!

Zenobia lowers her sword, glaring at him.

Zenobia So we were. (*to Timagenes*) I strip you of your office. Get out.

Timagenes Thank you, Majesty.

Zenobia Thank literary criticism. Not previously known for its valour.

Timagenes bows to Longinus and Wahballat and exits.

Yedibel.

Yedibel Majesty?

Zenobia Your views on the war?

Yedibel The heroic struggle of a downtrodden people against imperialism and servitude, Majesty.

Zenobia I appoint you First Minister. (*to Longinus*) Once more we are grateful to you for your guidance. Please accompany us to the Temple of Bel, where we shall put the holy relics on display.

Zenobia, Malik, Longinus, Zabdas, Yedibel and the courtiers exit. Wahballat lags behind to be near Porphyry, who is putting the books away.

Wahballat What caused that explosion, do you suppose?

Porphyry Let's just say I don't think the five sources of sublimity had a great deal to do with it.

They laugh. Zabdas returns.

Zabdas Majesty, your mother requests your presence at the Temple, in a certain tone of voice we both know well. I should hurry along if I were you.

Wahballat (*sighs*) Oh, public duties, such a bore. Until tomorrow, then, Porphyry?

Porphyry Tomorrow, Wahballat.

They shake hands, and Wahballat leaves.

Zabdas You have the King's confidence . . .

Porphyry How is your leg?

Zabdas I can't fight. But I can walk. Thanks to you.

Pause. Zabdas sits on the couch on which Longinus lay.

Porphyry And . . . how is your heart, Commander?

Zabdas You are good with secrets, aren't you, boy? Let me tell you something. (*He hesitates, but goes on.*) King Odainat and I were friends. Friends since boyhood. But the day he married Zenobia, something died between us. Because I wanted his wife. I never married. I gave my life to the service of my friend – in order to be near *her*. And then, one day – pff! – he is gone. And I have not the courage to act. Fine soldier, me. Is there anything . . . you could do for my condition?

Porphyry You mean – a magic potion? Slip it in her drink?

Zabdas Aye. Turn her gaze toward me.

Porphyry Do you think I am a sorcerer?

Zabdas You have powers not given to most men. Help me.

Porphyry I know nothing of love.

Zabdas Just get her to notice me once in a while!

Porphyry I can give you no potion, for none exists. But may I give you some advice? Don't do as she wants.

Zabdas What?

Porphyry Contradict her.

Zabdas Are you daft?

Porphyry Be difficult. Be prickly. Show her your mind is your own.

Zabdas All my life I have learnt to obey. Now I should be insubordinate? – How do you know this will work?

Porphyry I don't. I've never tried to seduce a Queen. (*He finds on the floor the cochlis brooch dropped by Longinus.*) Is this yours, sir?

Zabdas No. But I feel that I've seen it before.

Porphyry You take it then.

Zabdas (*pocketing it*) I will try your advice. It has merit.

Porphyry Good luck, Commander. In love and war.

They shake hands.

SCENE EIGHT

Rome. A military map-room. Aurelian is tossing a coin. He is with Pertinax, a Prefect, and a number of other generals.

Pertinax All the lands of the East have fallen to Zenobia. Three legions have been lost: the Third Gallica, the Fourth Scythica, and the Sixteenth Flavia Firma. She swept them away like the autumn leaves.

Aurelian What, with a handful of brigands?

Pertinax The Bedouin cavalry are fierce opponents, Emperor.

Aurelian A bunch of cunts on camels. With knives between their teeth.

Prefect Still, they control Asia Minor.

Aurelian Not for long.

Probus enters.

Probus. Take a look at this.

Aurelian flips him the coin.

Probus Syrian currency?

Aurelian The other side.

Probus (*turning the coin over*) Bloody cheek!

Aurelian She has proclaimed herself Empress. Her face on my coin! And her brat she calls 'Augustus'.

Probus Where did it come from?

Pertinax The Mint at Antioch.

Aurelian The Mint at Alexandria is also in her hands. So we can kiss goodbye to fiscal reforms. If any fucking Arab can make money, what's the point of curbing the issue at home? We might as well use pebbles from the street! Inflation will soar! And all those bent Senators will snigger in their sleeves.

Probus You can't let a woman do this to you.

Aurelian (*spits*) I know that.

Prefect So what do you propose?

Aurelian Tie the bitch's legs to elephants' tails, and split her like a rabbit for the pot.

Probus I take it the time for diplomacy is past?

Aurelian I should learn to stick to what I'm good at. Pertinax – how long to march to this desert?

Pertinax We calculate a hundred and twenty days.

Probus Emperor, you are used to fighting in the bogs and forests, where water is plentiful, and cover secure. This terrain is very different.

Aurelian I will adapt.

General 1 Even the maps are guesswork!

Aurelian There is no choice! What am I supposed to do, let some perfumed nomad take a third of the Empire, and shove it up my arse? Without the provinces we are nothing; Rome is just a vessel, into which their products pour. Gold from Spain, tin from Britain, amber from the Baltic – how could we live without any of this? The Empire *is* the world. I will not see it fracture. Nor can I tackle our domestic problems, until the frontiers are secure. That (*the coin*) is an act of rebellion. (*to Pertinax*) Set the wheels in motion.

Pertinax How many legions?

Aurelian We must leave sufficient troops on the Rhine and the Danube, and for the defence of Rome. We will draw upon our allies in the East. Say, six legions plus auxiliaries.

Prefect Forty thousand men.

Probus The Palmyrenes have seventy thousand.

Aurelian Yes, but I'm talking about soldiers.

Prefect One trained Roman's worth two sun-worshippers any day of the week.

Pertinax The supply line's going to be our biggest headache.

General 1 That and the Persian clap.

Pertinax Siege machinery?

Aurelian Yes.

Probus You're going to haul catapults through the mountains of Cilicia?

Aurelian With my teeth if necessary. To your business, gentlemen. Let us begin this work.

Pertinax Emperor, we salute you.

Pertinax exits with the Prefect and Generals.

Aurelian . . . I feel better. This is what I know.

Probus You're going to war against a female.

Aurelian It's not just her on her own . . .!

Probus It is not honourable. It is tinged with shame.

Aurelian *Losing* is dishonour. I don't intend to lose.

Probus And when you win, what will you do with her?

Aurelian . . . I'm fucked if I know.

SCENE NINE

Palmyra. Zenobia's palace. She and Wahballat are on a balcony, facing upstage, taking the salute from a march-past of soldiers and a cheering crowd. Wahballat now wears robes of imperial purple, a garland on his head. Zenobia has purple swathes attached to her army uniform. Malik waits within. As the cheering continues, Zenobia and Wahballat acknowledge it, shouting to be heard over the din.

Wahballat This adulation is exhausting. I'm completely fagged.

Zenobia The spontaneous joy of the people cannot lightly be dismissed. I love this city, look at it. The evening sunlight playing on the avenues of stone. Isn't it wonderful, what we've built?

They turn and come inside.

Wahballat You did it, mother. Not I. You have created your Utopia. Poets and thinkers flock here like migrating birds.

Zenobia Strange, though, how when you've achieved what you most desired, it does not satisfy . . .

Wahballat What do you mean?

Zenobia Nothing. But I never have time to read the books. They all seem so irrelevant.

Wahballat One day books will be written about you. I daresay you'll read *them*.

Zenobia I will presumably be dead. (*She has an idea.*) Malik, fetch the philosopher.

Malik exits. The people outside cheer.

Listen . . . The crime of the Romans has been answered. And they have no riposte. They are silent! Now *we* are the noise at the centre of things. We pulse with collective energy, the envy of the world. But you look glum. Why are you glum? You always sulk at parties.

Wahballat I spend so much time as the figurehead of the nation . . . I am way behind with my work.

Zenobia You would rather be in some dusty study, than living the life of a god?

Wahballat Well, yes, actually.

Zenobia What's so attractive about it?

Wahballat Oh, nothing. The company of friends.

Zenobia . . . Wait a minute. You have gone soft on the Greek boy.

Wahballat We get on awfully well, do you see –

Zenobia Are you sleeping with him?

Wahballat I don't know what you're talking about, mother.

Zenobia It wouldn't surprise me . . . the Greeks are famous for it.

Wahballat Look here, we're just jolly good friends!

Zenobia Yet you find him attractive –

Wahballat I do, yes, I do –

Zenobia A man loves women. Do you want to be a man?

Wahballat I was rather hoping to avoid the issue –

Zenobia What?

Wahballat – until I've made my mind up.

Pause.

Zenobia Malik castrated himself when he was twelve.

Wahballat Goodness me! Why?

Zenobia For a job in the royal household. Is that how you wish to be? Like him? (*She draws her sword and offers it to him.*) Here.

Wahballat Now let's not get over-dramatic –

Zenobia Well if you're only half a man, dispose of the bits you don't need!

Wahballat I told you, I'm undecided!

Zenobia I cannot abide indecision!

Wahballat Well, I'm not chopping my thing off just to make you feel better!

Zenobia All right, I'll do it for you.

Wahballat No!

She pursues him with the sword. Malik and Longinus enter.

Longinus You wished to see me, Majesty?

Zenobia I have a commission for you. *The History of the Palmyrene Wars.*

Longinus They are over?

Wahballat (*gloomily*) We won.

Zenobia I want a comprehensive record, in the epic style, of all our gains and conquests. With descriptions of the battles. And the heroes of the day.

Longinus I am to write this?

Zenobia Yes, you, the Sublime Longinus, in your inimitable syntax.

Longinus One is not sure one has the sensibilities of an historian, Majesty.

Zenobia Then apply the sensibilities of the poet. Elaborate. Apostrophise.

Wahballat Periphrasis, Longinus.

Longinus I know what it is, thank you.

Zenobia You have parchment? You have ink?

Longinus Plenty of ink.

Zenobia Then begin.

Longinus With the greatest respect, I – (*realising he has no choice*) Where would be the most appropriate starting point? The hour of your Majesty's birth?

Yedibel enters in a hurry, with a dirty, exhausted Bedouin scout.

Zenobia Minister? You were not announced.

Yedibel I bring bad news – a Roman army has crossed the Bosphorous! This scout rode day and night to warn us!

Scout They march like devils! Never eat, never drink! At night each soldier takes a shovel, and fortifies the camp – a city springs up in the desert, ringed around with stakes! They are not just Romans, but a western coalition – as well as the Gothic legions, the Dalmatian cavalry, and the Moesians and Pannonians, they have Celts, Britons, Spaniards – and they bring siege engines! Huge instruments of war! Ballistas, catapults, battering rams! And the Emperor Aurelian is riding at their head!

Zenobia . . . So he is coming. Good. The final test. The reckoning. (*She exchanges a look with Malik.*) – Yedibel, conscript ten thousand men, and begin the building of a wall.

Yedibel A wall, Majesty?

Zenobia A wall around the city. Four storeys high, with towers, checkpoints, sally-ports. An insurmountable wall. I must alert Zabdas.

Longinus Should we not postpone the *Chronicles of Zenobia* until we have tried conclusions with the Romans, Majesty?

Zenobia No. You will march with us, to report at first-hand on the death-throes of an Empire. You will stand in the front line of history, and trumpet the cause of the East!

Zenobia exits, with Malik, Yedibel and the scout. Longinus is dismayed.

Longinus The *front line . . .*? I'm a *philosopher*!

Wahballat You're a slave, old man. – I take it Porphyry will remain behind, to continue my tutorials?

Longinus Porphyry? No, I need him! For the book!

Wahballat I need him.

Longinus You think I can write it on my own?

Wahballat I need him. That is an imperial command. You may go.

Longinus bows and exits.

I need him . . . like the cactus needs a single drop of rain . . . to yield a gorgeous flower.

Malik enters.

Malik Emperor, a council of war has been summoned. Zabdas has a strategy – to allow the invaders deep into our land, and confront them in the harshness of the desert, which we know well – and where they will die like dogs, he says.

Wahballat And what do you think? How do the Romans look?

Malik Oh, the Praetorian Guard have a dazzling uniform, apparently.

Timagenes enters, furtively.

Timagenes Emperor, I beg an audience.

Wahballat Timagenes!

Timagenes I have been ostracised. I am a jackal, on the fringe of society. And why? Because I plead for peace. Wahballat, you are not a warmonger. It is time to oppose belligerence and hate! These Romans are connoisseurs of death. They will break us, crush us in their fingernails like so many lice – mounds of corpses will line the colonnades – the courtyards of the palaces will run with Arab blood! We can stop this!

Wahballat How?

Timagenes Overthrow the Queen.

Wahballat Oh dear.

Malik advances threateningly on Timagenes.

Timagenes Think hard! You could prevent a slaughter! (*He exits.*)

Wahballat Oh dear, dear, dear . . .

Malik looks at Wahballat.

SCENE TEN

The Roman lines at Emesa, in the desert. Night. Torches blazing. Standards stuck in the ground. Aurelian and Probus, wrapped up against the cold. Dogs and horses in the distance.

Aurelian What is that town behind their lines?

Probus Emesa.

Aurelian Any interesting features? Or just another stinking pisspot Arab hole?

Probus There is a temple to the sun-god. Popular in these parts.

Aurelian (*looking at the sky*) Not long till dawn. When the sun's rays strike the temple, we'll begin. I get a tingle in my balls, two hours before a battle. Very nice. How about you?

Probus No.

*A squad of heavily-armed soldiers – Cato, Antoninus,
Philip and Syrus – enter and sit, waiting uneasily for
daylight. They don't see the Emperor.*

Cato Watch out for scorpions.

Antoninus Scorpions?

Cato Yeh.

Philip Fucking Arab secret weapon.

Cato Fucking right.

Antoninus Scorpions and women. Now I've seen it all.

Philip Yeh, both got a sting in their tail.

Laughter.

Syrus (*indicating the Palmyrene lines*) Not this one. She
doesn't put it about.

Cato Oh, you're full of shit, Syrus.

Syrus No, it's definite. Some of the lads caught a
straggler, back at Antioch. Interrogated him. All done
right professional. Said he served in Zenobia's infantry,
though you'd never of guessed. Miserable looking
specimen, all bandy legs and earrings.

Philip Yeh, and his fingernails ripped off.

Laughter.

Syrus Well, what he says is – this is through a translator,
like, 'cos he don't speak no civilised tongue – just jabbers
like an ape, incofuckingherent – what he says is, this
Arab, before he lost the will to live and begged to kiss
the Emperor's arse, he says his Queen as he calls her is
totally what's the word? – chaste. She doesn't shag.

Antoninus What is she, frigid?

Philip Dried up and decommissioned.

Syrus No, it's energy, you see. You expend your energy, your bodily fluids, when you have it away with the opposite sex. Not her. She saves it all for fighting. Fucking coiled like a spring. Fucking killing machine. She'll cut your cock off for a trophy – hang it round her neck. Death with tits, mate, I'm telling you.

Cato You'll stand firm. But I pity the bloke who has to kill her.

Philip He's going to look a bit sick.

Antoninus Like running a spear through your mother . . .

Syrus Don't get no medals for that, eh, Cato?

They fall silent. Aurelian and Probus approach.

Aurelian Legionnaires . . .

Cato (*quietly*) Officers.

The squad snap to attention.

Aurelian Did you see it?

Cato See what, sir?

Aurelian It passed among you, a moment ago.

Cato Nothing passes us without a challenge, sir.

Aurelian Are you blind? I saw it clear as day!

Antoninus The enemy, sir?

Aurelian No, not the enemy – a friend! Divine in form, and radiating fire! An image of the sun!

Cato (*puzzled*) Don't think it come this way, sir.

Aurelian I saw the god. You must have, too.

Cato Yeh, well –

Probus The Emperor says you saw it.

Cato The Emp –

Syrus Hail Aurelian!

Soldiers Hail!

Aurelian A manifestation of the sun on earth. A moving spirit, a guiding light. This is a sign. Our cause is blessed.

Cato We shall not fail, then, shall we, lads?

Aurelian Not with the Sun God at our side.

Probus Hail Aurelian!

Soldiers Hail!

Probus Move out.

The soldiers leave at a run.

What did you see – apart from the normal corona of daybreak in the desert?

Aurelian I saw victory. And so did they. – Here is the plan. When the heavy cavalry charge our centre, which they will as their opening gambit, our battalions of horse are to break and run.

Probus Run?

Aurelian Run! Retreat in disarray! And let them follow.

Probus You are ordering the imperial cavalry to break ranks?

Aurelian Yes I am, Probus, and I don't want a debate about it!

Pertinax enters.

Pertinax Emperor.

Aurelian What?

Pertinax Envoys from the Palmyrenes, sir. They make a strange request.

Aurelian Go on.

Pertinax They say the clash of arms can be avoided – that no lives need be lost. If you will –

Aurelian What, man?

Pertinax Meet Zenobia face to face. Unarmed and alone. To hear a proposition.

Aurelian When and where?

Pertinax Dawn. Out there.

SCENE ELEVEN

Dawn on the battlefield. Drums and trumpets sounding as the two armies prepare. Zenobia enters with Malik, who carries a magnificent treasure-chest, which he sets down.

Zenobia Will he come?

Malik I see him.

Malik looks towards the Roman lines. Zenobia looks away.

Zenobia Describe him.

Malik He's the one in the purple, presumably?

Zenobia Yes!

Malik Pity. The other is tall, dark and gorgeous.

Zenobia And Aurelian?

Malik Well . . .

Zenobia He has no deformity, at least? Reassure me. It's important.

Malik Why? You only want to kill him. – He is average-looking, of average height. A powerful step. Piercing eyes.

Zenobia That will do.

She turns and watches as Aurelian and Probus enter from the other side. They stop and face the Palmyrenes.

Probus Two platoons of crossbows have you covered. I am right behind. Give me your sword.

Aurelian hands over his sword. Zenobia gives hers to Malik.

Zenobia Withdraw.

Malik He may kill you.

Zenobia He may try.

Malik exits.

Probus She is bold, the Amazon.

Aurelian So?

Probus I don't want anything to happen to you.

Aurelian Fuck off, Probus.

Probus exits. Aurelian approaches Zenobia, who stays by her treasure-chest.

Zenobia Take a look in the chest, Emperor.

Aurelian Is it full of snakes?

Zenobia You march with impunity across my land. You lay waste my crops, butcher my herds. Your columns of crunching steel and brass turn sandy tracks to sheets of glass. You have no right to do this. Yes, perhaps it is a vipers' nest. Open it, if you're a man.

Aurelian You open it. If you're a woman.

Zenobia (*laughs*) You doubt my femininity? I have five children. How many do you have?

Aurelian None.

Zenobia I doubt your manhood, then.

Aurelian I have no wife.

Zenobia I know.

Aurelian You call it your land. It is not. It belongs to the Empire of Rome.

Zenobia Surely what belongs to the Empire is what the Empire can control?

Aurelian Which is why I am here. – Your proposal?

Zenobia . . . There is no need to break up the world.

Aurelian You surrender?

Zenobia (*smiles*) No. You?

Aurelian No. I never have yet.

Zenobia These are the facts. I rule the East; you rule the West. But I hold the balance, between law and anarchy. Unless you crush me, I will drive a thunderbolt through everything you know.

Aurelian Then I must crush you.

Zenobia Open the chest. There are no snakes.

Aurelian kneels and opens the chest. It is jammed full of treasure, fantastic jewellery, goblets, gold. He lifts up handfuls of the stuff.

It is for you.

Aurelian For me?

Zenobia My wedding gift.

Aurelian Love-tokens on the field of war . . .?

Zenobia There will be no war. If we marry. If we jointly reign.

Aurelian Marry?

Zenobia Just politics. No passion.

Aurelian drops the treasure back in the box.

Aurelian This is a joke, am I right? Syrian sense of humour?

Zenobia I have no sense of humour. My son has always said. I propose a very modern marriage. No need to exchange pleasantries at breakfast, no need, Emperor, to keep your mistresses a secret, to fake love for the sake of diplomacy. We meet only for the intercourse of government.

Aurelian We run the Empire together? (*Zenobia nods.*) From Rome?

Zenobia Where else? And the years will pass in peace. Perhaps one day when we are old, we'll find we talk as friends. Give me your hand, and it's done.

Aurelian . . . If I marry, I must consummate the act.

Zenobia Unnecessary.

Aurelian Vital. Or Rome will laugh at me. The legends of your beauty are for once not inexact. Yes . . . I could go to bed with you. My face between your legs . . . yes, I can picture it.

Zenobia That is not part of the deal.

Aurelian Oh, you will not fuck a peasant, to save the world from war? It's true what they say, then, is it?

Zenobia What?

Aurelian You have so far unsexed yourself, your snatch has turned to sand?

In a flash, Zenobia pulls a knife from a hidden scabbard. But Aurelian's just as quick, and in the same instant he has his hidden knife in his hand. They go into a clinch, each holding a blade to the other's neck. It happens very fast, there's no circling around.

Well, you'd make an obedient little wife, wouldn't you?

Zenobia You insult me. You will die. My treasure will line your burial place.

Aurelian I'll give it to the whores on the Aventine, when I have beaten you. You cannot buy yourself an Empire, cunt!

They slowly back away from each other. Probus runs on.

Probus Aurelian!

Zenobia Sound the attack!

A snap blackout, followed immediately by –

SCENE TWELVE

*– a huge explosion. We're in Palmyra. Smoke wafts
across the stage. Porphyry staggers on. Porphyry's
clothes have been partly ripped away by the blast. A
breast is revealed: Porphyry is a woman. Wahballat
enters, coughing.*

Wahballat Porphyry? Are you safe? Are you – (*He sees
her.*)

Porphyry Made a discovery . . . sulphur added to nitre
and charcoal causes an . . .

Wahballat You are a woman!

Porphyry (*realising she is exposed*) Oh, no!

Wahballat (*angry*) Why have you deceived me?

Porphyry So that I could work.

Wahballat You are a woman. Oh, thank the sun and the
moon! A woman!

He embraces her and they kiss.

Act Two

SCENE THIRTEEN

Emesa. Longinus sits on a high rock overlooking the battle which rages below. He has his pen and ink.

Longinus 'Fleet-footed Zenobia'? . . . Been done. 'Sword-swinging Zenobia'? . . . Well yes, but literal, literal. 'Death-dispensing Zenobia'? . . . Sounds like a backstreet apothecary. – Oh, send me an epithet, please! (*Reads back.*) 'As the avenging army of Palmyrene zealots smote the Romans hip and thigh upon the gore-drenched fields of Emesa, something-something Zenobia, mighty Queen of the East, raised her standard with a something-something cry . . .' Hours! Hours on one wretched little line! They'll have changed the course of history half-a-dozen times before I have conquered this sentence! Composition is a curse; I should have stuck to reviewing. At least one can nod off after lunch.

Zabdas enters, dragging his bad leg up to Longinus' look-out point.

I congratulate you, Commander. The alien foe is routed. Brave-breasted Zenobia, blood-bolted from the fray, stands sovereign still on Syria's sacred soil. – Ah! (*He scribbles it down.*)

Zabdas What are you talking about?

Longinus They've run away, haven't they?

Zabdas Aye, they've run away, half a day's ride they ran, and us in hot pursuit. But then they turned, re-formed,

and cut us down like reeds. That withdrawal was a feint.
Aurelian is smarter than I thought.

Longinus You wouldn't call it a victory, then?

Zabdas No, I'd call it a thrashing.

*Longinus carefully crosses out all the lines he has just
written.*

Longinus What a waste of limpid prose. Pearls tossed at
oblivion. (*He sighs, and looks down.*) Those divisions
down there – they *are* ours, aren't they?

Zabdas No. We've got to pull back or we're finished.

*Longinus immediately gets up and starts packing his
things. Zenobia enters, with a squad of Palmyrene
soldiers protecting her. All are bloody and fatigued,
some are wounded. One is a signaller: his instrument
a long, booming horn.*

Signaller, sound the retreat!

Zenobia (*angrily*) On whose orders?

Zabdas On my orders, Majesty. We are defeated. We
must re-group in Palmyra.

Zenobia We are not defeated! Not while I can fight!

Zabdas You cannot fight their shock troops on your
own.

Zenobia Zabdas, has your backbone turned to jelly?
I countermand your order!

Zabdas We will be surrounded in a minute! Signaller,
do as I say!

Zenobia What is the matter with you? Are you defying
me?

Zabdas (*aside*) Oh, you notice?

Zenobia We go onwards! Never back!

Zabdas We go where I say, in battle.

Zenobia Come here! – and let me smash your other leg!
If you want to desert, you can crawl!

Zabdas (*aside*) I have crawled for long enough. – Your
orders are ill-judged, and I won't obey them. If we fall
back to Palmyra we can sit out their siege. They will
never survive in the desert.

Longinus There's a phalanx of archers, marching up my
hill. They are priming their crossbows. They're Romans!

Zabdas Right, move out!

Zenobia Stand and fight!

Zabdas (*to Signaller*) Sound your horn, man!

Longinus Run!

Zenobia (*to Zabdas*) I will have you crucified for this!

*As the signaller blows his horn, and all except
Zenobia begin to retreat off the hill, a hail of arrows
rains down on the stage. The signaller is killed
instantly. Zenobia is hit in the upper thigh, and falls.*

Zabdas Guard the Queen!

*The remaining soldiers, holding up their shields,
manage to pull Zenobia off. The signaller remains
where he fell.*

Her precious life! Protect her!

All exit amidst a tumultuous noise of battle.

SCENE FOURTEEN

Aurelian outside Palmyra, mopping his brow in the desert heat.

Aurelian What a beauty. Look at her. Enough to make you come in your sleep! What a piece of work . . . A defensive wall that size, encircling the city? How many men? How many days? With a fortification like that, they can hold out for months. Years maybe. While we catch rats in the desert. I will bring up my mantlets, and slingshots of fire; my mangonels will rain death on their children. But still they have this wall.

And the tigress, caged inside it. Who seeks to humiliate me.

There must be a way . . . When I shut my eyes the sun's still there. It's burnt a path into my brain and made my skull its orbit. Inextinguishable, yes, invincible, the sun, their god of life. I will claim it for Rome. I will be the Sun Unconquered.

SCENE FIFTEEN

Palmyra. Night. Zenobia lies on a couch; Zabdas kneels at her side.

Zabdas They withdrew at dusk. The wall was not breached. There are many dead and wounded. But the wall was not breached. Zenobia . . . you and I have fought skirmishes of our own, for which I find I shed unfamiliar tears. I have never meant to offend you. I love you more than the beat of my own pulse. And you proposed – aye, proposed! – to a Roman! And would have married him! I am torn down. I am rubble. Please, as a memento of my aching heart, accept this little token of my love.

He offers her the cochlis brooch. Pause. Zenobia
doesn't move. Then she snores lightly. Zabdas sighs,
then hides the brooch as Malik leads in Wahballat and
Yedibel.

Yedibel Where are her physicians?

Malik She will have no physicians!

Zabdas (*approaching them*) She sleeps.

Yedibel Sleeps? Or is she dying?

Malik (*upset*) The wound is inflamed. It weeps. I can do
nothing for her.

Zabdas Not dying, please!

Yedibel We will all be butchered!

Wahballat Porphyry could treat her.

Zabdas Yes – that boy has a gift!

Malik She won't see him, Commander! No man, she
says, may touch so delicate a place!

Wahballat I'll persuade her.

Zabdas Find Porphyry first.

Wahballat (*to Malik*) Come, I'll show you!

Malik and Wahballat exit.

Yedibel We could go over to the Romans . . .

Zabdas No! Never let me hear you talk of treason! I will
cut out your liver and feed it to my dogs, if you betray
Palmyra! The Queen will live!

Zabdas exits. Yedibel watches Zenobia sleeping.

Yedibel I wonder what you dream of . . .?

He picks up the cochlis brooch and admires it. As Wahballat enters he tucks it inside his cloak.

Wahballat Leave us.

Yedibel exits. Wahballat gently wakes Zenobia.

Mother. It's Wahballat. How do you feel?

Zenobia (*drowsily*) Are we besieged?

Wahballat Yes. But Zabdas says they can't last out for long. They have no supply lines. They'll starve.

Zenobia If Zabdas had any guts, we'd not be captive in our own city.

Wahballat But Zabdas –

Zenobia Zabdas is a traitor! We should have fought on!

She tries to get up, and falls. Wahballat helps her back on to the couch.

(*Groans.*) Oh . . . it hurts . . .

Wahballat The wound is rancid. It will kill you.

Zenobia It will not kill me, don't be absurd.

Wahballat It will kill you, mother! But there is someone with a cure. A doctor. Not a man.

Zenobia Not a man? What is it, a witch?

Wahballat Look here, I'm trying to save your life! – Porphyry is coming.

Zenobia I said no men!

Wahballat Porphyry is a girl.

Zenobia A girl? . . . Why does she disguise herself?

Wahballat She's a scientist, and a jolly good one, too. Women are not allowed to practise science, neither here nor in Athens. So she pretends to be a boy.

Zenobia Watch your step. Who knows what other counterfeits the imposter's capable of.

Wahballat She has a true heart.

Zenobia And a false face.

Wahballat But will you see her? (*She indicates that she will.*) – Malik!

Malik enters.

Send in Porphyry, please.

Malik makes a sign, and Porphyry enters and bows. Malik exits.

You have your bag of medicine?

Porphyry Yes.

Wahballat Use all your skill.

They touch hands for a second, and Wahballat leaves.

Zenobia My son says you are female. Prove it.

Porphyry takes Zenobia's hand and puts it between her legs.

So you have soft, moist places too. You bleed. You can bear children.

Porphyry Yes.

Zenobia But you don't paint your cheeks, nor dab scent on your wrists.

Porphyry No.

Zenobia Examine my wound. You dissemble well. I was fooled. Your master too. And poor Wahballat brought to a crisis of sexual identity. I take a rather dim view . . . (*Indicates that she should explain.*)

Porphyry My work is important to me. Wahballat understands.

Zenobia Do you love him?

Porphyry Yes.

Zenobia Enough to give up your work?

Porphyry . . . Must it come to that?

Zenobia My son must have a wife. He must breed, or why, tell me, why have we bothered? If you adore him so terribly much, and he likewise dotes on you, well, we'd better have a wedding, hadn't we?

Porphyry Are you jealous of us?

Zenobia Jealous?

Porphyry Of two people in love.

Zenobia You think that, do you?

Porphyry The glint of cruelty in your eyes. (*examining her*) Is the arrow-head inside?

Zenobia No. I cut it out.

Porphyry I will put on this ointment. It's a by-product of the crystallisation of seaweed, that I've treated with essence of sulphur. An iodide, if you want the technical term. Brace yourself. It will hurt.

Zenobia Not as much as running from the Romans.

Porphyry treats the wound.

Tell me about your master. I think he dissembles too. I would have thought the man who wrote 'On the Sublime' could have come up with something rather better than the eight pages of sub-Homeric doggerel that so far constitutes the history of my life, wouldn't you?

Porphyry Keep still, please. Longinus is a good man.

Zenobia There are no good men.

Porphyry He tries hard.

Zenobia He has tricked me, hasn't he?

Porphyry is silent.

If he discovers your sex, you know, you cannot remain as his pupil.

Porphyry Please . . . Majesty . . .

Zenobia No more work. No more philosophy. Just cooking, and a brat clamped on your nipple.

Porphyry I can't give up now! I'm so close!

Zenobia Then answer my question. And I will keep silence. We can reconsider the matter when Wahballat comes of age. Did Longinus write 'On the Sublime' or did he not?

Porphyry (*sighs*) No, he didn't. The manuscript turned up in a library in Athens, and I made a fair copy.

Zenobia So who's the true author?

Porphyry Nobody knows. It's over a hundred years old.

Zenobia . . . A fraud. And I took his advice!

Porphyry (*dressing the wound*) This must be dressed with a fresh poultice three times a day, and I have prepared a potion that I want you to drink. I hope it will prevent the infection from spreading.

Zenobia You mean it might on the other hand kill me.

Porphyry My art is in its infancy. But I don't think you will die, Majesty.

Zenobia I assure you I will not! (*She manages to stand.*) How long till dawn? (*Calls.*) Captains! Report!

Yedibel enters at a run with Malik and Wahballat.

Yedibel Majesty, a letter from the Emperor!

Zenobia Read it.

Yedibel 'From Aurelian, Emperor of the world, to Zenobia and her allies in war. I command you to surrender. If you do so, your life, Zenobia, shall be spared, and together with your children you shall live in a place of my appointing. Your jewels, your gold, your silver, your silks, your horses and your camels shall be forfeit to the Roman treasury; otherwise our enmity shall be forgotten, and the people of Palmyra may preserve their rights as citizens of Rome.'

Wahballat What do you make of it?

Zenobia He's bluffing. His horses are dying; they won't eat camel-thorn. His men are plagued by insects, and delirious in the sun. He has no friends in the desert. Yedibel, what form of reply do you advise?

Yedibel Well, er, the prospect of not actually dying at the point of a Roman sword is, well, tempting, Majesty, but –

Zenobia But you will not die if he goes away. Not immediately, that is.

Yedibel Quite so, Majesty, and my advice to you is that the imperialist aggressor must be resisted; the small nation's voice must be heard.

Zenobia Oh, my voice will be heard. It will ring in his ears for the rest of his days.

Wahballat . . . I see we're feeling better. Thank you, Porphyry.

Zenobia This youth is not like other men. His touch is free of indelicacy. His company pleases me. (*to Porphyry*) I appoint you Royal Physician. I want to see you every day. (*She dismisses Porphyry with a wave of her hand.*)

Porphyry (*bowing*) Majesty. (*She exits.*)

Zenobia Yedibel – our allies stand firm?

Yedibel The Armenians lost an entire squadron in this morning's raid, but yes, yes, otherwise they are solid.

Zenobia Ensure they're well supplied. We can't afford to lose our friends. Will the Persians support us?

Yedibel They cannot decide. They have no love for the tribe of Odainat.

Zenobia Send another runner. With coffers full of gold. Now leave me. I have a letter to write.

Wahballat Shall I call Longinus?

Zenobia No. I will do it.

> *Wahballat and Yedibel exit. Malik brings a pen and parchment to Zenobia's couch.*

. . . What shall I say to him, Malik?

Malik Well, I think you can skip inquiring after the health of his relatives and so on and so forth –

Zenobia Malik.

Malik I myself would first decide the colour of the ink. If you want to infuriate the silly old tart, I'd suggest a regal purple. If you want to vent your anger, a vile, splenetic red. Blue will look cool and commanding, unmoved by his arrogant tone. Black for death, as in, his. Green to deceive him, and imply you've lost your wits. Everything rests on your appraisal of the man's personality.

Zenobia I rather liked him, as a matter of fact.

SCENE SIXTEEN

Night. Aurelian enters his tent.

Aurelian Bring my breastplate! Hone my sword! – With one stroke I'll finish it, and we can all go home! – I will shaft her, good and hard, right up to the hilt.

> *Probus, Pertinax and the Prefect enter. Probus has Zenobia's letter.*

Probus No, I don't think so.

Aurelian But she requests it! Single combat! She's begging to be slain!

Probus She knows it is not politically possible for you to accept.

Aurelian I don't give a toss about politically possible – I want to win! Victory is victory, isn't it? Come *on*, Probus!

Pertinax You might lose.

Aurelian Bollocks!

Probus I have seen her with a knife-blade at your throat.

Pertinax She is strong, and quick.

Probus And devious.

Aurelian And I am old and knackered, my sword-arm limp and flaccid, drooping like a geriatric's prick, this is what you're telling me? You're telling me I can't win a fight with a slag in a sandpit? What's she going to do, scratch my fucking eyes out? Fuck it, you lot are losing your edge. Are we soldiers, or poofs in fucking armour?

Probus Nobody is questioning your martial expertise. Your skills put our finest gladiators in the shade. But I hardly think, Emperor, that butchering this upstart will bring us the accolades we long for. I hardly think that winning a war this way will speed the course of your inevitable deification.

Aurelian It is not just a war. It is the reunification of the world. I can live with a little shame.

Prefect If you kill a woman, Emperor, the victory is tainted. We will march home with our tails between our legs. And if you – say you stub your toe against a stone – the sun blinds you for a second – she gets in a lucky blow – where are we then? No, this action must be decided by military might, not a degrading tussle between the Emperor of Rome and some Syrian courtesan. We're not in ancient bloody Greece, with minotaurs and fuck knows what; this is as you say a war for the preservation of civilised society. So do it the civilised way.

Pertinax Besides, how do you know you can trust her? What if she comes with hunting dogs, tigers, birds of prey that know her call? What if she does magic?

Aurelian Magic?

Prefect Oriental witchcraft.

Aurelian Fuck, I hadn't thought of that. Strange practices they have here . . . strange fruit . . . the heat, the incense . . . invading your brain . . .

Probus Sir, this letter scripted in ridiculous gold leaf is designed precisely for the effect it has achieved. We are suddenly unsure of ourselves. She means, with this hysterical gesture, to undermine our morale. Don't give her the pleasure.

Aurelian I would give her the pleasure of a fist up her arse.

Probus We all would.

Pertinax Bit of luck we all will.

They laugh. Aurelian relaxes.

Aurelian All right. What's the alternative?

Prefect I've got a deal going with some Arabs, the Tanukh I think, not the locals, nomads. No allegiance to Palmyra. They will guard the supply routes back to Antioch. For free use of Zenobia's wells, when we liberate the city. No jewels, no gold. Just a drink for the camel. Any good?

Aurelian Well done. Give them the water, Prefect. If it means we can eat.

Pertinax I think we should fight at night.

Probus At night? No one does that.

Pertinax Exactly. Bring up the battering-rams under the stars. Disconcert the fuckers.

Aurelian I like it. And we'll play music.

Probus Music?

Aurelian Marching music! All night long! Be like trying to sleep on a parade ground! – Probus?

Probus The Armenians are wavering. Give them a push, and they'll turn. They owe nothing to Zenobia. If we pay more, they'll fight for us.

Aurelian Do it. We're going to break this bitch. Here's something odd that happened. I went into the temple, you know, on the Acropolis at Emesa, temple of the sun. Temple of Heliogabalus. Beautiful fucking thing. Stained glass like a mermaid's tears, and the last of the light coming through . . . beautiful. – I saw it again.

Probus The vision?

Aurelian Great shimmering ball of flame, streaks of pure fire all around it. I went down on my knees. It floated. Over my head, as I prayed. I was not harmed. I was favoured! The Sun God fights beside us.

Prefect I have seen it too. I think I've seen it. And some of the men.

Aurelian One light, in the heavens. One force, and that is us. When we smash this wall . . .

SCENE SEVENTEEN

Wahballat's library. Night. He and Porphyry lie on the floor, on a makeshift bed surrounded by books. A tray of food nearby. The insistent sound of the battering rams, hammering at the walls, and Roman martial music far in the distance.

Wahballat Happy?

Porphyry Yes. (*She kisses him.*)

Wahballat It's puzzling, isn't it? Outside a war is raging, men cascade in blood. Yet here I am in paradise. The happiest days of my life. No system of philosophy can explain this to me.

Porphyry When you find the one person in the world that you want to be with . . . that you can share things with . . . all the rest is vapour, swirling gas . . . The battering rams are your pounding heart, the missiles airborne kisses . . . Put you and me together, gently heat, and look: essence of love.

Wahballat Our love is doomed.

Porphyry Don't say that.

Wahballat How long can they keep it up? (*the Romans*)

Porphyry For ever. I don't care.

Wahballat The sky will crack open, and the wells will run dry. It's finished. Palmyra is dying.

Porphyry But we have our work! Let them make history; they are insects, scrabbling in the dung. We are close to our goal. The medicine worked on your mother; the formulae fall into place. As long as the walls keep the Romans out, we can sift through the secrets of matter. And soon we will have knowledge, of everything and nothing, and we will look down on their bickering like bored, impassive gods!

Wahballat But it's my home.

Porphyry I am your home. Come inside me and be safe.

Wahballat My love . . .

> *They kiss. A secret door in the bookcase creaks, sticks, and starts to open.*

Porphyry What's that?

Porphyry and Wahballat leap up as Timagenes enters through the secret door.

Wahballat You may not enter!

Timagenes pulls a knife. Porphyry and Wahballat back away. Timagenes sees the food, and falls on it, eating ravenously.

Timagenes Do you see where your lethargy has brought us? There is no food out there! But the dictator's son does not go hungry.

Wahballat How did you get in?

Timagenes There are passageways hidden throughout the palace. Tunnels, underground bunkers. I know them all. – You must act now, before it's too late!

Porphyry What does he want you to do?

Wahballat Stage a coup against my mother.

Timagenes Take command! Negotiate a truce!

Porphyry (*to Wahballat*) No, you can't! The Romans will not let me work! I need Zenobia in power!

Timagenes Wahballat, don't listen! Call a halt to the killing!

Porphyry But I'm so nearly there! The ancient doors swing open! Oh, Wahballat, don't ruin everything we've struggled for . . .

Timagenes A bloodless revolution, that's all – and the westerners will leave us in peace.

Wahballat (*torn*) Give me room to think!

Timagenes There is no time! How can you sit here reading books, blind to the catastrophe of a once-great city?

Timagenes grabs Porphyry and holds the knife to her throat, backing away towards the secret door.

The boy comes with me, until you come to your senses!

Wahballat Let her go!

Zenobia enters, completely recovered from her wound. Timagenes is distracted. Wahballat throws himself at him. Porphyry gets clear as they struggle. Wahballat, fighting like a man possessed, gains the upper hand. He corners Timagenes with the knife.

Zenobia Kill him.

Wahballat . . . I can't, mother.

Zenobia Weakling!

Wahballat Timagenes is not a fool. The war is going badly.

Timagenes Children are dying of starvation! The longer we resist, the greater the Romans' anger will become. Eventually they'll wear us down, and then destroy us all.

Zenobia You know nothing! What do you know? We are winning!

Timagenes My family are under the bombardment!

Zenobia Help will come soon from the Persians!

Timagenes The Persians? You are dreaming, surely! You have been dreaming for four years! You dream you are a strategist – you dream you have an army – you even dream you have the blood of Cleopatra! It is all fantasy, Zenobia, motes of dust!

Zenobia Fantasy? I have shed my blood, I have watched my blood drain down in the soil of my native land! And you call it fantasy? Do you not know how great we are?

We had poetry before the Greeks! Architecture before the Romans! We built the first cities! Invented the alphabet! We awoke at the dawn of civilisation – and you would have us lost in the sleep of history? One small nation stands up to the West, and you say we are dreaming? (*drawing her sword*) You cry defeat. You die.

Wahballat stands in her path.

Wahballat Go, Timagenes. Go.

Zenobia What, with a knife in your hand?

Wahballat It's how we do things now, isn't it?

Timagenes makes his escape.

Zenobia I have old men and boys on the battlements. If they can pick up a spear, they can fight. Join them.

Wahballat You didn't bring me up to be a fighter.

Zenobia Things have changed. The sky is dark with their arrows. Their battering rams are rattling my teeth!

Porphyry We are scientists. We have no interest in the art of war.

Wahballat What do you want here?

Zenobia I want my philosopher!

Wahballat We work without him. Leave us.

Zenobia (*in a fury*) Longinus!

Zenobia exits. Porphyry is already back at work.

Wahballat Gosh, I didn't know I could do that.

Porphyry Our time is short. Prepare the chemicals.

SCENE EIGHTEEN

Aurelian, Probus and the Prefect stand looking up at the wall. The battering rams and martial music continue in the background.

Prefect Why do these bastards always resist? Why don't they accept the inevitable?

Aurelian Perhaps they've forgotten we're here.

Probus . . . We need new weapons.

Prefect Nothing wrong with our weapons.

Probus They're predictable. What we do is always predictable. Here's our attack, here's their defence. We've done it for hundreds of years! They resist because they know how to resist. We need something against which resistance is simply unimaginable.

Aurelian What's on your mind, Probus?

Probus I'm not sure, sir. A weapon of destruction.

Aurelian I like it when young men dream.

Probus There is so much destruction in nature. The power of the lightning bolt, the blast of the volcano . . .! If we could harness that, we'd soon demolish their brickwork.

Prefect I've been using battering rams for my entire career, and they haven't let me down yet.

Aurelian frowns thoughtfully at Probus.

SCENE NINETEEN

*On the walls of Palmyra. Yedibel looks down. Longinus
joins him.*

Longinus She wishes to see me?

Yedibel Those soldiers below.

Longinus The ones marching out of the gates?

Yedibel Know who they are?

Longinus Not definitively.

Yedibel They are Armenians. Our chief allies. They are
changing sides. You spoke for war, Longinus. Your
current position is unenviable. For a small remuneration,
I will try to save your life.

Longinus What do you want?

Yedibel Well . . . something like this, perhaps?

He shows the cochlis brooch.

Longinus That's mine!

*Longinus makes a desperate grab for it and they
struggle. Meanwhile Zenobia appears further along
the battlements.*

It's mine! It's my insurance!

Zenobia Longinus!

*Longinus succeeds in getting hold of the brooch.
He breathlessly approaches Zenobia, concealing the
brooch as he goes. Yedibel exits.*

I relied on you. And you have betrayed me!

Longinus August Queen, I do not, with respect, recall being consulted about any Armenians.

Zenobia Not the Armenians! I mean this! (*She flourishes her copy of 'On the Sublime'.*) You presented yourself as a philosopher of genius! You plagiarised an ancient text, and claimed it as your own.

Longinus I rehabilitated a neglected work, found gathering dust in a cellar. Common academic practice.

Zenobia You stole it! And I thought you were an intellectual!

Longinus I am an intellectual!

Zenobia You have made me look a fool! You will pay for this!

Longinus I know you killed your husband.

Zenobia What?

Yedibel, Zabdas and Malik enter on the battlements.

Zabdas Armenian mercenaries! Daft to use them!

Yedibel Now we're weak on the eastern ramparts!

Zabdas I say abandon the wall! We can fortify the palace, and hold out there. Your orders, Majesty – ?

Zenobia 'On the Sublime' is a fraud.

Malik Majesty, nobody cares about the Sublime! We are all on the verge of extinction!

Zenobia Well, Longinus is to blame for that!

Longinus holds up the brooch.

My brooch . . .! I gave that to my husband!

Longinus She killed him.

Zenobia I did not kill him!

Longinus I was by his side when he perished!

Yedibel You killed Odainat?

Zenobia No!

Yedibel And led us into this?

Longinus She poisoned his wine! I saw it! This jewel is the proof!

Zenobia No . . .

Yedibel It's over. Surrender.

Zenobia How dare you oppose me! Cowards! Fight on!

Malik Majesty! Come!

Zenobia (*draws her sword*) I am not running!

Yedibel Zabdas! Disarm her!

Zabdas draws his sword without much enthusiasm.

Zabdas Zenobia – please –

Zenobia I am not running! I will fetch help!

Zenobia swings and cuts into Zabdas' good leg. He drops.

Malik Come, now!

Zenobia and Malik exit.

Yedibel Guards! Arrest her!

Yedibel exits after them. Longinus approaches Zabdas.

Zabdas The brooch . . . give it to me . . .

Longinus (*handing it over*) And then . . .?

Zabdas Throw me from the battlements! Skewer me on
their spears! That would fix it! This rat, that gnaws at
my heart. Oh, the vermin of emotion!

SCENE TWENTY

*Aurelian's tent. He and Pertinax examine a map. An icon
of the Sun God is prominently displayed. The Prefect
and a centurion bring in Timagenes, his hands bound.*

Prefect Came over to our lines. Claims he knows how to
breach the wall.

Aurelian Does he, indeed? You see the blessing of the
sun? (*turning to Timagenes*) Who are you?

Timagenes I was First Minister in the government of
Palmyra – until I fell from grace.

Aurelian And now you would have your revenge . . .?

Timagenes I would see the war ended. My people are
dying.

Aurelian Mine are dying too. So fucking what?

Timagenes I can find the secret conduits, that perforate
the wall. I can show you how to take the city. It gives me
no joy to do so, Emperor. Just end it, swiftly. And be
merciful.

Aurelian Oh, I am merciful, my friend, I am as welcome
as rain in August, me. You will lead us to Zenobia?

Timagenes Zenobia has fled, last night, upon her
swiftest camel.

Aurelian To?

Timagenes To cross the Euphrates, and recruit fresh forces.

Aurelian Pertinax, take a platoon of horse, and try and head her off.

Pertinax leaves at a run.

SCENE TWENTY-ONE

Wahballat's library. Night. He is sleeping on the make-shift bed. Porphyry enters in great excitement, carrying a flask of bubbling liquid of the deepest red.

Porphyry (*gently*) Wahballat – wake up! Wake up, my darling . . .

Wahballat I'm so tired . . .

Porphyry You will never be tired again. Or frail, or sick. I think I've done it!

Wahballat You've done it?

Porphyry If my calculations are correct – this is the elixir!

Wahballat Are you saying . . . we can outlive the war . . . outlive the Romans? We can be together for all time?

Porphyry Try it!

Wahballat Kiss me first.

They kiss.

Porphyry Drink.

Wahballat (*looking at the potion*) I trust you.

Porphyry I love you. I will never hurt you. Drink.

Wahballat drinks a long draft of the elixir.

Wahballat How do we know if it works?

Porphyry Ask me again in a thousand years.

Wahballat Now you.

Porphyry takes the flask. But before she can drink, the squad of Roman soldiers from Scene Ten burst into the library. They rush at Porphyry and grab her. She struggles. The flask is dropped to the floor, and smashes.

Cato Got one!

Antoninus Get the other!

Porphyry Run!

Wahballat dodges the soldiers and gets the secret door in the bookcase open. He looks back –

Run! Run!

Antoninus After him!

Wahballat exits. The soldiers halt at the secret entrance.

Philip It's pitch black, Cato.

Syrus Could be booby-trapped.

Cato Fuck it, leave him. Now, what have we here?

Philip Books. Lot of books.

Cato Books?

Syrus (*looking at one*) Arab writing. All squiggles.

Antoninus Any pictures?

Syrus Nah.

Cato Burn them.

Porphyry No!

A soldier hits Porphyry. Another starts to tear up a scroll.

Please! The wisdom of centuries!

Cato Put him with the rest. Await orders.

Porphyry is dragged out. Syrus tries to light a tinderbox.

Get a move on, Syrus. I want to see a fucking conflagration on the count of three. One – two –

SCENE TWENTY-TWO

Zenobia and Malik on the banks of the Euphrates.

Zenobia There must be a boat!

Malik There isn't.

Zenobia Not a raft? Not a hollowed-out tree?

Malik The river's as broad as an old whore's bum. We need a ferryman.

Zenobia Am I beaten by a stretch of yellow water? (*She sits disconsolately.*) Look at it. I hate it.

Malik A boat will arrive.

Zenobia Is this how it ends, Malik? All dreams, all ambitions, all desires – just washed away? Your whole life turned to mud? I had hoped to walk through Rome in triumph. Now I sit by a river in disgrace.

Malik There is no disgrace for you, Majesty. I have served you since the day you married. I knew you by your Aramaic name, when you were nothing, just a girl from the hills. Now the whole world knows Zenobia, Queen of the East. Even in defeat, she will be remembered.

Zenobia I am not defeated yet, believe me!

Malik No, and come what may, you must survive. You have so much to offer. Your beauty, and your will. A beacon for all women, for all time. You must survive.

Zenobia How can I reward you, Malik?

Malik I just want to see you happy. – Look! A boat! (*Waves.*) Over here!

Zenobia When I've crossed the Euphrates, I'll be happy.

Offstage, Pertinax and a squad of Roman soldiers arrive.

Soldier 1 (*off*) There!

Soldier 2 (*off*) By the river!

Pertinax (*off*) Take her alive.

Malik (*to the ferryman*) Hurry!

Pertinax and the soldiers run on and surround the Palmyrenes.

Zenobia I've always hated rivers.

Pertinax I arrest you in the name of Imperial Rome!

Zenobia I hate the sea too.

Malik Here they come, the tourists, looking for their souvenirs.

Pertinax Kill him.

Malik Oh, kill me in a moment. First I must dance for my Queen.

Malik dances. Zenobia watches with tears in her eyes. Malik flounces flirtatiously in front of the soldiers, who start to laugh.

Soldier 1 Fucking fairy.

The soldiers move in on Malik from all sides, their shields held before them. At the last moment, with the soldiers distracted, he calls out to Zenobia:

Malik Now!

Zenobia Malik!

Malik Go!

The soldiers stab Malik, who dies. Zenobia makes a run for it, drawing her short sword. The soldiers pursue her: two of them have spears, one has a net. She is cornered. She fights wildly, wounding one of the soldiers, but then they pincer her with the long spears, and finally throw the net over her. She screams in defiance as she is picked up and carried off.

SCENE TWENTY-THREE

Aurelian in Zenobia's palace, looking out at the city. Probus and Timagenes nearby.

Aurelian Most extraordinary town I've ever laid eyes on . . . Look at those towers! What are they?

Timagenes Burial places, Emperor.

Aurelian Bodies in the sky? Why?

Timagenes I could not say. Tradition.

Aurelian Good for you. Traditions are important. – And these marvellous temples – how many gods do you worship?

Timagenes All the gods, Emperor.

Aurelian No special one?

Timagenes No.

Aurelian How curious. But I must admit I'm staggered by your buildings. And this is a royal palace, all right. Look at the ceilings! The mosaics! Fancy living here, Probus? Nothing like it in Europe!

Probus No thank you, Emperor.

Aurelian Now traditionally at this point I embark on the customary orgy of destruction and smash this place to pieces, but I can't destroy such colonnades as those, can I? Act of fucking vandalism. I don't want to go in the books as the lunatic with the sledgehammer. So I am prepared to break with convention, and let them stand.

Pertinax enters with the Prefect and soldiers carrying Zenobia in the net. They tip her out at Aurelian's feet.

Pertinax The Queen of Palmyra is your prisoner. We got her at the river.

Aurelian What was she doing – having a paddle?

The Romans laugh.

Timagenes (*to Zenobia*) Forgive me, Majesty. I did it to save lives.

Zenobia spits at Timagenes.

Aurelian Now, now – no need for that. Timagenes, you have done us a service. Without you we'd be squatting in the sand from now till Saturnalia. For that fucking

238

wall is impregnable. You have my personal thanks.
However . . . I cannot love a traitor. I cannot reward a
traitor. For a traitor once may be a traitor again. It's a
sickness. And there's only one cure.

*Quickly, Aurelian draws his dagger and stabs
Timagenes, who dies.*

Remove him. Probus, throw your cloak over that
(*Zenobia*). I don't like looking at naked women. Unless
I've got my balls between their legs.

*The soldiers drag out Timagenes' body, and Probus
covers Zenobia with his cloak.*

Now leave us alone.

Prefect Not a good idea, Emperor.

Aurelian Perhaps not, Prefect, but it is a bloody order.

Probus She has the eyes of a viper.

Aurelian Out.

*Probus, Pertinax and the Prefect leave. Aurelian is
alone with Zenobia. She turns away from him. He
smiles.*

What's it going to be, then? Little torture? Little rape?
Where shall we begin? (*Pause.*) Lovely place you've got.
Pity I must knock it down.

Zenobia's eyes flash.

So there is blood, hot blood, behind the mask. There is a
human being in there somewhere.

Zenobia drops her cloak to the floor.

Put your tits away. I'm too old for all that.

Aurelian picks up the cloak and hands it to her.

Zenobia When are you going to kill me? Don't drag it out. I hate waiting.

Aurelian Not expedient, they say. My advisors. Do you have advisors? Such a pain in the arse. But I have to leave a caution. Some trace of my displeasure. Some guarantee of order in the world.

Zenobia We could have ruled the Empire together.

Aurelian That's true. But now I have it to myself.

Zenobia And you wish to humiliate me.

Aurelian Too fucking right I do. (*thoughtfully*) Outside Antioch – saw a bloke up a pole. Some kind of mystic or other. Sits in a barrel at the top. They send up bread and water on a string.

Zenobia I will throw myself off!

Aurelian You will be chained. You'll dangle.

Zenobia Then all the East will rise in my revenge! The tribes will be united in their anger!

Aurelian Then I keep you in darkness. I hide you away.

Zenobia And you will dream of me. The beauty in a dungeon. My face will sour your sleep.

Aurelian Your face I will disfigure!

Zenobia No!

Aurelian Look, I have to satisfy the appetite of Rome!

Zenobia And what do they crave? A little woman in the kitchen, with a spoon in place of a sword, crushing garlic instead of men's heads?

Aurelian Well, it might be a start!

Zenobia (*falling to her knees*) Please, valiant Emperor, take pity on me! I was misled, I was seduced by possibility – I was too weak to stand up to my subjects! A woman should not fight.

Aurelian Probus!

Probus enters immediately.

Have a listen to this.

Zenobia I wear my armour with shame, for I know it demeans my sex. You have vanquished me in combat, which is just, and now I ask you, if you can, to let me live in peace.

Probus Well, well, well.

Zenobia Let me cease to be a man. Give me skirts to wear! Let me do embroidery, gardening, *anything* – but please, let me survive!

Aurelian (*in a sudden fury*) Have you the slightest notion how much trouble you have caused? Half way round the fucking world, I came to muzzle you! And now you want to potter in your garden? I ought to cut your throat!

Zenobia I was given bad advice!

Aurelian I'll say you were given bad advice, anybody who gives that kind of advice deserves to meet a most unpleasant end!

Zenobia So, we agree.

Aurelian What the fuck do we agree on?

Zenobia They should be punished.

Aurelian Who should?

Zenobia My counsellors. My generals. Those who deluded me.

Aurelian You sacrifice your own best men –

Zenobia They caused chaos!

Aurelian – to save your worthless life?

Zenobia You must leave a caution. Rome's laws have been flouted. We had no king, no manly authority – but now you have come to discipline the wayward. You bring calm to a frenzied land. I welcome you.

Aurelian This is a load of cock!

Probus (*aside to Aurelian*) Cock, certainly, Emperor, but highly expedient cock. We need bodies, to be picked at by the crows. And our troops can be men again, husbands again, keepers of women.

Pause.

Aurelian What are their names?

Zenobia Yedibel, head of the government. Zabdas, commander-in-chief. And Longinus, a Greek, whose lust for war began the whole adventure.

Aurelian (*to Probus*) Wheel them in.

Probus exits. Pause.

When I was a boy, I used to lie in the woods all summer. Not a summer like you have, not an inferno of wind and dust, but green, pleasant. I spent a long time watching wasps. We had a lot of wasps. Now the female wasp is a terrifying beast. Know what she has to do when she gets pregnant? She has to find a nice succulent spider to paralyse with her sting, so she can lay her eggs within it. But some summers, spiders are scarce. And if she can't find one, her eggs hatch inside her, and these hungry little grubs can't tell the difference between a fat juicy spider and mummy wasp's womb, can they, so they just start chewing, eating her up, sucking at her organs till she drops dead on the ground.

Zenobia . . . What will you do with me?

Probus, Pertinax, the Prefect and soldiers enter, leading Longinus, Zabdas and Yedibel, who are roped together at the neck.

Aurelian Take you to Rome. – These are the men?

Zenobia Yes.

Aurelian Zenobia says you advised her. Is this so?

Longinus Emperor, I am a scholar by trade, and not given to meddling in matters of state. Whatever advice I may have offered to that lady was of a purely philosophical nature, concerning the problems of Being and Nothingness and the Emanation of the Universal Mind.

Aurelian Which one is he?

Zenobia Longinus.

Aurelian Longinus, what gods do you believe in?

Longinus It is all one and the same, Emperor, all the generation of some vital cosmic force, and I'd be more than happy to go into details with you one afternoon, if your curiosity is aroused.

Aurelian The Sun God is the only deity. Heliogabalus. Who won this war for us.

Longinus Yes, that's a perfectly valid point of view, and –

Aurelian I sentence you to death.

Longinus I have to tell you she murdered her husband. King Odainat.

Yedibel It's true!

Aurelian No. We did that.

Longinus *You* did it?

Aurelian Got a bit too uppity. Neutralised him. Your defence is concluded?

Longinus I have never profaned Rome!

Probus hands Aurelian a thin manuscript. He reads the title page.

Aurelian 'The Chronicle of Zenobia, Queen of the East, together with an account of her glorious stand against an evil Empire. By Cassius Longinus, scholar.' (*to Probus*) Execute them on the palace steps.

Longinus But Emperor – !

Aurelian And get a decent crowd!

Probus Prefect.

As the Prefect starts to march the prisoners out, two soldiers enter with Porphyry captive.

Prefect Eagle-bearers of the Third Legion, report!

Soldier 1 It's a girl, sir. Cut its hair off. Says it's the servant of the Queen, and demands to be brought here.

Aurelian A girl?

Porphyry Yes.

Longinus You're a girl? Well, that explains your lack of concentration!

Aurelian Speak.

Porphyry I am the Queen's handmaiden. I have served her all my life. I bathe her feet in goats' milk; I beautify her eyes. I tried to escape dressed as a boy; but now I am caught, I must serve my mistress. She needs me. Let me go with her, to the very end.

Aurelian This is your maid?

Zenobia She is devoted to me. I must have her. Bring her with me to Rome.

Aurelian You can't have a bath on your own?

Zenobia No.

Aurelian Fucking hell, Probus, this is turning into a charade. They'll be packing their underthings next. (*to Zenobia*) All right. (*to Probus*) Let's do our work.

All exit except Porphyry and Zenobia. Zabdas reaches out to touch her but is pulled roughly away.

Porphyry Thank you.

Zenobia You saved my life. I save yours.

Porphyry You could not save Zabdas?

Zenobia Why should I?

Porphyry He's been in love with you for twenty years.

Zenobia In love with me?

Porphyry I think I gave him some bad advice.

Zenobia Zabdas . . .? No, not Zabdas . . .

Zenobia weeps. Porphyry comforts her.

SCENE TWENTY-FOUR

Palmyra. Wahballat moves furtively through the city.

Wahballat I've got to find her. Perhaps she escaped! How can I live without her?

*A squad of Roman soldiers marches through.
Wahballat hides until they are gone.*

They burnt the library! Smashed the apparatus! All our discoveries, lost!

He comes upon Longinus, Yedibel and Zabdas. They have been crucified (not with nails, with ropes). All three appear dead.

A curse on my maniac mother, who brought down this blood-storm in the desert!

Zabdas, however, is still alive.

Zabdas Say nothing against her.

Wahballat Zabdas!

Zabdas The greatest Queen our land has ever seen. I loved her, Wahballat.

Wahballat I love Porphyry.

Zabdas She is taken to Rome with your mother.

Wahballat Rome!

Zabdas They have gone. They left a garrison.

Wahballat But why did they take Porphyry?

Zabdas Your mother asked for her. Wahballat – I am dying. I must confess to you.

Wahballat Confess what? That you loved my mother?

Zabdas No. That I killed your father. I poisoned Odainat.

Wahballat But – you were his friend!

Zabdas I coveted his wife. I thought she would be mine. But I lacked . . . something. What did I lack? – Take this.

You should have it.

Zabdas, dying, drops from his hand the cochlis brooch. Wahballat stares at it.

Wahballat This was my father's. My mother gave it him. She is to blame for everything! I should open my veins, and let her sap run out! She has stolen my love from me! And I will have revenge.

Wahballat exits, with the brooch.

SCENE TWENTY-FIVE

Rome. Gratus and Quintinius, holding garlands of flowers. Aurelian and Probus enter, still in their military uniforms. The Senators bow.

Gratus We greet you with garlands, Aurelian, Conserver of the World! The Empire is secure from East to West. You have worked wonders in a few short years.

The soldiers accept the garlands.

Aurelian I asked you here, Senators, because I need your assistance.

Quintinius Delighted to be of service, Emperor.

Aurelian Quintinius. You're a builder, right?

Quintinius Well no, not personally – I mean I don't get muck on my hands – but I have a little outfit, yes –

Probus – refitting half of Rome.

Aurelian I have an Imperial Commission for you.

Quintinius (*thrilled*) Emperor!

Aurelian I want to build a wall.

Quintinius Garden wall? Wall to hang pictures?

Aurelian A wall around the city. A fortification.

Quintinius Phew! Take a few days to do an estimate.

Aurelian No need for an estimate.

Quintinius Always have an estimate. So the customer knows where he stands.

Probus In this case, there is no need.

Quintinius Why not?

Aurelian You're paying for it.

Quintinius I'm what?

Aurelian As a gesture of revitalised civic responsibility, you are offering your services to the public good. We need a wall. The Juthungi and Allemani are beaten, for now; but they may come out of their forests again.

Probus And who knows where the next threat will arise?

Aurelian We must be prepared.

Quintinius Er, I might have to refuse this contract, Emperor, as we have a heavy run of orders just at present.

Aurelian Then I will put you on trial for embezzlement. I can prove your involvement in the scandal at the Mint.

Probus Documents with your signature. Testimony of the staff.

Aurelian My people have been working, while we have been away. Now, a team of surveyors is waiting outside. They will give you the specifications. Thank you for your generous co-operation. Oh, and Senator – do a lovely job.

Quintinius leaves, downcast.

You're very quiet, Gratus.

Gratus I'm not a businessman at all. I just give parties, really.

Aurelian (*smiles*) From you all I need is advice.

Gratus Oh – excellent.

Aurelian I have brought back Zenobia, Queen of Palmyra. I have her in a dungeon on the hill. Thought you might like a peep in through the bars.

Gratus That would be a very considerable fillip, Emperor, thank you.

Aurelian Thing is, I have to work out what to do with her. I can't kill her, obviously.

Gratus No, no.

Aurelian And yet, I have to demonstrate that I will not have people snap at my bollocks with impunity. An example must be made.

Gratus Quite so.

Aurelian Well, you have experience of these affairs. You dreamt up revels for Gallienus. Very artistic, so I hear. Me, I'm just a soldier. I wouldn't know a wild bacchanalian jamboree from a kiddies' harvest festival. I like to stay at home.

Gratus I think you're thinking of a Triumph.

Aurelian Am I? Yes, I think I am.

Gratus An exquisite parade of the conquered and their rare, exotic treasures, through all the major thorough-fares of Rome. A monumental statement of our health and wealth and power.

Aurelian Sounds fucking marvellous.

Probus Organise it.

Aurelian and Probus exit quickly.

Gratus (*sighs*) I don't think I heard the magic words 'Reimbursement for your trouble.' I don't think a budget was discussed. Oh, why is there a shortage of good assassins whenever you really need one?

SCENE TWENTY-SIX

Zenobia's house of imprisonment. She enters wearing her armour, and bedecked from top to bottom in the most magnificent jewellery, very like that which she offered to Aurelian. But she is also shackled hand and foot with enormous golden chains, too heavy for her to lift on her own. Porphyry, now dressed as a girl, follows behind to help carry the chains. The sound of a restless crowd outside. Gratus enters, fussing like a couturier.

Gratus Divine, utterly divine. Never seen anything like it! Cost me an absolute packet, but who could place value on a spectacle like this? Your beauty alone is worth the outlay.

Porphyry How long will it take?

Gratus Nine hours. First come twenty elephants, and two hundred more ferocious beasts, including four tigers, and, I believe, a giraffe. Eight hundred pairs of gladiators, for the Colosseum tomorrow. And then the captured prisoners; and then you. Immediately behind you is the Emperor, in a chariot drawn by four stags, which once belonged to the King of the Goths. When we reach the Capitol, Aurelian will slay the stags as an offering to

Jupiter. The entire army marches past, and lastly, rather as if we were prisoners too, I regret to say, the full body of the Senate. It is a Triumph without parallel, and it is Aurelian's.

Porphyry Afterwards, what happens to her?

Gratus Nothing ill, I sincerely hope. This public abasement I think should be enough. We are justly famed for our parades, but also for our hospitality and, yes, gracious living.

Aurelian and Probus enter. The Emperor wears a purple tunic embroidered with palms, covered with a purple toga embroidered with stars. On his head a laurel wreath.

Aurelian Gratus, you've surpassed yourself.

Probus Let the people marvel at the enemies of Rome. Let them see what monsters we have tamed.

Gratus This lady is no monster, I am sure.

Aurelian You should have seen her on the field at Emesa. Are we ready?

Gratus One more thing.

Gratus takes a crude placard with 'Zenobia' written on it, and hangs it round her neck.

Aurelian How does it feel? You content?

Zenobia I'm still here.

Aurelian Walk.

Porphyry picks up the golden chains, and she, Zenobia and Gratus exit. A roar from the crowd.

I wait for the chariot?

Probus It's outside. A slave will stand behind you, holding over your head a golden crown, and whispering constantly in your ear that all human glory is fleeting.

Aurelian Too bloody true, boy. See you tonight. (*He makes to leave.*)

Probus Aurelian – (*He looks around to make sure they are unobserved, then kisses Aurelian full on the lips, and holds him close.*) Well done.

Aurelian smiles fondly at Probus.

Aurelian No bastard laughed at me, did they?

Aurelian exits. An even greater roar from the crowd.

SCENE TWENTY-SEVEN

The dining room of Gratus' luxurious villa in Tivoli: three couches arranged around a table inlaid with ivory. Porphyry enters, well-dressed in women's clothes. She places a vase of flowers on the table. Gratus enters.

Gratus Everything set for this evening?

Porphyry It's all in hand, sir. The wild boar is on the spit; the oysters and eels are coming from the market; the wine is opened.

Gratus Do you know how to purify wine?

Porphyry No sir, I'm sorry, I don't.

Gratus Drop the yolk of a pigeon's egg into it – it draws the impurities down to the bottom of the flask.

Porphyry That's very intriguing. Why do you suppose that happens?

Gratus I haven't the faintest idea.

Porphyry (*wistfully*) Cooking holds its share of mysteries, doesn't it?

Gratus I'm not particularly interested in cooking. It's eating I'm interested in. Have you got the African snails?

Porphyry Yes.

Gratus The walnuts and figs from the cellar?

Porphyry And the dormice in honey.

Gratus Mmm . . . Tell cook not to season the dishes with salt; unwashed sea-urchins are better.

Porphyry And the best ones come from Cape Misenum, if I'm right?

Gratus You're learning fast, Porphyry. The serious banquet is composed mainly of soft food, the kind that will putrefy fast. Money must be spent. A lot of important people are coming.

Porphyry I understand.

Gratus She is dressing?

Porphyry She looks wonderful.

Gratus Oh, how right you are. She looks magnificent, every hour of the day. I am a lucky bastard, aren't I?

Porphyry Very lucky, sir.

Gratus I am going to the baths, so I shall be relaxed at feeding time. Please inform her. – Is it raining? It looks like rain.

> *Zenobia enters. She does indeed look magnificent, a sophisticated Roman matron, wearing the finest silks, and make-up, and a string of pearls.*

My treasure . . . My little desert bloom . . .

Zenobia kisses Gratus, then shows off her clothes.

Zenobia Will I do?

Gratus Exquisite.

Zenobia The pearls are adorable. So generous of you, Septimus.

Porphyry I will just check on the pastries. (*She exits.*)

Zenobia Did you know Cleopatra once swallowed a pearl worth ten million sesterces?

Gratus No!

Zenobia Yes! Dissolved it in vinegar. She bet her Roman lover she could prepare a feast more costly than he might ever imagine.

Gratus She was right. But please – don't eat your pearls, my darling.

Zenobia (*laughs*) I shan't. As long as you've got me something tasty.

Gratus I have for you a very special treat. A lamprey, caught before spawning – for its flesh is softer then – and served on a bed of livers, from plaice and bass and turbot.

Zenobia And to follow?

Gratus Sow's udders.

Zenobia I can hardly wait.

Gratus Nothing is too perfect for my luscious Arab queen. I was going to the baths but . . . you in that dress, it's just . . . you make my mouth water. I would eat you up, and to hell with the dinner.

Zenobia You may do what you like with me.

Gratus May I really?

Zenobia I am your wife.

Gratus I want you.

Zenobia Yes.

Gratus Later.

Gratus kisses her, and gropes her lewdly. She seems to quite enjoy it. She moans a little as she kisses him passionately. He buries his head in her bosom.

Zenobia Now go to the baths. Refresh yourself.

Gratus I adore you, Zenobia.

Zenobia I know.

He leaves, blowing kisses. Zenobia is rearranging her clothes as Porphyry returns, carrying sticks of lighted incense which she places around the room.

Porphyry You seem happy.

Zenobia I am. The cream of Roman society is coming to my table. The meal will be a dream, a work of art. The talk will be of lechery, philosophy, and fashion. And the wholesale price of bricks if Quintinius is on his usual form. Of course I am happy! My husband treats me well.

Porphyry Things have turned out comfortably.

Zenobia Things have turned out better than I ever thought possible. I live in Rome! I have a villa! Why, I have a hundred pairs of shoes!

Porphyry But the price is high.

Zenobia The past is forgotten. A miasma of heat and sand. You know what they say here? 'A happy people has no history.' Live for the present, Porphyry. We're in Tivoli. Try and have fun.

Porphyry I am trying.

Zenobia Well, try a little harder, dear, you're giving me a headache. That long face. Those droopy shoulders. Why are you so distracted?

Porphyry . . . I lost something.

Zenobia Well go and look for it! Heavens!

Porphyry Yes, ma'am.

> *Porphyry exits. Zenobia wafts around the room, humming cheerfully to herself. Aurelian enters, in civilian clothes. She doesn't see him at first. He watches her. His head and shoulders are wet with rain.*

Zenobia Emperor!

Aurelian I stood in the atrium. Nobody came.

Zenobia They're all in the kitchens. Preparing a feast.

Aurelian The fat Senator loves to entertain.

Zenobia Will you stay? Be our guest of honour?

Aurelian What are you having?

Zenobia Sow's udders. And the vulva for Gratus. His favourite.

Aurelian The man eats the cunt of a pig. How can you live with him?

Zenobia Please, stay for dinner.

Aurelian I disapprove of gluttony. This advertising of wealth, socialising for prestige. And soldiers don't dine like civilians. A biscuit and water will do me.

Zenobia But you can't eat alone!

Aurelian I will not be alone. And at your groaning
tables, isn't it forbidden to discuss politics or war?
I don't do small-talk. Compulsory good humour is alien
to me.

Zenobia It's easy once you've got the hang of it. (*A cloud
passes momentarily over her face.*) I have been and
admired your Temple of the Sun. It is a masterpiece.
So – how to put it? – sunny.

Aurelian I have introduced the cult of Heliogabalus to
Rome. It was that or Christianity, which gives me a pain
in the tits. Turn the other fucking cheek and whatnot.
No, we'll go with the sun. – Your boy, Wahballat.

Zenobia What of him?

Aurelian He led an insurrection in Palmyra. The
remnants of your army, the Bedouins and sheikhs, rose
against my legions. I sent Pertinax. Today a courier
informs me he has razed the city to the ground. I thought
you'd want to know.

Zenobia (*shocked*) All destroyed?

Aurelian Smashed to bits. I'm sorry. I liked it.

Zenobia The whelp! He did that on purpose! You caught
him, I hope?

Aurelian No.

Zenobia You should have.

Aurelian But still we have the trade-routes. The caravans
plod on. Gratus should be pleased. He can still buy his
cinnamon, his ginger and cloves, to stuff inside some
carcass.

Porphyry enters.

Zenobia (*to Porphyry*) Palmyra has been wrecked.

Aurelian I must get home. Have a good party. I hope the wine you give this husband is less potent than the wine you gave your first.

Zenobia I did not kill Odainat.

Aurelian Well neither did we. I checked the files. His classification was positive; a staunch ally of Rome.

Zenobia Then who – ?

Aurelian An enemy? A friend? Does it make a difference?

Aurelian exits. Zenobia sits with a glazed look.

Porphyry So some distant town is rubble . . .

Zenobia My home . . .

Porphyry This is your home. This is where you sleep and eat. The men lie on the couches, leaning on their left elbows, eating with their right hands, talking; the women sit at the table, and smile. I eat with the slaves in the kitchen.

Zenobia It's a system. It works.

Porphyry (*suddenly angry*) But why have you chosen to accept it?

Zenobia . . . Were I a man you would not ask. It would pose no problem.

Porphyry You are such a disappointment!

Zenobia There are walls, you know, there are limits and constraints, on what is available to us!

Porphyry I tear down walls! It's what I do!

Zenobia I build them. There's our difference.

Porphyry I'm leaving you.

Zenobia (*surprised*) You can't.

Porphyry I have heard of a secret society, here in the heart of Rome – Rome, where we thought there was no science! – a group of researchers dedicated to cutting things up, and then cutting them up again, and then cutting and cutting, down to the smallest particle – and how far can you go? At the very end, do you find the first principles of life?

Zenobia Have you noticed it is raining? How wonderful! It rains!

Porphyry What has happened to you?

Zenobia I just learnt to live with the weather.

Porphyry That's the one thing I don't want to learn.

Zenobia (*sarcastically*) Oh, would you like me to end it all? An asp, perhaps? – Don't be so romantic.

Porphyry I'm going to find Wahballat. (*She turns to leave.*)

Zenobia What, still, you think of *him*? – Oh, my dear, I'm sorry. He's dead.

Porphyry No . . . that's impossible . . .

Zenobia The Romans killed him.

Porphyry (*screams*) No!

She runs out. Zenobia sits alone, hard and distant. After a moment she gets up, and begins to go around the room, plumping up the cushions on the sofas. The sound of heavy rain.

SCENE TWENTY-EIGHT

Palmyra. Windy. Huge chunks of masonry lie on the ground, overgrown with weeds. The sound of sheep. Wahballat enters, dressed as a shepherd.

Wahballat I tend my flock. We live in huts. The desert wind torments us. Nothing left now of the great metropolis. Just jagged columns pointing at the sky – the drifting sands of history. Sometimes I dream of my alchemist lover. In the past, when I was young. But I never grew up. Never came of age. I've tried to kill myself several times. Pointless.

> *Two explorers enter, Dawkins and Wood. They wear the clothes of Englishmen of 1750. Wood has a sketch-pad. Wahballat hides.*

Dawkins We've found it! God bless us, we've found it!

Wood The ruins of Palmyra!

Dawkins Start drawing, Mr Wood!

Wood It exists! It truly exists!

Dawkins The city of Palmyra . . .! The architecture of your dreams!

Wood We shall have etchings that will be the talk of London.

Dawkins All those miles of nothing – then suddenly, this! The home of Zenobia, who rose against Rome in what? – two-seventy AD? – damn near fifteen hundred years ago!

Wood And it's ours, Mr Dawkins. We're first.

Dawkins Draw! Draw everything in sight!

Wood begins to sketch. Wahballat moves, and they see him.

A shepherd.

Wood What's that he's got round his neck?

Dawkins A gem.

Wood There's treasure here?

Dawkins (*to Wahballat*) May we take a look, sirrah? At your jewel?

They close in on Wahballat, who panics, and tries to escape. They grab him. Dawkins rips from his neck the cochlis jewel of Odainat.

Wood Where is it? Where's the treasure?

Wahballat (*in Arabic*) Leave me be! I am nothing! (*He runs off.*)

Dawkins Damn! That's the end of our fortune.

Wood I believe, Mr Dawkins, these ruins will make us rich.

Dawkins You're right. Draw, man! They'll build houses in this style in Piccadilly, when they've read our book!

Wood Must have been something to see.

Dawkins Must have been a miracle. (*He gazes at the jewel.*)

Wood What will you do with it?

Dawkins I think . . . I'll donate it to the British Museum.

The End.

THE TURN OF THE SCREW

screenplay
based on the story by
Henry James

The Turn of the Screw was first produced by United Productions in association with Martin Pope Productions and WGBH/Boston for Meridian Broadcasting. The film was first screened on ITV on 26 December 1999.

Miss Jessel Caroline Pegg
Miss Jodhi May
The Master Colin Firth
Mrs Grose Pam Ferris
Flora Grace Robinson
Cook Jenny Howe
Miles Joe Sowerbutts
Peter Quint Jason Salkey

Director Ben Bolt
Producer Martin Pope
Executive Producer for WGBH/Boston Rebecca Eaton
Executive Producers Michele Buck, Jim Vaughan

Casting Director Kate Rhodes James
Make-up Designer Roseann Samuel
Costume Designer Sheena Napier
Music Composer Adrian Johnston

Associate Producer Helga Dowie
Editor Jerry Leon
Production Designer Pat Campbell
Director of Photography David Odd

Characters

The Master
Miss
Flora
Miles
Mrs Grose
Luke
Cook
Groom
Gardener
Maids

Miss Jessel
Peter Quint

London, 1850s.

Late at night. The oily surface of the Thames,
cluttered with debris.

We tilt up to see a figure, dimly lit by the gas-lamp she
is standing under.

It's a young woman (Miss Jessel, but we don't know
this yet).

She stands at the parapet, looking down at the murky
river. She wears an expression of abject misery.

A hansom cab clatters past her across the bridge, but
there are no other bystanders.

The woman steadies herself on the standard of the
gas-lamp, and climbs with difficulty on to the parapet.

CU her face as she stands looking down at the river.
She contemplates a miserable end.

She jumps. We see her skirts billow out like a parachute.

The dark shape of the woman hits the water. The river
quickly swallows her up.

CUT TO

A pleasant day. A young woman whom we shall call
Miss, dressed in clothes of good quality, but simple in
style, crosses a busy London thoroughfare. She checks an
address written on a sheet of paper.

Well-dressed Londoners pass by. Miss approaches an
expansive mansion.

CUT TO

Miss sits timidly in the opulent drawing room of a gentleman we shall call The Master. She's so nervous she's perched on the edge of her chair. The room is filled with fine furniture, paintings, decorative Chinese vases, Indian tapestries – it's luxurious, exotic, elegant and quite unlike anything she's ever seen before. There are sizeable sprays of white lilies in several prominent places.

Her manners are perfect but she is clearly unused to company of this kind. Standing before the fire, an elbow perched languidly on the mantlepiece, is The Master. He is extremely handsome, charming and rich. Aged in his mid-thirties, he's been around the block a few times, and he knows how to keep a young lady very keenly entertained. His clothes are exquisite, his manner soft and approachable. He has deep, dark eyes and a mischievous smile. He behaves quite formally towards her, as the situation demands, yet also seems able to draw her into his confidence.

The Master I have indeed read your letters of reference, and they are indeed impeccable. But this would be your first position?

Miss Yes, sir. It is the first time I have left home.

The Master (*smiles*) Nonetheless, you have some experience . . .?

Miss When I responded to your advertisement I believe I gave details of my work in the village schoolroom. I would venture to say I have a better than average grounding in all the major subjects.

The Master I don't doubt it. You seem eminently qualified for the post.

Miss Thank you, sir.

She looks around the room, pleased with her good fortune. The Master moves to sit before her, not too far away. He frowns.

The Master The children in question are my nephew and niece, to whom I am guardian. My brother died on active service in India – and his wife, the year before, from Yellow Fever.

Miss I am very sorry to hear it.

He acknowledges her condolence, shutting his eyes for a few seconds, as if in prayer. She bows her head slightly, but watches him from under her eyelids. He is certainly very attractive.

The Master So I am, as I say, a bachelor. I have not a pennyworth of paternal understanding. And I travel a good deal.

Miss (*impressed*) Do you?

The Master I am abroad much of the year. I've therefore installed these youngsters in my country place in Essex. It is at Bly that I require a governess.

Miss I have no preference as to location.

The Master You do not? Splendid!

He gives her a dazzling smile, then stands and goes to a spray of white lilies, which he smells with evident pleasure. Then this seems to remind him of something, and he peers glumly out of the window, hands thrust deep in pockets.

I must say I pity the poor chicks. Left with no Mama or Papa to protect them. I assure you I've done what I can.

Miss Oh, I'm certain you –

The Master There was at first a young lady in charge there, who did for them most beautifully. A very proper person, as we thought. A Miss Jessell. But we had the misfortune to lose her.

Miss She left?

The Master I am sorry to say she died.

A pause as this sinks in. Miss looks at the floor, blinking.

Miss (*quietly*) Of what did she die?

The Master It's not a matter I feel inclined to discuss. But . . . we miss her, nonetheless; the children especially miss her. I have tried to get down to Bly as often as practically I might, but the awkward thing is, my own affairs take up all my time. And besides, I have not the patience for children. (*Pause.*) I will be frank with you. I have seen several candidates for the post of governess. But none has yet engaged. For each, the main condition has proven prohibitive.

Miss looks up at him. He elaborates.

The main condition of the job is that you will never trouble me – but never, never. Neither appeal nor complain nor write about anything; but meet all questions yourself, receive all moneys from my solicitor, take the whole thing over and *leave me alone*. The minute you arrive, you will naturally have full authority. It really is imperative that I am not disturbed.

Miss nods, considering.

As for the boy, he is away at school. After the . . . unpleasantness, I put him there. He is only ten, but what else could be done? He will be in your custody during the holidays.

Miss I haven't yet said that I'll engage.

The Master You would do me the greatest favour. You would lighten a burden. I should remain forever in your debt.

As he says this he takes hold, lightly, of her hand. He squeezes it and releases it. Miss looks as if a high-voltage current has passed through her. She gazes into his eyes. He doesn't break away.

I am asking you to assume the management of my family affairs. I would not ask, had I not the highest estimation of your abilities. May I place my confidence in you?

Miss (*in a whisper*) I don't know, I . . .

He smiles one of his special smiles.

The Master May I?

CUT TO

Essex.

It's a summer's day, but overcast and grey, threatening rain. Through the gently rolling farmland of North Essex – Constable country – rides Miss in an open one-horse carriage, driven by the Groom. Her trunk is lashed to the luggage rack.

The Groom is a middle-aged countryman of sour demeanour, dressed entirely in black, with bushy white whiskers. He concentrates on the pot-holed lane ahead, paying no attention to his passenger, his mouth set in a lugubrious scowl. Miss looks downcast; she imagines she may be entering a long, dark tunnel.

The carriage approaches Bly. It's a medium-sized country house, not too grand or ostentatious, but significantly huge nevertheless. Bits of the house were

*built at different periods; most conspicuous is a tower,
with battlements at the top, which has been added to
the east wing at some point. Below the house, at some
distance across the pristine lawns, is a large lake.
Flanking the lawns are tall trees, and to the side by the
tower are ornamental gardens.*

Miss visibly brightens. It's nicer than she had expected.

*Two young Maids appear in two separate upper-storey
windows, watching the approach of the carriage on the
driveway below. They see Miss look up at them.*

Mrs Grose (OOV) Gertie! Anne! Down here at once!

*The Maids come running down the stairs, joining at
the bottom the rest of the staff, who are moving
outside. They are summoned by Mrs Grose, the
housekeeper. She is a woman in her early forties,
uneducated and accustomed to hard work, with a
kindly face. She has a good, ample figure and dresses
neatly in her starched working clothes.*

Come along now, quick! Get in line!

*As the carriage pulls up at the front entrance of Bly,
the Maids join the rest of the staff who are lined up
on the driveway. Here we have Cook, a lady of
obligatory rotundity, the two young Maids, the
houseboy Luke, the ancient Gardener, and the
curmudgeonly Groom.*

*As Miss descends from the carriage, Flora, aged
eight, appears in the doorway. She's very beautiful,
and clutches a small posy of flowers.*

Welcome to Bly, Miss.

Miss Thank you, Mrs Grose.

Mrs Grose I got the staff out for your inspection.

Mrs Grose escorts Miss to the beginning of the line: Cook. Miss extends her hand, and Cook, not expecting this, shakes it, and smiles. Miss passes along the line, shaking everyone's hand, even the Groom at the end.

Miss This is everyone?

Mrs Grose Yes, Miss.

Miss turns towards the house – and there is Flora, grinning, her hair cascading in ringlets, her face a picture of innocent fun.

(OOV) And this is Flora.

Flora advances to Miss, drops a slightly shambolic curtsey, and offers the posy of flowers.

Flora (*smiling*) These are for you, Miss.

Miss smiles back at the girl.

Miss Will you show me around my new home, Flora?

CUT TO

Flora leads Miss up the main staircase. The walls are lined with oil portraits of the patriarchs of the family. Miss notices a conspicuously new painting: it's The Master, smiling affably, a vase of white lilies visible in the background. Flora tugs her onwards.

Miss I must say, it is a most agreeable residence. Your Uncle has provided for you well.

Flora Yes – isn't he sweet?

CUT TO

Miss and Flora enter the schoolroom. It's austere, with a double desk facing the teacher's table, a blackboard, a bookshelf, maps of the Empire pinned to the walls. Miss scans the room quickly. She approves.

Flora When shall we begin?

Miss Lessons commence tomorrow.

Miss barely has time to look around further before Flora grabs her hand and tugs her out through the door. The girl has golden hair and wears a blue frock. Miss likes her more and more.

CUT TO

Miss and Flora peep into the master bedroom. It has a splendid four-poster, and the walls are lined with wood-panelled cupboards. But all the furniture is shrouded.

Flora This is my Uncle's room.

Miss His bedroom?

Flora giggles.

CUT TO

A dark, stone-flagged passageway. Flora's feet patter on the floor as she scampers along it. She turns to speak over her shoulder to Miss, who is following.

Flora Come on, Miss!

Miss Where are we going?

Flora A place I found. No one ever comes here!

Flora disappears around a corner. She leads Miss up a long, stone staircase, which twists and turns. They climb and climb. Daylight filters in through slits in the walls. Towards the top they have to fight their way through ancient cobwebs.

Flora and Miss emerge through a little wooden door and find themselves on top of the tower. There's a terrific view of the lake and the woods, with open farmland beyond. It's clear from this aspect that we're very, very out of the way here – there's no sign of any other habitation.

Flora skips up to the battlements. Miss stays away from the edge.

Miss Do be careful, Flora.

Flora Why? (*She laughs, tossing her rich, curly hair in the breeze.*)

CUT TO

Miss has been given the best suite in the house, two large interconnecting rooms. The bedroom has a vast state bed, picture windows opening on to the grounds, plenty of room to move, and a pair of tall mirrors. Miss's trunk stands opened and partly unpacked in the middle of the floor. We can see through to her sitting room, where there is a writing table, and a sofa in front of the fire.

Miss studies herself in a triple-panelled full-length mirror. There's a knock at the door.

Miss Come.

Mrs Grose enters. She carries a vase of flowers which she stands on a side-table.

Mrs Grose Is everything to your satisfaction, Miss?

Miss It is more than satisfactory, and not at all what I had been led to expect! (*She laughs, looking into the mirror.*) I confess, I have never seen myself in one of these before!

Mrs Grose (*nervously*) Flora was polite?

Miss Her manners are commendable –

Mrs Grose Thank you, Miss.

Miss – under the circumstances.

Mrs Grose I have done my best.

Miss I can see that, Mrs Grose. I can certainly see that. You have done admirably. I am sure we shall on every question be quite at one.

Mrs Grose curtseys and turns to leave. But then she turns back:

Mrs Grose Oh, Miss, I am so glad you are here!

Mrs Grose leaves the room. Miss frowns at her rather over-enthusiastic response.

CUT TO

Later that day. On the lawn, in front of the house, Miss lies on a blanket, asleep. A little way off, Flora plays happily, making a daisy chain, humming to herself.
A call comes from across the lawns:

Mrs Grose (OOV) Miss!

Miss opens her eyes. The first thing that swims into view is the tower; then gradually she pulls into focus the rest of the house. She sees Flora playing nearby,

and then she pinpoints the sound that woke her:
Mrs Grose is coming across the grass, carrying a tray.

I brung some lemonade, Miss. It's nice and cold.

Miss (*rubbing her eyes*) Am I dreaming? Or is it real?

Mrs Grose pours lemonade, and gives a glass to Flora
and a glass to Miss.

Mrs Grose It's real all right. And I'm real. And Flora's
real.

Flora has wandered a little way off, out of earshot.
The women look at her. Miss sips her lemonade.

What think you of her, then?

Miss She is an angel.

Mrs Grose (*smiles*) She is that. (*She turns back towards*
the house.)

Miss There is something I wish to ask you. Tell me
about the lady who was here before.

Mrs Grose The last governess? Well now, let's see,
I suppose she was young and pretty, Miss, like you.

Miss (*trying to hide a smile*) He seems to like us young
and pretty.

Mrs Grose Oh, he did. I mean he does.

Miss (*confused*) I beg pardon?

Mrs Grose has transparently said something she ought
not.

You said 'he did'.

Mrs Grose Did I?

Miss To whom were you referring?

Mrs Grose (*flustered*) Why, the Master! – Please, Miss,
I must get on.

*And Mrs Grose hurries into the house. Miss stares
after her, frowning. Flora comes to Miss and gives her
the daisy-chain she has made.*

CUT TO

*In Miss's bedroom, the two Maids are making up a small
bed for Flora, at the foot of Miss's bed. They place in it
Flora's collection of china dolls.*

CUT TO

*Supper in Mrs Grose's parlour. This is where most of the
children's meals are taken, at a polished table. The Maids
serve as Miss sits with Flora and Mrs Grose. It is Mrs
Grose's domain, and she has pride of place.*

Mrs Grose Now that Miss is settled here, Flora, you
shall move out of my room, and into hers.

Flora (*clapping her hands and speaking with her mouth
full*) Goody!

Miss (*sternly*) We are at table, Flora.

*Flora is immediately subdued. A cool pause. Miss tries
to make amends:*

Well, at the end of the week I am to meet your brother.

Flora's eyes light up at the thought.

(*to Mrs Grose*) Does he look at all like her?

Mrs Grose My, yes, he's gorgeous, you will be quite
carried away by him!

Miss (*smiles*) I'm afraid I'm rather easily carried away.

Mrs Grose (*laughs*) Are you?

Miss Yes. I was quite carried away in London.

Mrs Grose At your interview . . .?

Miss nods, smiling still, but now also embarrassed.

Well, Miss, you're not the first, and I daresay you won't be the last.

Miss has to turn away. Secretly, she sighs. Flora giggles.

CUT TO

The Master's bedroom. The door opens quietly, and Miss looks in. She surveys the room, then slips inside, closing the door quietly behind her. She stands in the centre of the room and stares at the bed.

Miss goes to one of the wardrobes, and tentatively opens it. There are rows of suits on hangers. Her eye alights on a splash of colour: the Master's waistcoats. He goes for what at this time might be called a flamboyant style. Miss runs her fingers over the rich material.

CUT TO

Evening, the light fading. In the garden, white lilies are growing. Miss bends to touch the head of one, and smell its perfume. She plucks the flower and walks on through the garden with it cupped in her hands. We hear the rooks in the trees.

As Miss approaches the house, she stops in concern. Before her is the tower, and a man is standing on its summit. It's not someone we've seen before. He is young, thin, wearing good clothes but no hat; his hair is red. He looks directly down at Miss, who, though apprehensive, returns his stare. The man leans on the parapet with both hands on the ledge. After a few moments he looks away from Miss, and scans the garden. He moves to another corner of the tower. Miss watches, immobile.

The man looks down at her once more, with an expressionless but somehow malign set to his features. All the sounds of evening seem to drop away – there's an intense hush. Miss holds her breath. Then the man turns and walks to the far side of the tower, and suddenly she can see him no more.

CU Miss: she is half-frightened, half-fascinated.

CUT TO

Next morning. Miss descends the stairs to the hall. She is deep in thought. Luke approaches her, bearing a letter on a silver tray.

Luke The morning post for you, Miss.

Miss takes the letter without really noticing it, and Luke starts to go.

Miss Oh, Luke?

Luke turns back, a little reluctantly.

Were there any visitors last evening?

Luke (*surprised*) Visitors? No, Miss.

Miss dismisses Luke. She looks at the envelope, preoccupied. Mrs Grose approaches her.

Mrs Grose (*smiling*) Have you a letter, Miss?

Miss It is the Master's hand.

CUT TO

Miss is pacing the floor in her sitting room, shaking her head in dismay. She reads a note from The Master.

The Master (VO) 'This, I recognise, is from Miles' headmaster, and Miles' headmaster's an awful bore. Please deal with it for me. I don't want to know!'

> *She goes over to the writing table, where there lies another letter. She picks it up and reads it through, not for the first time.*

Miss Oh, dear, Miles!

CUT TO

Mrs Grose's parlour. She's in a state of shock. Miss paces the room, holding her letter.

Mrs Grose Expelled?

Miss Yes.

Mrs Grose Miles, expelled?

Miss Dismissed from the school.

Mrs Grose (*struggling to comprehend*) They won't take him back after the holidays?

Miss They absolutely decline.

Mrs Grose But why?

> *Miss, uncertain how to reply, places the other letter on the table in front of Mrs Grose.*

(*shaking her head sadly*) I can't read, Miss.

Miss Oh. I'm sorry.

Embarrassed, Miss picks up the letter, and reads it again.

Mrs Grose What does the headmaster say?

Miss He gives no particulars. Simply expresses regret that it's impossible to keep him. Which can mean only one thing: that he's an injury to the others.

Mrs Grose (*offended*) Master Miles! An injury!

Miss But if he has done something *bad* . . .

Mrs Grose He is not bad! He is scarce ten year old!

Flora knocks and appears in the doorway, holding up her schoolbook.

Flora Excuse me, Miss, I've finished.

Mrs Grose goes to her.

Mrs Grose You might as well say *she* is bad, bless her! – Run along, Flora, Miss'll mark your work later.

Flora skips out, and Mrs Grose closes the door.

Meet him first, and then decide.

Miss So you have never known him to be bad?

Mrs Grose Oh, I didn't say *that*! He is a boy, after all!

Miss Then you have known –

Mrs Grose Yes, Miss, I have! And I thank God for it too! A boy with no spirit is no boy for me!

Miss You like them with the spirit to be naughty . . .? Well, so do I!

Mrs Grose laughs happily; they seem to agree on everything.

But not to the point where they contaminate –

Mrs Grose Eh? What's that?

Miss Where they corrupt –

Mrs Grose I can't follow you, Miss. Children are children, that's all.

CUT TO

Evening. Miss enters the kitchen. Cook is with the two Maids and Luke. They are all laughing as Miss enters, at which moment the laughter suddenly ceases.

Miss Good evening.

Cook Good evening, Miss.

The others murmur their 'good evenings', without much enthusiasm.

Miss I should like to know whether there were any persons here from the village, yesterday at about this time . . . any tradesmen, say . . . young men?

Cook None whatever, Miss.

They all shake their heads.

Miss Are you positive?

Cook (*darkly*) No one comes here from the village.

CUT TO

Miss climbs the winding stone steps up the tower. She pushes her way through the cobwebs and out on to the top of the tower. She pauses to catch her breath. Her eyes dart about nervously. There's no sign of anyone having been there.

Miss forces herself to walk forwards to the parapet. She leans her hands on it, in the same manner as the man she saw previously. She shivers as she looks down.

CUT TO

In the schoolroom, two days later. Miss is chalking up some simple long division on the blackboard. Flora sits at her desk, watching, pencil in hand.

From outside, on the driveway, comes the sound of the post-horn. A carriage pulls up outside the house. Flora, forgetting herself, jumps up and runs to the door.

Flora It's Miles!

CUT TO

Flora runs out of the front door and down the steps. The carriage comes to a halt and Miles leaps down. Miles is 'incredibly beautiful'; he has an open, honest face, floppy hair, long limbs, gentle hands.

Miss appears in the doorway behind Flora, watching intently. Flora and Miles embrace happily. They seem very genuinely pleased to see each other. They whisper briefly, Flora glancing back towards Miss as she does so. Then, hand in hand, they turn and walk towards Miss, as the Groom struggles to unload Miles's trunk from the carriage. Flora releases Miles's hand.

Miss Hello, Miles.

Miles extends his hand in a very adult fashion, beams her a brilliant smile, and speaks clearly and politely:

Miles I'm delighted to make your acquaintance, Miss.

They shake hands. He certainly doesn't look like trouble. Miss breathes an inward sigh of relief. Miles turns to Flora and they grin cheerfully at each other. Mrs Grose appears at the door behind Miss. Miles spots her and waves gaily:

Mrs Grose!

CUT TO

Miss and Miles enter the hall, followed by Mrs Grose and Flora.

Miss Had you a good journey?

Miles First class, thanks. I hope you're settling in all right. I think you'll find Bly's a jolly nice place.

Miss (*smiles*) I'm sure I shall.

CUT TO

Supper in Mrs Grose's parlour. Miles now sits next to Flora, opposite Miss. Mrs Grose presides and the Maids serve. Today there are scones. Mrs Grose takes one from the three-tiered cake-stand. Miles immediately offers the jam-pot.

Miles Care for some jam Mrs Grose?

Miss watches approvingly. The boy's manners are impeccable.

CUT TO

The schoolroom, next day. Miles and Flora sit side by side at the desk, concentrating hard. Miss is giving them a history test.

Miss Battle of Waterloo.

Miles (*shoots his hand up*) Eighteen-fifteen!

Miss acknowledges the correct answer.

Miss Battle of Trafalgar.

Miles (*shoots his hand up*) Eighteen hundred and five!

Miss Who won that great sea battle, Flora?

Flora We did, Miss.

Miss smiles indulgently at her, then looks to Miles for the right answer:

Miles (*shoots his hand up*) Admiral Nelson, Miss!

CUT TO

Some days later. High summer. On the lawn are Miles and Flora, in light, breezy clothes, playing tag.
Under the shade of the trees sit Miss and Mrs Grose. The remains of a picnic are spread out on a tartan rug. Miss watches the children closely as they race happily past.

Miss The charge is grotesque. It doesn't live an instant! *Look* at him!

Mrs Grose turns to look at Miles.

Mrs Grose What will you say to his Uncle, then?

Miss hadn't really thought this far ahead.

Miss Nothing. I am pledged not to trouble him. Not on any account.

Mrs Grose What will you say to his school?

Miss Nothing.

Mrs Grose (*smiling*) And to the boy himself?

Miss (*laughing*) No, nothing! We have the entire summer. Unless he has something to hide, he will be frank with us.

Mrs Grose I'll stand by you, Miss.

Miss Thank you. We'll see it out!

Mrs Grose We will.

Miss stands, picks up her skirts, and runs to join in the game with the children. Mrs Grose watches with satisfaction.

CUT TO

The picnic party push through the undergrowth by the lake and arrive at a rickety, half-rotten jetty, with a flat-bottomed boat moored to it by a long rope. There are oars in the boat. Miss gasps in surprise. Flora claps her hands with delight. Miles pulls on the painter, and turns to Miss as the boat comes in to the jetty.

Miles All aboard, Miss!

Miss Oh, I couldn't . . .!

Miles holds the boat close to the jetty with his foot. He and Flora form a line and both give a smart naval salute. Mrs Grose laughs.

Mrs Grose Go on – where's the harm?

Miss shrugs: 'Why not?' Lifting her skirts, she steps gingerly into the beautiful old boat.

CUT TO

The middle of the lake. Miles rows, quite competently, as Flora and Miss sit together in the stern. It's very still and quiet on the water.

Miles Where do you come from, Miss?

Miss From a tiny little village in Hampshire, Miles. My father's the parson there.

Flora And have you brothers and sisters?

Miss Oh yes, two brothers, and four sisters, and I'm the youngest.

Miles Good heavens, there are loads of you!

Miss (*laughing*) Yes, that's why I have to work!

Flora This isn't work, though, really and truly – is it?

Miss lies back and trails her hand lazily through the water. She's relaxed and content, and she likes their company.

Miss No. Really and truly, it isn't.

A pause. Miss looks up, and sees both the children apparently looking towards the same point on the shore, among the trees, fifty yards away. Miss looks too, but can see nothing. The children continue to stare. Then they break off and notice Miss considering them intently, with a puzzled frown.

Flora That's where the heron lives.

Miles I wonder where he's gone?

CUT TO

*Evening. The light is just fading behind the closed curtains
in Miles's bedroom. He is in bed, in his nightgown, hair
brushed and face scrubbed, with a book open in his lap.
He reads by the light of a single candle. There is a knock
and Miss enters. She stands by the open door.*

Miss Time to blow your light out.

Miles puts his book aside.

Miles Goodnight, Miss.

Miss Did you say your prayers?

Miles Absolutely, yes.

Miss Goodnight, then.

Miss slips out of the door. Just as she's closing it:

Miles Miss? – I had the most marvellous day. Thanks so
much.

And Miles blows out his candle.

CUT TO

*Sunday. Dressed in their best clothes, Miss, Miles, Flora
and Mrs Grose walk to church. They are followed by
Cook and the staff. They come down the driveway away
from the house, and exit the park through the high
wrought-iron gates. The church bell is tolling in the
distance.*

CUT TO

The church party walk along a country lane. The children are ahead, the adults behind. Miss is thoughtful; she turns confidentially to Mrs Grose.

Miss Did my predecessor see anything amiss in the boy?

Mrs Grose She never said.

Miss And was she . . . particular?

Mrs Grose . . . About some things, yes.

Miss But not all?

Mrs Grose She's dead, Miss. I won't speak ill of her.

Miss Quite right, Mrs Grose, quite right.

They approach the village church through the graveyard. Miss still looks like she's turning things over in her mind.

Did she die here, at Bly?

Mrs Grose No, she went off.

The church bell stops ringing.

Miss Went off to die? What do you mean? She was taken ill, and went home?

Mrs Grose (*curtly*) She was not taken ill, no, she went for a holiday, to which she had a right, and the next thing I know, the Master says she's dead.

Miss But of what?

Mrs Grose He never said! (*She hurries towards the church door.*) We'll be late for service, Miss!

Mrs Grose disappears into the church. Miss remains a few moments in the graveyard, pondering.

CUT TO

The drawing room. Miles and Flora sit side by side at the piano, playing a duet. Miles takes the more difficult bass part; he plays well. Flora's task is to bang in some high notes with one finger, which she does with a giggle.

Outside, evening is falling. Miss sits at a big oak desk, listening to the music. Mrs Grose enters with a tray of lemonade. They both turn to look at the children, across the room.

Mrs Grose Miles is very gifted, isn't he?

Miss Yes. But the curious thing is, that he has never, not once, in all these weeks, spoken of his school. Never mentioned a friend, or a master, or anything . . .

CUT TO

Miss is about to enter Mrs Grose's parlour. She hesitates at the door as she hears the children whispering. She peeps in. Miles and Flora are sitting in their usual places, their heads bent towards each other, in earnest discussion.

Miss enters. The children spring apart, looking guilty. One of the Maids stands against the wall behind them. Miss takes her seat at the table, across from them. Flora leans towards Miles and whispers in his ear.

Miss (*sternly*) Flora, what is this secret that we may not openly discuss? I do not approve of secrets. Let that be firmly understood.

*Flora blushes. Miles nods to the Maid, who brings
from the sideboard an extravagant cake, with pink
and white icing, which she sets down before Miss,
who is greatly surprised. The children laugh and clap
their hands.*

Miles It's for you, Miss.

Flora We asked Cook to bake it.

Miles We thought you deserved a treat.

*Miss is a little overcome, and astonished at their
generosity.*

CUT TO

*Another Sunday. From outside, we see Bly in the pouring
rain, as a summer storm batters the building.*

*There's a distant crack of thunder. We go in closer, to
see Miles and Flora's faces peering out of the grown-up
dining room window, watching the rain.*

*Inside the grown-up dining room, Miss joins Flora and
Miles on the window-seat. They're slightly grumpy
because they've been trapped inside all day. Miss is
sewing up a hole in a pair of gloves.*

Miss Has it eased at all?

Flora No, Miss.

Mrs Grose approaches them, also in her Sunday best.

Mrs Grose 'Tisn't good to miss church.

Miss We shall go to evening service, if the rain permits.

CUT TO

*A little later, Miles, Flora, Miss and Mrs Grose emerge
cautiously from the front door. They look up at the sky.
It's still raining, but much more lightly.*

Miss Let's risk it.

> *They make their way down the front steps, followed
> by the staff. But then Miss stops.*

Oh! I have left my gloves. Walk on, I'll catch you up!

> *And Miss scampers back into the house. The children
> stop.*

Mrs Grose (*to the children*) Go with Cook. I'll wait for
Miss.

CUT TO

*Miss comes quickly into the grown-up dining room, and
straight away spies her gloves on a chair by the window.
At the same moment she registers a person on the far
side of the window, looking in. She catches her breath,
frozen to the spot. It's the red-haired man she saw on the
tower.*

    *He's standing outside on the terrace, in gentle rain.
His face is close to the glass; he's still not wearing a hat,
but a fancy waistcoat is clearly visible. He stares directly
at Miss, who returns his gaze. After a few seconds he
breaks away, and intently examines several other points
in the room, as if looking for something, or someone.*

CUT TO

Miss comes tearing out of the side door, and arrives on the terrace outside the dining room. There's nobody there. She spins round and scans the garden: no sign of anyone. It's hard to see where he could have gone, without being spotted. Miss goes up to the window and puts her face close to it, as the man had done. She sees Mrs Grose come into the dining room. Mrs Grose looks up and sees Miss's face at the window, and instantly turns white with shock.

Mrs Grose's POV from inside the dining room. Miss's face at the window is streaked with rain; her hair has partly come adrift from under her hat; her stare has a harrowing intensity.

Mrs Grose hurries around the corner of the house on to the terrace where Miss still stands outside the window.

Mrs Grose What in the name of goodness has happened? You're as white as a sheet!

Mrs Grose comes closer.

Miss There was a man. Standing here, looking in. An extraordinary man.

Mrs Grose What extraordinary man?

Miss I haven't the least idea! He was awful!

Mrs Grose Then thank heavens the children didn't see him! Normally they'd be sat right there! (*She points into the dining room.*)

Miss At this hour?

Mrs Grose It's tea-time!

Miss Of course, the rain . . .!

Mrs Grose Have you seen this fellow before?

Miss Yes, once, weeks ago – on the tower.

Mrs Grose What was he doing up the tower?

Miss Looking down at me.

Mrs Grose Was he a gentleman?

Miss No . . . No.

Mrs Grose Someone from the village?

Miss No. I checked.

Mrs Grose Why didn't you mention it?

Miss I'd no wish to scare you.

> *Now Mrs Grose does indeed look scared. The scene*
> *plays with gathering pace.*

Mrs Grose Why, what is he?

Miss He's a horror.

Mrs Grose (*wide-eyed*) A horror?

Miss God help me if I know what he is!

Mrs Grose You saw him at the window, and you ran
out?

Miss Yes, I came to meet him.

Mrs Grose I couldn't've done that.

Miss (*with a nervous laugh*) Nor me! But I've my duty.

Mrs Grose To the children . . .

Miss Yes.

Mrs Grose What is he like?

Miss Like nobody.

Mrs Grose Nobody?

Miss He has no hat.

CUT TO

Miss sits damply in front of the fire in her sitting-room. Mrs Grose drapes a shawl over her shoulders. We get a sense that the door is securely locked, and they talk in low voices. Their conversation continues as if without pause.

Miss He has red hair, very red, close-curling, and a pale face, with rather queer whiskers, as red as his hair. His eyes are sharp, and strange.

Mrs Grose's expression registers increasing dismay.

He gave me a sort of sense of being a music-hall man. I've never in fact seen one, but he was much as I suppose them to be. Tall, active, erect – but not a gentleman, not ever a gentleman.

Mrs Grose But handsome –?

Miss Remarkably. And dressed in very fine clothes, that don't quite seem to be his own.

Mrs Grose (*in a whisper*) They're the Master's.

A nasty pause. Mrs Grose looks giddy.

Miss . . . You *know* him?

Mrs Grose It's Quint.

Miss Quint?

Mrs Grose Peter Quint. The Master's valet.

Mrs Grose shuts her eyes. Miss draws her breath in sharply.

Miss Go on.

Mrs Grose He never wore his hat, but he did wear – well, there were waistcoats missed. When they were both here, last year. Then the Master went. And Quint was alone with us.

Miss And what became of him?

Mrs Grose God knows.

Miss When did he leave?

Mrs Grose He didn't leave. He died.

Miss (*stunned*) Died?

Mrs Grose He's dead.

CU Miss as she takes in this information. It goes very quiet, just the coals hissing on the fire.

He was found one morning, icy it was, on the road from the village. He'd taken a wound to the head. They think he came late from the public house, and being in liquor, slipped and fell. That's what they think. But with the life Peter Quint led, well, you never know, do you?

Miss (*softly*) But I *saw* him.

Mrs Grose Yes, Miss.

Miss You do believe me?

Mrs Grose Yes, Miss.

Mrs Grose is clearly very upset. She wrings her hands. Miss seems possessed of a strange conviction. Her eyes burn, and she paces the room.

Miss I think he was looking for someone. (*She thinks hard.*) He was looking for little Miles. Miles would customarily have been there. He wants the child.

Mrs Grose Heaven forbid! He shan't have him again!

Miss Again? They were together before?

Mrs Grose They were always together. Don't blame Miles. It was Quint's fault. Quint spoiled him. Quint was much too free.

Miss Too free? With my boy?

Mrs Grose Too free with everyone. When the Master left, Quint was in charge.

Miss (*in fury*) A serving man? In charge of my innocent babies? With influence over their lives? And you say this fellow was bad?

Mrs Grose Well, I knew it, but the Master did not. He was *vile*.

> *Miss paces for a moment, thinking hard, with a steely expression.*

Miss I see what I must do. I must protect our little creatures from this . . . thing. I must interpose myself between him and them, with all the weapons of my faith. For I'm certain he will come to us again.

CUT TO

Some weeks later. Miles and Flora leave Mrs Grose's parlour and walk along the hall. Mrs Grose marches behind them. They're like prisoners under escort.

Miles and Flora ascend the staircase, past the portrait of The Master. Waiting for them at the top is Miss. Mrs Grose stands at the bottom as they climb up.

The children file past Miss on their way to the schoolroom.

Miss throws a questioning glance down to Mrs Grose: 'Anything?' Mrs Grose shakes her head: 'Nothing.' Miss turns to follow the children into the schoolroom.

CUT TO

In the schoolroom, the children have a thick atlas open on their desk. Miss is writing on the blackboard as she speaks. She writes 'Sea of Azov' underneath 'Russia'.

Miss The Sea of Azov is situated at the northern end of the Black Sea. Its principal port is Taganrog. – Have you found it, Flora?

CUT TO

Tea in Mrs Grose's parlour. Lessons are over for the day. Miles, Flora, Miss and Mrs Grose at table, one of the Maids serving.

Flora Miss, may we play outside after tea? I should so like to, now that summer is nearly gone.

Miss Miles? Does that suit you?

Miles I should prefer to read my novel, actually, Miss. It's terrifically exciting. It's all set in darkest Africa, where there's a plot to –

Miss I would not wish to stop you from reading. Well . . .

She's uncertain what to do. Mrs Grose comes to the rescue.

Mrs Grose My duties this afternoon are light. I will sit with Miles.

Miss smiles her thanks.

CUT TO

Miss and Flora walk slowly across the lawn. It's a pleasant afternoon. Miss carries a needlework bag and a parasol.

Flora And you can be – the Empress of all the Russias!

Miss (*smiling*) What does the Empress of all the Russias do?

Flora The Empress of all the Russias does – whatever she likes!

Miss May she sit? May she sew?

Flora Of course! – So long as she reviews the Navy, when it sails from Taganrog . . .
  Miss laughs lightly to herself.

CUT TO

Miss has seated herself on a rug overlooking the lake, and has taken a piece of embroidery from her bag. Flora sits on the ground maybe five yards away from Miss, busy with several pieces of wood, engrossed in a game. She's trying to work a long thin piece of wood into a small hole in a stout flat piece of wood, to represent the mast of a ship. She struggles to push it in. Flora seems in a world of her own. Miss glances at her and continues her embroidery.

Flora (*playing*) She's the finest warship on the Sea of Azov . . .

  Miss keeps her eyes on her needlework.

Flora Set the mainsail! The Empress is coming aboard!
Hey, you scurvy dog – what's the matter with you?

(Sings)
What shall we do with the drunken sailor?
What shall we do with the drunken sailor?
What shall we do with the drunken sailor,
Early in the – (*She suddenly stops.*)

*Miss smiles to herself, still not looking up. She slowly
becomes aware that Flora has gone very quiet. Miss
looks up. Flora is staring intently at the far side of
the lake. Miss turns and looks in the same direction.
She sees nothing but the water and the trees.*

   *Miss turns back to Flora, to discover that the girl
is now staring at her. It could be that Miss's troubled
expression and darting eyes have aroused her concern.
They gaze at each other for a few moments, then
Flora turns back to her warship.*

Look lively there!

*Miss turns and, again, looks across the lake. We pick
out, in long shot, a young woman (Miss Jessel)
standing on the far side of the lake. She is hatless,
dressed all in black, and as pale as death. She appears
to be watching Flora. Miss lets out a little gasp.*

   *Miss looks again at Flora, who has her back to the
lake, and is still trying to force the little stick into its
hole. She continues her imaginary game, all innocence.*

You'll be made to walk the plank, if you don't wind that
capstan! Come along now! The Empress expects every
man to do his duty!

*Flora looks up and sees Miss staring at her in a
particularly frightful way. Flora gives Miss her
sweetest little blue-eyed smile.*

Miss suddenly leaps up and grabs Flora's hand and drags her violently away from the lake. Flora is astonished and confused.

Miss runs across the lawn, back towards the house, half-dragging Flora by the hand. Flora stumbles, trying to keep up, with no idea what's happening.

Miss runs in through the front door, still tugging Flora behind her. She hauls the girl up the stairs.

Miss hauls Flora along the landing and into the schoolroom. Miles sits with his feet up on his desk, engrossed in his storybook. At Miss's table, Mrs Grose is dozing contentedly.

Miss Mrs Grose!

Miss practically throws Flora into the room. Miles gets his feet down double quick. Mrs Grose wakes with a start and immediately stands up.

(*to the children*) Do not dare move!

Miss beckons Mrs Grose insistently, and together they leave the room. Miss shuts the door firmly. The children stand, ramrod-straight, staring at each other in fright.

Miss and Mrs Grose confer in whispers on the landing. Miss is much distracted.

Mrs Grose What in the world is it?

Miss Flora can see.

Mrs Grose See what?

Miss You know what.

Mrs Grose (*horrified*) She told you?

Miss No, that's the worst of it – she *keeps it a secret!*

Mrs Grose He appeared again?

Miss No, a woman, in black, pale and dreadful. A figure of unmistakeable evil. She fixed the child with her awful eyes, with a kind of furious intention.

Mrs Grose To do what?

Miss To corrupt her.

Mrs Grose Did you know the woman?

Miss No. But you do. And so does the child.

Mrs Grose is stopped in her tracks.

It was my predecessor.

Mrs Grose Miss Jessel?

Miss Miss Jessel. Do you doubt me? Ask Flora – she'll confirm it! (*changing her mind*) Oh, no, for God's sake, don't! She'll only lie!

Mrs Grose (*alarmed*) My dear, my dear – she is an innocent girl! We must keep our heads, you know!

Miss glances at her, suddenly worried. Has she made a mistake? She turns back into the schoolroom, where Flora and Miles are still standing to attention, afraid to move a muscle. Miss goes straight to Flora, and puts her arms around her.

Miss There, there! What a lot of commotion! Let's all get back to normal, shall we?

Miss kisses Flora, who relaxes a little. Miles is watching intently. He's puzzled. Miss shepherds the pair of them out of the door.

CUT TO

A game of cricket on the lawn. Flora is bowling. Miles is in to bat, in front of a makeshift wicket. Miss is deep in the outfield, standing and watching, not really paying much attention to the game.

Flora lobs an underarm ball towards Miles, who gives it an almighty whack. The ball sails high, coming down directly over Miss.

The Children Catch, Miss! Catch!

Miss sees the ball dropping out of the sky. She cups her hands and shuts her eyes, and somehow catches it. The children are jubilant. They run towards her, clapping.

Miles I say, well done! First rate! – You're in to bat.

Miss tosses the ball to Flora, and takes the bat that Miles offers her.

From an upper window of the house, Mrs Grose watches the cricket game below. She's in Miss's bedroom; behind her, the Maids are re-making Flora's bed. Mrs Grose smiles warmly, glad to see that all appears to be well.

Miss takes up her position with the bat. She stands at the wicket, waiting nervously, as Miles and Flora have an earnest, whispered discussion at the bowling end. It begins to annoy her.

Miss (*calls*) May I ask what you are talking about?

Miles (*with a smile*) Tactics.

Miss looks suddenly worried. Flora takes up a fielding position close to the wicket. Miles is preparing a massive run-up to bowl. He comes tearing in towards

304

the crease, and launches a fast full-toss. Miss doesn't even see it as it smashes into the wicket.

Howzat!

Flora Oh, rotten luck!

Miles Fine effort for a novice.

Flora reaches up to put her arms around Miss' neck, and pulls her face down, and kisses her.

Flora You're jolly game, Miss! We do have such *sport* with you!

CUT TO

Early evening in the drawing room. The curtains are drawn, and candles burning, as a game of charades is in progress. Flora and Mrs Grose sit on the sofa, trying to guess what Miles is acting out. Everybody is laughing at his antics – except Miss, who sits apart, sewing, not joining in. Miles holds up two fingers and then spins round and round, quickly.

Mrs Grose Second word: twist?

Flora Spinning top?

Miss Dizzy? Swivel?

Miles shakes his head. They're not getting it. He changes tack. He begins to act the part of a ghost. He waves his hands going 'Whoo . . . whoo . . .' in a scary manner. Flora and Mrs Grose keep laughing. Miss freezes in horror as Miles directs his performance at her. She stares at him as he rolls his eyes. Mrs Grose glances at her, troubled. Suddenly, Miss gets up and hurries from the room. She can't take it any longer. The game suddenly comes to an abrupt halt.

CUT TO

On the landing outside the bedrooms. Mrs Grose watches from the top of the stairs as Miss ushers Miles and Flora into their respective bedrooms. One of the Maids stands at each doorway, with a candle to light the children to bed.

Flora Goodnight, Miles.

Miles gives Flora a brotherly hug and a kiss on the cheek.

Miles Sleep tight, my dear.

Flora Goodnight, Miss.

Miles Goodnight, Miss.

On impulse, Miles puts his arms up around Miss's neck and kisses her on the cheek.

You may have first bat tomorrow if you like.

The children enter their bedrooms. Miss joins Mrs Grose and they descend the stairs.

Mrs Grose Well, I have to say, I think they love you very much. They're so sweet to you.

Miss Too sweet, perhaps.

CUT TO

Miss and Mrs Grose enter Mrs Grose's parlour. The table is laid for supper.

Miss In these two months I have lived with Miles he has never, once, been bad. He's been a little prodigy of goodness. Yet you claimed, when that awful letter arrived, that you'd known him to be naughty. Tell me now what you meant.

Mrs Grose (*reluctantly*) It was during the time with Peter Quint. They were perpetually together. It weren't fit. I had a word with Miss Jessel, and she told me to mind my business. So I had a word with Miles.

Miss And what did he say?

Mrs Grose I don't think I can repeat it. He denied this and that. He used words.

Miss He lied? About going with Quint?

Mrs Grose Well, Miss Jessel didn't mind, you see. She didn't forbid it. I suppose it suited her. She had the girl, he'd the boy.

Miss (*sickened*) And they *met*?

Mrs Grose (*in turmoil*) I don't know, I don't know!

Miss You do know, you poor thing, only you haven't my dreadful boldness of mind.

Mrs Grose No, that I haven't.

Miss And then Jessel had to go because she was with child?

Mrs Grose nods furtively.

But Miles covered, and concealed, their liaisons . . .

Mrs Grose He was a small boy, Miss, some things are only natural –

Miss Not lying! I will not have lying 'natural'!

A pause. The supper has been quite forgotten. Miss is again quite agitated.

307

No wonder you looked so queer when I showed you the letter from his school.

Mrs Grose Well, if he was as wicked as they say, how is he such a cherub now? And Flora too?

Miss I am wondering if it is all part of their deception. Perhaps they communicate with each other! Perhaps every day! And divert our attention with their games, and nonsense!

Mrs Grose No, they're just playful . . .

Miss Playful? And if they grow up to lead lives of wickedness and debauchery . . .? Will you still call them playful? If their souls are damned?

CUT TO

Miss's bedroom, late at night. Flora sleeps at the foot of the bed. Miss gently smoothes the hair back off Flora's face, and closes the white lace curtain around her bed.

Later, Miss lies in bed, asleep. She sits up sharply as she hears a noise outside her door. She notices that the window is open, and the breeze moves the curtain. The noise comes again. A footstep on the boards? Without further thought, she slips out of bed, takes up a candle, goes to the door, and slips outside.

She walks purposefully along the landing, holding aloft the candle, which doesn't spread much light.

She comes to the head of the stairs. There's a tall window by the turn in the staircase, half way down. She begins to descend, and then, in the moonlight stealing through the window, she discerns a figure.

She goes on down with no apparent show of fear. As she gets closer to the window, her candle illuminates Peter Quint.

Quint turns slowly and looks at her. He seems to recognise her, as she does him. They are only a few feet apart, and he is clearly a 'living presence'. The corners of his mouth curl up in a faintly malicious little smile. Miss stares back at him without emotion. After a few seconds, Quint swivels round and walks down the staircase. Miss stays where she is. Very quickly he disappears into the gloom.

CU Miss. She hasn't moved. Her eyes are ablaze.

CUT TO

Daytime. Miss walks along the terrace in front of the house with Mrs Grose, who is chilled by her account.

Mrs Grose He came up the stairs?

Miss As large as life.

Mrs Grose . . . Are you sure?

Annoyed, Miss stops and confronts her.

Miss Do you accuse me of making it up? I described to you, in detail, two persons whom I had never seen. You must trust me, Mrs Grose!

Mrs Grose I do, Miss, I do.

CUT TO

The middle of the night. Miss lies awake in her bed. Again, she thinks she hears a noise. She rises and pulls on a shawl, passing the sleeping Flora.

Taking her candle, Miss prowls the house. She finds nothing.

She returns to her bedroom. She immediately goes to Flora's bed. The white curtains are drawn around it, making it seem as if Flora's within. But some instinct makes Miss draw aside the curtain. The bed is empty.

At that moment the curtain sways in the breeze, and Miss notices Flora's bare legs, beneath the hem of her nightgown, under the curtain – she's peering out of the open window.

Flora emerges from behind the curtain. She looks grave.

Flora Where have you been?

Miss Were you looking for me?

Flora Yes.

Miss You thought I would be walking in the grounds?

Flora Well, I thought *someone* was.

Miss drops into a chair, feeling the pressure. Flora comes and sits on her knee, snuggling up. Miss regards her with great suspicion.

Miss Did you see anyone?

Flora Of course not.

They stare at each other. Then Miss lifts Flora, and puts her back in bed.

CUT TO

Next day. Miles and Flora work in the schoolroom. Miss, at her desk, attempts to mark their books, but she's drooping with tiredness. Miles watches her intently.

CUT TO

Another night. Miss rises from her bed and takes her candle. She passes Flora's bed, and checks that the girl is there. She goes on out of the bedroom door.

As she turns on to the landing, she comes face to face with Miss Jessel, making her way towards the bedrooms. Jessel appears to see Miss. Jessel immediately turns and descends the stairs.

Miss hurries after the figure. She gets to the head of the stairs just in time to see Jessel turning the corner, mid-way down.

Miss skips down the stairs as fast as she can. But when she gets to the bottom, Jessel has disappeared into the darkness of the house.

CUT TO

Sunday. Mrs Grose and Miss walk along the lane to church. It's windy. The leaves are beginning to turn yellow and fall from the trees. At a distance behind them walk Miles, Flora, Luke and the two Maids, all in their Sunday best.

Miss stumbles over a pot-hole in the lane. Mrs Grose catches her arm as Miss struggles to her feet. It's an effort.

Mrs Grose Are you hurt, dear?

Miss No, just tired.

CUT TO

Late at night. Miss has fallen asleep, her book face down on her chest. Flora gets out of her bed, slips behind the curtains, and opens the window.

The noise and the draught wake Miss. Looking to the window, she sees the girl's bare legs beneath the curtain.

Miss slips quietly out of bed, takes up her candle, and with great caution slips into her sitting room. Flora doesn't notice anything, doesn't move from her post.

We go with Miss into the sitting room. She makes for the window and quietly draws back the curtain. She presses her face to the glass.

On the lawn below is Miles. He stands still, wearing his nightgown, and staring upwards, above Miss, in the direction of the top of the tower. Miss is astonished. She cranes her neck, but from her position, she can't see what the boy is looking at.

Shielding her candle from Flora, she hurries out of the bedroom.

Miss quickly makes her way downstairs. She comes on to the terrace above the lawn where Miles stands. He hasn't moved; he still gazes up to the top of the tower. Miss looks upwards but there's nothing there, nothing but the full moon. Miles turns and stares impudently at her.

Miss You are in your nightgown!

Miles (*matter-of-factly*) So are you, Miss.

Miss is suddenly embarrassed. She takes Miles' hand and they walk towards the front door. He goes without fuss.

Miss and Miles climb the stairs, hand in hand.

Miss and Miles enters Miles's bedroom. He gets obediently into bed. She closes the door and leans against it.

Miss I think the time has come to tell me.

Miles Tell you what, Miss?

Miss The truth, Miles.

Miles I'm perfectly willing to tell you that – only I'm not sure if you'll understand.

CU Miss. A look of satisfaction flickers across her face: she thinks she's got him now, he will have to admit what he sees.

Miss Try. Why were you out there?

Miles Well . . . so that you'd think exactly what you're thinking at this minute.

Miss Which is?

Miles (*with a sweet smile*) That I am *bad*.

This is so unexpected, and such a defeat, that Miss has to make an effort not to cry.

Miss And are you?

Miles Oh yes. When I want to be. I left the house at midnight. I haven't slept at all. It was all planned. Flora was to wake you. So she opened your window. And you took the bait!

Miss (*a whisper*) I see.

Miles When I'm bad, Miss, I really am extremely *bad*.

He grins cheerily. In low spirits, and utterly exhausted, Miss kneels by the edge of his bed.

Miss But why, Miles? Why?

Miles Because you ought to know, my dear, what I'm capable of.

Miles takes Miss's face in his hands, and plants a kiss on her forehead.

Just think what I could do if I wanted!

CUT TO

Miss 'Just think what I could do if I wanted'! – his precise words.

Miss and Mrs Grose are sitting on the terrace overlooking the lawn. It's a blustery day in early autumn. Before them, the children are ambling up and down. Miles has his arm around Flora's shoulder, and is reading to her from a book of fairy-tales as they parade back and forth, out of earshot of the adults.

I see things very clearly now. If you'd been with me on these recent nights, you'd understand. The four of them perpetually meet. And nothing proves it better than the children's silence. Never a word – not one word! – never an allusion to either of their old friends – the pair who have plied them with evil. Oh, we can sit and watch them showing off, pretending to be lost in a fairy-tale – but all the time they are secretly talking of horrors. They're talking of the dead restored to them.

Mrs Grose is looking at her in complete astonishment. Now she examines the children closely. They do seem to be whispering to each other, and glancing over their shoulders occasionally at the adults, but this could perhaps be on account of Miss's increasingly weird behaviour. She continues, coolly and dispassionately:

314

They have not been good – they have been absent. They don't answer to us. They answer to *them*.

Mrs Grose looks sickened.

CUT TO

The schoolroom. It's raining outside. Miles and Flora sit at their desks, as bright-eyed and attentive as ever. Miss paces back and forth.

Miss William Shakespeare was born in fifteen sixty-four in Stratford-upon-Avon. Which of you may tell me something about his work?

Miles puts his hand up.

With what are you familiar, Miles?

Miles *Hamlet*, Miss. I chanced upon it in the library.

(*He recites.*)
Angels and ministers of grace defend us!
Be thou a spirit of health, or goblin damned,
Bring with thee airs from heaven or blasts from hell,
Be thy intents wicked or charitable,
Thou com'st in such a questionable shape
That I will speak to thee.

Flora Ooh, Miles, that's scary.

Miles is pleased with himself. But Miss is seething.

Miss Are you having sport with me?

Miles (*innocently*) No, Miss.

Flora I thought it was jolly good, Miss.

Miss I will not be teased! Do you imagine I am easy prey?

Flora I don't know what you mean, Miss.

Miss (*sarcastically*) You don't know what I mean.

Flora No, Miss.

Miss glares at them. Miles still seems eager to please her.

Miles I've read *Macbeth*, too, Miss.

CUT TO

Miss is in the drawing room, running her finger along the bookcase shelf containing several volumes of Shakespeare, looking for a book. Finally she locates it – the copy of Hamlet. *It does exist. She hefts it in her hand, feeling its solidity.*

The door opens and Mrs Grose comes into the room. She's clearly on a mission.

Mrs Grose Am I disturbing you, Miss?

Miss Not at all.

Mrs Grose Only I been thinking.

Miss raises an eyebrow. This is a novelty.

You must write to their uncle in London. That'd be for the best.

Miss Are you suggesting that I inform him his house is poisoned and his niece and nephew mad?

Mrs Grose But if they *are*, Miss?

Miss And if I am too, I suppose you mean? That would be charming news to be sent him by a person in whom he has placed his confidence, and specifically asked that she give him no worry.

Mrs Grose But he might help!

Miss Help? He won't help, you silly woman, he'll have me locked up as a lunatic, and leave the field free for the Devil! No, what we need is *proof*.

Mrs Grose How on earth are we to get that?

Miss I wish I knew! My eyes have been closed. I no longer see. But they do. And they see *more* – things terrible, unguessable, from dreadful passages in the past! Oh, I long to come to the point, to speak the names: 'Where is Peter Quint? Where is Miss Jessel? I know they're here, you little wretches! What infernal lessons do they give you?'

Mrs Grose (*horrified*) But you can't say that! They are so trusting! It would break their hearts! And what if you are . . . if you are . . .

Miss Wrong?

Mrs Grose . . . Yes!

Miss . . . Then we shall work by stealth. Await our opportunity.

CUT TO

Miss walks in the grounds, down by the lake. Autumn is well advanced now, and most of the leaves are off the trees and scattered across the park. It's cold, and the lake is crested with waves. She goes to the spot where she saw Jessel before, and stares across the water to the far shore. There's nothing unusual there.

Miss walks slowly across the lawn, back to the house. In the distance the Gardener is raking up leaves.

From the window of Miles's bedroom, Flora and Miles watch her. Their faces are expressionless. Miles places his hand on Flora's shoulder, protectively.

CUT TO

Tea in Mrs Grose's parlour. Miles, Flora, Miss and Mrs Grose.

Miles Miss, may we write to our uncle?

Flora We should so like to see him.

Miss considers this. Are they trying to trick her? She glances at Mrs Grose, who averts her eyes.

Miss Your uncle has asked not to be bothered. He is engaged on work of vital importance.

Flora Oh, we wouldn't be any bother.

Miss . . . Very well. You may write. Leave your letters in the hall for Luke to take to the village. Now, if you have had sufficient, you may leave the table.

Miles and Flora fold their napkins, stand up, carefully push their chairs under the table, and then come around to Miss's side. They each kiss her on the cheek as they go out.

Flora Thank you, Miss.

Miles Thank you, Miss.

They leave the room. Mrs Grose pours Miss more tea.

Mrs Grose He's never once wrote to them.

Miss (*sighs at her dullness*) That is part of the flattery of his trust of myself.

Mrs Grose gives her a curious look.

CUT TO

In the schoolroom, Miles and Flora are each writing a letter. They approach the task seriously, taking great care not to smudge their ink.

CUT TO

Miles lays their freshly-sealed letters on the big oak table in the hall. A moment later Miss appears. She goes to the table, picks up the two letters, tucks them into her pocket, and returns straight upstairs.

CUT TO

In Miss's bedroom, a close shot of her hand opening a small drawer, depositing the letters inside, closing it, and locking it with a tiny key.
   She catches sight of herself in the full-length mirror. She looks haggard; her hair is a mess; she's engaged upon an act of dishonesty. She certainly wouldn't want the Master to see her like this.

CUT TO

The walk to church. There's a frost on the ground, and the air is bright and sharp. The church bells ring out through the cold. Miss walks with Miles at her side; ahead of them are Flora and Mrs Grose, and all the staff. Miles is wearing a fancy waistcoat similar to the style we've seen on Quint: his uncle's tailor has attired him. He seems very grown-up, suddenly.

Miles I say, my dear –

Miss Yes, Miles?

Miles When in the world am I going back to school? I'm not sure it's good for a chap to be constantly with a lady.

Miss (*tries to laugh*) And always with the same lady?

Miles Of course she's a jolly perfect lady, that goes without saying. But I'm getting on, don't you know . . . And you can't say I've not been awfully good, can you?

Miss No, I can't say that, Miles.

Miles Except just that one night, when I . . . went out.

Miss Oh yes. But I forget what you did it for.

Miles Why, just to show you that I could! And I can again.

Miss stops him, and bends to look him straight in the eye.

Miss I do know that. But you won't.

Miles . . . Then when *am* I going back to school?

Miss Aren't you happy here? Don't I teach you well enough?

Miles Oh, it isn't that.

They enter the churchyard through the wicket gate. Flora and Mrs Grose are just entering the church, along with Cook, the two Maids, and Luke.

Miss What, then?

Miles (*blurts it out*) I want to see more life! I want my own sort!

Miss There aren't many of your own sort, Miles! Except maybe Flora!

Miles You compare me to a *girl*?

Miss Don't you love sweet little Flora?

Miles Of course I do, and you as well, and it's a good thing too, for if I *didn't* –

Miss Yes?

Miles Does my uncle think what you think?

This change of tack stuns Miss. The bells have stopped ringing.

Miss How do you know what I think?

Miles Well, I don't, for it strikes me you never tell me. But I mean does he know?

Miss Know what?

Miles The way I'm going on.

Miss I don't think your uncle much cares.

This is hard for Miles.

Miles Don't you think he can be made to?

Miss How?

Miles Why, by coming down, by coming here.

Miss But who'll gct him to?

Miles I will! I'll go to London!

Miss I forbid you!

Miles Well, I shall!

Miss Miles, you must not!

Miles Well, I intend to! And then we'll see!

Miles looks at her with an air of triumph, then turns and marches off into church. Miss looks like she's

been punched. *She leaps up, grabs her skirts, and
starts to run – out of the churchyard, back along the
lane. The sound of a hymn starting up in the church
follows her.*

*Miss runs through the wrought-iron gates and up
the driveway towards Bly.*

*She races in through the front door and heads for
the stairs. The house is empty and quiet.*

*Miss enters her bedroom. From under her bed she
drags out her trunk. She pulls open the lid, then goes
to her chest of drawers and starts to fill the trunk
haphazardly with clothing.*

*A few minutes later. Miss is forcing down the lid of
her now-overflowing trunk. All her drawers, cupboards,
wardrobes are open – but she's packed in a frenzy, and
there are still possessions of hers strewn about. She
suddenly remembers something, and turns to the door.*

She runs down the stairs towards the schoolroom.

*Miss enters the schoolroom with a purposeful air,
and starts to gather up her books from the bookcase.
But then she sees, sitting at her table, head in hands,
Miss Jessel. Miss stands stock still. Miss Jessel weeps
bitterly, her beautiful face lined with care. Slowly, she
stands, and turns to face Miss head on.*

Miss You terrible, miserable woman.

CUT TO

*Mrs Grose, Miles and Flora approach the house along
the driveway. They are followed at a distance by the rest
of the staff.*

*Mrs Grose enters the schoolroom and sees Miss sitting
at her table, head in hands, in the same attitude in which
we have just seen Miss Jessel.*

Mrs Grose Miss?

Miss looks up. Her hair is a mess, her eyes piercing.

(*worried*) What happened to you?

Miss I came home . . . for a talk with Miss Jessel.

CUT TO

Miss's sitting room. Mrs Grose pours her a glass of sherry.

Mrs Grose Do you mean she spoke?

Miss It came to that.

Mrs Grose What did she say?

Miss That she – the suicide, I think I may presume – suffers the torments of the damned. And, to share them, she wants Flora. But it no longer matters.

Mrs Grose Doesn't it?

Miss I have decided to summon the Master.

Mrs Grose Oh, Miss, in pity do!

Miss Miles thinks I am afraid to do so. Well, he shall see he's mistaken. I am wise to his strategies. His uncle shall see this.

She takes from her pocket the Headmaster's letter.

Mrs Grose From the school?

Miss (*nods*) The Master shall have it straight from me, that I can no longer undertake to educate a child who has been expelled –

Mrs Grose For heaven knows what!

Miss For wickedness. What else can it be? Is he stupid?

Untidy? Infirm? No. He is wicked. I shall take the initiative, he shall stand to account, and that will open up the whole thing.

Mrs Grose (*sighs*) Ah, Miss . . .

CUT TO

Miss sits at the table in her sitting room. Her suite has been restored to its usual impeccable order. Night, but she's still fully dressed. Before her, beneath the lamp, is a blank sheet of paper. She holds her pen, but cannot think what to write. She's been there a while.

She stands, and wanders through to the bedroom. Flora is asleep in the little bed. Rain batters the windows – the weather has turned rough. Miss takes up a candle, and goes out of the door.

Flora's eyes flick open. She's awake. She watches Miss leave.

Miss walks along the landing with her candle. The door to Miles's bedroom is slightly ajar. Miss stops and listens.

Miles (*breezily*) I say, you there, come in!

Miss pushes the door open. Miles sits up in bed, in the dark, wide awake. Miss takes a few steps in, illuminating the room with her candle.

Miss How did you know I was there?

Miles Do you fancy you made no noise? Why, you're like a troop of cavalry!

Miss glances quickly around the room.

Miss You weren't asleep?

Miles No, I lie awake and think.

Miss What is it that you think of?

Miles Why, you, of course, my dear.

Miss I'd frankly rather you slept.

Miles But then there's that other business.

Miss What other business?

Miles The way you bring me up. Keep me from school. And all the rest.

Miss All the rest?

Miles Oh, you know!

Miss sits down on the edge of the bed, and places her candle on the bedside table. Once again, she glances around the room.

Miss You shall certainly go back to school – but not to the old place – we shall find a better one. How was I to have known that this troubled you so, when you've never spoken of it before? Never mentioned a word about your schooldays?

Miles smiles sweetly. She suspects him of playing for time.

Miles Haven't I?

Miss No. I'm in the dark. I thought you were happy with things as they are.

Miles I'm not. I want to get away. I want to be with some chaps. I think my uncle should come down, and you should completely settle things.

Miss If we do, you may be sure he will take you away from Bly.

Miles But that's exactly what I want! And you'll have to tell him – tell him how you've let it all drop. My schooling and so forth. You'll have to tell him a tremendous lot!

Miss And what will *you* have to tell him?

Miles is silent. Miss gets down on her knees beside the bed, clutching his hand.

Dear little Miles, dear little Miles . . .

Miles I'm not little.

Miss What happened before?

Miles Before what?

Miss Before I came.

He gazes straight into her eyes. We get the impression of the possibility of unimaginable evil. Miss is almost weeping.

Dear little Miles, I only want to help you!

Miles appears not to comprehend what on earth she's talking about.

I'd rather die than hurt a hair of you! I just want you to help me to save you!

The windows fly open, and a terrible blast of icy air comes howling through the room. The candle is blown out.
    A moment later, all is calm. The room is still. Miss raises her head from her hands to find everything is dark.

(*whispers*) The candle's gone out.

Miles The wind did that, silly.

CUT TO

The schoolroom. Next day. Miss, Miles and Flora, who is now very wary of Miss. Outside, it's grey and damp after the night's rain.

Miss Who can tell me how many ounces there are in a pound?

Flora (*cautiously*) Sixteen, Miss?

Miss How many pounds in a hundredweight?

Miles A hundred and twelve, Miss!

Miss How many pounds in a ton?

Miles Two thousand, two hundred and forty, Miss!

Miss Excellent, Miles. You are on good form today.

There is a degree of sarcasm in Miss's voice, but Miles beams with pride. Miss consults her watch.

I believe it is time for luncheon.

CUT TO

Miss, Miles and Flora descend the stairs together. Miss takes a letter from her pocket. Miles watches with discreet interest as she lays it casually on the hall table.

Miles May I play for you after we've eaten, Miss? I've been practising something new.

CUT TO

In the drawing room, after luncheon. A big fire is burning. Miss sits in an armchair, relaxing as Miles plays the piano for her. He's rehearsed a complex piece and is performing it beautifully. Flora sits in another chair, somewhat less interested.

The music is of a strange, dreamy nature, wistful and elegiac. Miss enjoys it.

Miss drifts off into a peaceful reverie, lulled by the music. She closes her eyes.

Close shot of Miles's hands at the piano keys. He plays with a dexterity and assurance that one would think impossible in a child.

CUT TO

Close shot of Miss lying back in the armchair. Her eyes are closed. Suddenly she opens them, frowning. She glances quickly around the room. Flora has gone. Pull back as Miss sits bolt upright and interrupts Miles.

Miss Miles!

He stops playing, a little annoyed, and turns to her.

Where's Flora?

Miles shrugs, and laughs lightly, and picks up again from the bar where he stopped.

Miss immediately stands and leaves the room.

CUT TO

Miss comes into the hall, where she meets Mrs Grose going in the opposite direction.

Mrs Grose Oh, Miss, have you written the letter?

Miss Yes. – Have you seen Flora?

Mrs Grose I thought she was with you.

Miss (*highly agitated*) I'll look upstairs, you look down.

Miss races upstairs. Mrs Grose scurries off down a corridor.

CUT TO

Miss peers into the schoolroom. No sign of Flora.
Miss goes through her bedroom. She's not there either.

CUT TO

Mrs Grose looks into the kitchen. Cook is at the range.

Mrs Grose Has Flora been this way?

Cook shakes her head. Mrs Grose hurries out at what is, for her, great speed.

CUT TO

Mrs Grose and Miss meet again in the hall, Miss coming fast down the stairs. We can still hear Miles's piano playing coming from the drawing room. Mrs Grose holds her arms wide: 'She's nowhere.'

Miss (*with certainty*) She's gone out.

Mrs Grose Where to?

Miss To that woman!

Mrs Grose She's with *her*?

Miss is running for the front door.

Miss Come on!

Mrs Grose What about Miles?

Miss He'll be with Quint!

Miss is outside. Mrs Grose is in a flap. She hesitates at the door. Miss barely glances back at her as she races down the front steps.

Go to Miles if you prefer!

Mrs Grose hastens to join Miss. They run across the lawn towards the lake.

Mrs Grose You think she's by the water?

Miss Yes!

They arrive by the side of the lake. There's no sign of Flora. They halt, panting, disappointed. Mrs Grose has a brainwave:

Mrs Grose The boat!

The two women push their way through the dank shrubbery towards the old jetty. When they arrive there, the boat is gone. Miss peers across to the far side of the lake.

Miss She's gone over.

Mrs Grose All by herself?

Miss She's not by herself.

*With as much speed as they can muster, Miss and Mrs
Grose scramble their way along an overgrown path
around the side of the lake.*

*On the far side there is a grassy stretch between the
water and the trees, and alongside this a little inlet.
On the other side of the inlet is a slight hillock. Mrs
Grose and Miss come out of the woods to find the
boat hauled up on the mud in front of them.*

At that moment Flora comes out of the trees.

Mrs Grose There she is!

*Flora stands and smiles innocently at them. Mrs Grose
runs towards her; Miss lags behind. Mrs Grose goes
down on her knees and takes Flora in her arms,
hugging her tightly, smothering her neck and hair with
kisses. Miss hangs back.*

Oh, my precious, where have you been?

*There is a clear contrast between Mrs Grose's
instinctively maternal behaviour and Miss's reticence.
Miss is so disbelieving of Flora that she seems cold
and indifferent to the child's predicament. She sees
Flora looking up at her over Mrs Grose's shoulder;
she's not smiling now.*

Flora Where's Miles?

Miss I'll tell you if you'll tell me.

Flora Tell you what?

Miss (*violently*) Where is Miss Jessel?

Mrs Grose (*bawls*) No, Miss, you can't, not to a child!

*But Miss's attention has been caught by a figure
beyond, and partly to the side of, Flora and Mrs Grose.
Across the inlet, on the little hillock, stands Miss
Jessel, watching them. Miss clutches at Mrs Grose.*

Miss She's there! She's there!

Dazed and blinking, Mrs Grose stares in the direction in which Miss's finger points. But Miss's attention is caught by Flora, who, after flicking a casual glance over her shoulder, fixes Miss with a grave, hard stare.

(*to Flora*) She's there, you unhappy little thing, she's there!

Mrs Grose is frustrated and angry.

Mrs Grose Where on earth do you see anyone?

Miss can only gape at her, shocked to her boots. She swivels again to gaze upon Miss Jessel. She manhandles Mrs Grose around until she too is pointing in the appropriate direction.

Miss Look, woman, look! Directly in front of you! She's as real as you or I!

Mrs Grose groans deeply and bends to Flora.

Mrs Grose There's no one there, and poor Miss Jessel's dead and buried, isn't she, my sweet? It's all a mistake – we'll go home as fast as we can.

Mrs Grose and Flora, holding hands, stand apart from Miss. Flora fixes her with 'her small mask of disaffection'. Miss' face falls, as the full extent of her defeat – and Jessel's triumph – sinks in.

Miss Flora?

Flora I see nobody. I never have. I think you're cruel.

Flora buries her head in Mrs Grose's skirts, and lets out a hideous wail.

Oh, take me away from her!

Miss . . . From *me*?

Flora Yes, you bitch, from you!

Mrs Grose (*in horror*) Oh!

> *Mrs Grose starts to tug Flora away. Miss stands miserably in the mud, glancing from time to time at Miss Jessel, who seems to be gloating over her.*

Miss Oh, now I understand. *She* is speaking through you. – Take her away, Mrs Grose, take her, go on! Go!

> *As she speaks, Mrs Grose and Flora are making their way back along the overgrown path by the side of the lake. Miss sinks to her knees in the boggy ground.*

I've done my best, but I've lost you . . .

> *She lets out a deep sob, and slumps forwards on to her hands, her head hanging down.*

CUT TO

> *The Maids and Luke dismantle Flora's bed and remove it from Miss's bedroom.*
> *Miss enters the room just as they are carrying the bed-frame out. They ignore her. The room looks big and empty now.*

CUT TO

> *Night. Miss sits in her sitting room, staring hollow-eyed into the fire, with her hair down and a shawl around her shoulders. There are no candles burning. Her lips are pursed.*
> *Indistinctly, from far off in the house, we occasionally hear a child's cries and shouts: it's Flora.*

A light knock at the door. Miss doesn't respond. The door opens and Miles comes in, still fully dressed, and carrying a candle. Miss glances at him without expression, then resumes gazing into the flames.

Miles takes the chair opposite Miss. He makes no attempt to speak to her. They sit there in absolute stillness. We stay with them for a long time – as long as it will hold.

CUT TO

Mrs Grose Miss, Miss! Wake up, Miss!

Miss struggles up out of a deep sleep. She's in her bed, and Mrs Grose is standing over her, shaking her shoulder, trying to rouse her. It's early morning.

Flora's ill!

Miss gets immediately out of bed, reaching for her wrap. Mrs Grose stands firmly in her way.

No, Miss, she doesn't want you! She's had a most feverish night. She asks me every three minutes if I think you're coming in. I'm awful sorry.

Miss at once relaxes. She takes a seat.

Miss Of course, I see, I see perfectly. I have challenged her, I have cast doubt on her. Oh, I did put my foot in it, didn't I? She'll never speak to me again.

Mrs Grose No, Miss, she do say she won't.

Miss I think you'll find that's the root of her 'illness', Mrs Grose. Take a seat, please. Flora will be fine.

Mrs Grose sits, uncertainly.

Naturally you accept her word that she saw no one by the lake.

Mrs Grose What else can I do?

Miss Nothing! You're dealing with the cleverest little creatures. The demons had such wondrous material to work with, they've made them even smarter than they were before!

Miss laughs harshly. Mrs Grose looks at her with some apprehension.

And now she'll attempt to discredit me with her uncle. – I know what you must do. Leave here at once, and take Flora with you.

Mrs Grose To London?

Miss Anywhere! Just away!

Mrs Grose I will. Because I can't stay. Not no longer.

Miss (*leaping at the possibility*) Why not? Have you *seen* something?

Mrs Grose I've *heard* something. From the child. Really, the most shocking, appalling language you could ever have imagined.

Miss Oh, I can imagine! – About me?

Mrs Grose, her eyes cast down, nods.

Thank God!

Mrs Grose looks up in surprise.

It proves my point, I think!

Mrs Grose I must get the little ones away. Far from Bly. Far from *them*.

Miss (*jubilant*) So you do *believe*?

Mrs Grose Yes, I do.

Miss It occurs to me that my letter raising the alarm will have reached town ahead of you.

Mrs Grose No. Your letter never went. I asked Luke if he'd took it. He said he'd never seen it. Master Miles –

Miss Do you mean Miles stole it?

Mrs Grose (*nods*) I reckon he did! So his uncle shan't discover how naughty he's been!

Miss Oh!

Mrs Grose And I reckon that's what he done at school. He stole.

Miss is almost deliriously happy.

Miss Take Flora with you. But leave the boy with me.

CU Mrs Grose. She looks deeply worried by this. But Miss shepherds her swiftly out of the door.

CUT TO

Miss looks down from her sitting room window as Mrs Grose leads Flora by the hand out to the carriage. The Groom is sitting up, ready to drive, and the luggage is packed.

Miss frowns darkly as she sees Miles run out behind Flora and talk to her for a second. They embrace, whispering to each other.

CUT TO

On the driveway, Flora glances up over Miles's shoulder towards Miss's sitting room. She sees Miss at the window, and her pale, haggard face shows abject fear.

Mrs Grose hurries Flora into the carriage, then turns back to Miles.

Mrs Grose Be good now.

They drive off. Miles waves forlornly at the departing carriage. Then he too looks up to see Miss, at her window, staring down at him with an icy expression.

CUT TO

Miss walks along the corridor towards the kitchen. She holds her head high, and exudes authority.

She enters the kitchen. Cook and the Maids are preparing food at the table. Miss speaks to them quite sharply.

Miss Miles is late for his lesson.

Maid He said he was going for a stroll, Miss.

Miss He did, did he?

Cook Where is little Flora, Miss?

Miss She is indisposed. Mrs Grose has taken her to London. But I remain, and I run a tight ship.

Cook Yes, Miss.

Maid Yes, Miss.

Miss Master Miles and I will take dinner in the grown-up dining room, Cook.

Cook nods her acknowledgement.

CUT TO

Miss's sitting room, late in the day. She kneels in prayer.

Miss (*prays*) Never before did I comprehend the true nature of evil. But victory requires only another turn of the screw of human virtue. Success will depend on my rigid will. With Your aid, Lord, I'll wring it out of him. I will bring him to You. He'll confess. And if he confesses, he's saved.

CUT TO

Evening. Miss descends the staircase. She passes once again the portrait of the Master.
  She hears Miles playing the piano in the drawing room. It's the same piece that he played to lure her away from Flora. Miss hardens herself for the trial to come.

CUT TO

Miss sits in the grown-up dining room, waiting for Miles. The table is laid with the best silver cutlery. The two Maids stand waiting to serve; the food is cooling on the sideboard.
  Miles saunters in. For the first time, he has his hands in his pockets. He wanders through the room, turning his back on Miss, and stares out of the window – the very window where Miss saw Peter Quint.
  Miss signals to the Maids to serve. Plates of meat are placed on the table.

Miss Come here and take your mutton, Miles.

Miles I say, my dear, is Flora really very ill?

Miles sits opposite Miss. The Maids serve vegetables.

Miss She will presently be better.

Miles Are you sure she was fit enough to travel?

Miss Certainly. She will see a good doctor in London. And a journey away from Bly is exactly what she needs. Away from the source of her affliction.

Miles (*chewing his meat slowly*) I see, I see.

CUT TO

The meal has ended, and the Maids are clearing away the last of the dishes. Miss and Miles sit looking at each other. She is very tense and upright. As the Maids leave:

Miss That will be all.

The Maids curtsey and go out. Miles looks apprehensive. He gets up, and once again goes to peer out of the window at the dull, grey evening. Miss watches him intently. There is a barely-disguised chilliness between them.

Miles Well, now we're alone.

Miss Not absolutely alone. (*She forces a smile.*) We shouldn't like that!

Miles I suppose not. Of course we have the others.

Miss We do indeed have the others.

Miles But . . . they don't much count, do they?

Miss Don't they? Don't they count?

Miss goes to the sofa and takes up her embroidery.
It gives her something to do with her trembling hands.
Miles turns back to the window.

You had a nice stroll?

Miles Yes, thanks, I went for miles about. I've never been so free.

Miss Do you like that?

Miles (*cheekily*) Do you? – Oh I'm sorry. I ought not to mock, ought I? You are the one who is really alone.

Miss I greatly enjoy your company, Miles. Why else would I have stayed on? I'd like to think I am your friend. But I believe there is something you wish to tell me. I believe there is something preying on your mind. I know what it is. But I want you to tell me.

Miles bites his lip.

Miles . . . I'll tell you everything. I'll tell you anything you like. But not now.

He looks longingly out of the window at the gathering dusk.

Miss You want to go out again?

Miles Awfully.

Miss Why?

Miles I have to see Luke.

Miss' expression leaves us in no doubt that she knows this is a lie.

Miss (*sighs*) Well, you may go to Luke, if you will satisfy one small curiosity.

Miles appears to indicate his agreement. He faces her.
Miss concentrates on her needlework as she speaks.

340

Tell me if, yesterday afternoon, from the table in the hall, you took my letter.

Miss glances up, and sees Peter Quint at the window. He's outside, behind Miles, looking in. Miss leaps up, grips Miles tightly by the shoulders, and prevents him turning around.

Miles (*frightened*) Yes! All right! I took it!

Miss gives a low moan of satisfaction, pulls Miles close to her body, and enfolds him in a tight hug. Miles finds it hard to breathe. Miss keeps her eyes fixed on Quint, who holds her gaze, pacing slightly to left and right like a caged animal.

Miss Why?

Miles To see what you said about me!

Miss You opened it?

Miles nods. Miss pulls his face up to look into hers. She keeps glancing at Quint in the window. Miles tries to turn to see what she's looking at, but she grips his head in her hands, preventing him. She's clearly hurting him.

And what did you find?

Miles Nothing.

Miss No, nothing! Nothing, nothing! A request to meet your uncle! Nothing!

Miles (*very meekly*) Nothing.

Miss Did you steal other things at school, or merely letters?

Miles Did I what? *Steal*?

Miles blushes with embarrassment.

Miss Was it for that you were expelled?

Miles (*surprised*) You know I was expelled?

Miss I know everything! So – did you –?

Miles No, no! I didn't steal.

Miss shakes him violently. She screams into his ear.

Miss Then what did you do?

Miles starts to cry. He tries to look around the room, but Miss forces his face back into her line of sight. Her eyes flick up to establish that Quint is still witnessing her struggle. He shows no emotion, but watches intently.

Miles (*miserably*) I said things!

Miss Bad things?

Miles Bad enough to have me sent down, Miss!

Miss Who did you say them to?

Miles Just my friends!

Miss releases him slightly. He gasps for breath.

Miss (*sarcastically*) So, you are an innocent, Miles, are you?

Miles (*tearful and confused*) I don't know, Miss!

Miles turns to look towards the window, as it seems so much to obsess Miss. She leaps forward and grabs him again, preventing him. Miss glances at the window. Quint has gone. Miss turns back to Miles – but then something makes her look up again. Quint is back. But now he is inside the room. He advances slowly towards Miss and Miles. She backs away to the far wall, pulling Miles in front of her.

Miss (*to Quint*) No more, no more!

Miles (*cries*) Is she here?

Miss Who?

Miles Miss Jessel! Flora said, you see Miss Jessel!

Miss No. It's not Miss Jessel! But it's *here*! Right before us!

Miss forcibly spins Miles around, to face Peter Quint. But Miles, clearly, sees nothing. His eyes roam helplessly around the room.

Who is he? Say it!

Miles (*screams*) Peter Quint – you devil! Where? Where?

Quint seems to recognise his name. He seems shocked at hearing Miles pronounce it.

Where?

Miss pulls Miles tightly to her bosom, twisting him around, forcing his face hard into the fabric of her clothes. She focuses on Quint, who backs into the shadows and disappears through the following:

Miss What does he matter, now? *I* have you! He has lost you for ever! – You have lost him, Quint! I have him!

She grips Miles even tighter, her hands on the back of his head. He struggles, kicking his legs, but she's remarkably strong. She watches until Quint has entirely gone. Then, slowly, very slowly, she releases Miles, planting kisses on the top of his head as she does so.

As she releases her grip, Miles's head flops backwards. He's dead.

Miss rocks the boy's body in her arms, weeping.

*We see this picture in a shot through the window.
Then we pull back, to outside the house, pulling
further and further back until the whole façade of Bly
stands starkly against a leaden grey sky. At the bottom
of the lawn a bonfire, tended by the silhouetted figure
of the gardener, sends upwards a thin plume of smoke.
The End.*